Cultural Cleansing in Iraq

Cultural Cleansing in Iraq

Why Museums Were Looted, Libraries Burned
and Academics Murdered

Edited by
RAYMOND W. BAKER, SHEREEN T. ISMAEL
and TAREQ Y. ISMAEL

PlutoPress
www.plutobooks.com

First published 2010 by Pluto Press
345 Archway Road, London N6 5AA and
175 Fifth Avenue, New York, NY 10010

www.plutobooks.com

Distributed in the United States of America exclusively by
Palgrave Macmillan, a division of St. Martin's Press LLC,
175 Fifth Avenue, New York, NY 10010

British Library Cataloguing in Publication Data
A catalogue record for this book is available from the British Library

ISBN   978 0 7453 2813 3   Hardback
ISBN   978 0 7453 2812 6   Paperback

Library of Congress Cataloging in Publication Data applied for

This book is printed on paper suitable for recycling and made from
fully managed and sustained forest sources. Logging, pulping and
manufacturing processes are expected to conform to the environmental
standards of the country of origin.

10   9   8   7   6   5   4   3   2   1

Designed and produced for Pluto Press by
Chase Publishing Services Ltd, Sidmouth, England
Typeset from disk by Stanford DTP Services, Northampton, England
Printed and bound in the European Union by
CPI Antony Rowe, Chippenham and Eastbourne

This book is dedicated to the memory of
Professor Issam al-Rawi, Professor of Geology,
Baghdad University and Chairman of the Association
of University Teachers (AUT). Professor al-Rawi founded
the register of assassinated academics and worked tirelessly to
record the fate of Iraqi academics and experts in the wake of
the invasion of the Coalition Forces and dissolution of the
Iraqi state. Dr. al-Rawi was assassinated on October 30, 2006,
after being targeted to silence the truth.

CONTENTS

PREFACE

No reasonable person, even those critics most angry and disgusted with the Bush administration, would claim that the destruction of particular Iraqi cultural treasures or the assassination of specific scholars was the aim of the armchair "warriors" who planned and launched the war against Iraq. Nevertheless, the destruction was willful. The war planners quite consciously and deliberately aimed for the destruction of the Iraqi state. They did so because a strong Iraq was an impediment to American imperial designs and Israeli insistence on unimpeded regional hegemony. A strong Iraqi state cast a shadow on both visions. In willful violation of international law against preventative war and with complete disregard for its responsibilities as an occupying power, the United States and its allies have failed to protect Iraq's incomparable cultural treasures. Given the scope of the destruction that took place on their watch, it is hard to escape the conclusion that the occupiers understood that damaging the cultural underpinnings of Iraqi identity would also hasten the collapse of modern day Iraq. In just the same way, the apparent indifference and failure to respond to the decimation of the Iraqi intellectual class through targeted assassinations points to the conclusion that Iraq's occupiers and their allies had little interest in preserving the priceless human resources represented by Iraq's educated elite. Oil mattered and so Oil Ministry records were protected. The files of the Interior Ministry that would certainly have compromised both Americans and Israelis mattered and so they were protected. In contrast, priceless archaeological artifacts and leading scholars faced the looters and the assassins alone and undefended. The aim of this book is to demonstrate to the world in the most precise and accurate way that conditions created by the occupiers enabled the cultural destruction of Iraq. There were of course other criminals afoot in the mayhem unleashed by the invasion. However, the primary responsibility for this shameful, immoral and illegal chapter in modern history falls on the Bush administration that launched this war of choice to "remake" modern Iraq.

This book results from a collective effort of Iraqi and international specialists to provide a record of what Iraqis and the world have lost. As a group we shared a commitment to record and assess the cultural devastation and the killings of Iraqi scholars and intellectuals. It was that commitment that allowed so diverse a group to work together so smoothly. We are grateful for the exceptional hard work and dedication from our two research assistants: Candice M. Juby worked diligently to bring the chapters into conformity with the publisher's style, and Christopher Langille helped in a multitude of ways to bring the project to completion. We are especially thankful as well to Roger van Zwanenberg, the chairman of Pluto Press, who offered creative suggestions and asked hard and stimulating questions at all stages. Finally, we appreciate the decision of Edel el Moallem of Dar el Shorouk International to publish an Arabic version of our book in cooperation with Pluto Press for distribution in the Arab world.

The Editors
February 7, 2009

PART I

Formulating and Executing the Policy of Cultural Cleansing

1

ENDING THE IRAQI STATE

Raymond W. Baker, Shereen T. Ismael, and Tareq Y. Ismael

Just days after the devastating attacks of September 11, 2001, Deputy Defense Secretary Paul Wolfowitz declared that a major focus of US foreign policy would be "ending states that sponsor terrorism." Iraq was labeled a "terrorist state" and targeted for "ending." President Bush went on to declare Iraq the major front of the global war on terror. American-led forces invaded with the express aim of dismantling the Iraqi state.

Mainstream social science has yet to come to terms with the full meaning of "ending states" as a policy objective. Social science in the era of post-World War II decolonization has focused for the most part on the study of state-building and development. The primary axis of contention among development scholars and policy makers has been between one school espousing state-driven development models and a second advocating neo-liberal market approaches. Little has been written by either school on the question of state-destruction and de-development. Such outcomes have generally been seen as the by-products of war and civil-strife, rather than as desirable policy outcomes. Critical scholarship has challenged the adequacy of such dominant views. Critics draw attention to such phenomena as covert regime subversion, targeted assassinations, death squads, and ethnic cleansing. Such phenomena tend to be dismissed by the mainstream as representing criminal excess rather than explicit state policies. However, the preeminent superpower the United States, and its junior partner Israel, have had a hand in such activities for many decades. This important historical record of such activity tends to be reduced to CIA/Mossad excesses and the product of operating in a "tough neighborhood," plagued by supposed age-old conflicts and religious extremism. In light of Iraq, such dismissals or rationalizations no longer suffice. It is now imperative to recognize that there are precedents for violence aimed at undermining or destroying states, though it is the magnitude of the destruction in Iraq that makes unavoidable the recognition and analysis of state-ending as a deliberate policy objective.

The consequences in human and cultural terms of the destruction of the Iraqi state have been enormous: notably, the deaths of over 1 million civilians;[1] the degradation in social infrastructure, including electricity, potable water, and sewage systems; the targeted assassination of over 400 academics and professionals and the displacement of approximately 4 million refugees and internally displaced people. All of these terrible losses are compounded by unprecedented levels of cultural devastation, attacks on national archives and monuments that represent the historical identity of the Iraqi people. Rampant chaos and violence hamper efforts at reconstruction, leaving the foundations of the Iraqi state in ruin. The majority of Western journalists, academics, and political figures have refused to recognize the loss of life on such a massive scale and the cultural destruction that accompanied it as the fully predictable consequences of American occupation policy. The very idea is considered unthinkable, despite the openness with which this objective was pursued.

It is time to think the unthinkable. The American-led assault on Iraq forces us to consider the meaning and consequences of state-destruction as a policy objective. The architects of the Iraq policy never made explicit what deconstructing and reconstructing the Iraqi state would entail; their actions, however, make the meaning clear. From those actions in Iraq, a fairly precise definition of state-ending can now be read. The campaign to destroy the state in Iraq involved first the removal and execution of Saddam Hussein and the capture of Ba'ath Party figures. However, state destruction went beyond regime change. It also entailed the purposeful dismantling of major state institutions and the launching of a prolonged process of political reshaping.

Contemporary Iraq represents a fragmented pastiche of sectarian forces with the formal trappings of liberal democracy and neo-liberal economic structures. Students of history will recognize in the occupation of Iraq the time-honored technique of imperial *divide et imperia* (divide and rule), used to fracture and subdue culturally cohesive regions. The regime installed by occupation forces in Iraq reshaped the country along divisive sectarian lines, dissolving the hard-won unity of a long state-building project. The so-called sovereign Iraqi government, the Iraqi Governing Council (IGC), established by the Coalition Provisional Authority (CPA), was founded as a sectarian ruling body, with a system of quotas for ethnic and confessional groupings. This formula decisively established the sectarian parameters of the "new Iraq."

In parallel fashion the occupiers have redesigned the nationalistic and state-centered economy to conform to an extreme neo-liberal market model marked by privatization and the opening of the fragile Iraqi market to foreign capital, especially American. Nowhere is this more evident than in the dismantling of Iraq's national industries. The oil sector in particular has been opened to the domination of non-Iraqi, predominantly US companies. Iraq's national industries, the backbone of the country's autonomous national project, have been auctioned off through a wrenching process of privatization, plagued by corruption. Iraq's central bank has been prohibited outright from financing state-owned enterprise. With the collapse of trade tariffs and tax regimes, Iraq's private sector has been overwhelmed by foreign competition.

The political and economic reengineering of Iraq under occupation demands critical evaluation. The Iraq invasion, however, brings into view the equally consequential human and cultural dimensions of state destruction as a war aim. State-ending in Iraq was a comprehensive policy. However, its human and cultural dimensions have yet to be as fully documented and analyzed as an integral part of the destruction of the Iraqi state. The horrors of cultural destruction and targeted assassinations in Iraq are still seen for the most part as a mere consequence of war and social disorder. The mainstream narrative bemoans the loss of world class cultural treasures and views the murders of individuals through the prism of human rights violations as "collateral damage."

Such views obscure more than they reveal. Few would question that state-building has an integral cultural and human dimension. So too, we argue, does state-destruction. To be remade, a state must be rendered malleable. Obstacles to this goal in Iraq included an impressive intelligentsia committed to a different societal model and the unifying culture they shared. The actions of the occupying forces indicate that they understood that the emergence of the new Iraq would require liberation from the grip of the inherited intelligentsia and culture of a unified Iraq. Iraq under occupation would see both human and cultural erasures that advanced these goals. Thus, state destruction in Iraq entailed more than regime change and more than political and economic restructuring. It also required cultural cleansing, understood in the Iraqi case as the degrading of a unifying culture and the depletion of an intelligentsia tied to the old order.[2] The occupiers acted accordingly.

For this cultural and social dimension of state destruction, however, we do not have the same explicit policy directives as for the project of political and economic remaking. Nor was the process itself as straightforward. The cultural cleansing of Iraq was achieved in large part by inaction. The occupiers fostered and legitimated a climate of lawlessness with the wholly predictable consequence of weakening a unifying culture and eliminating an intelligentsia that had staffed Iraq's public institutions. One would be hard pressed to find an explicit admission of such aims from the architects of Iraqi occupation. Yet, the issues cannot be avoided simply in absence of an explicit policy declaration along these lines. The parallel cases of Bosnia, Palestine, and the 2008 Israeli rampage in Gaza make it imperative to put the cultural and human dimensions of ideologically-driven state destruction front and center. Talk of incompetent planning and "collateral damage" in the context of a global war against terrorism persuades many precisely because the very idea of deliberate cultural destruction and targeted murders on so wide a scale is so unthinkable to the mainstream.

Ironically, the unembarrassed ideological context within which Iraq was invaded makes it easier to challenge effectively the mainstream inclination to disregard cultural destruction as willed policy. State-ending in Iraq was explicitly intended to have an instructive effect. The invasion of Iraq had the larger purpose of demonstrating precisely how unchallengeable and unrestrained the shock and awe of American power would be to all those forces that stood in its way. Massive loss of life and cultural devastation were acceptable, if not outright desired. For the demonstration of the power of the sole superpower the deaths and depredations were in many ways the most chilling markers. At the same time, ideological forces that set and defined these objectives of state-ending in Iraq stepped out of the shadows and took center stage. To be sure, the real motives behind the assault were covered by the useful talk of "terror" and liberation. However, it was important for the demonstration effect that the assault itself and the havoc it caused be screened as fully as possible. Consequently, there could be no doubt as to what those forces were, no matter the dissimulations that screened their purposes. The ideologically driven aim of state-ending derived from a confluence of influences that included American neo-conservatism and its imperial ambitions, Israeli expansionism and its drive for regional domination, and Western multinationals and their relentless quest to regain control of Iraqi oil.

The Ideological Imperatives for a "New" Iraq

The cultural and social destruction of Iraq was foreshadowed by a decade of ideological statements and policy planning. And with the controversial Presidential election of George W. Bush in 2000, and the casus belli provided by the 9/11 terrorist attacks, this ideological vision was put in practice, Iraq representing the preeminent test case. The neo-conservative policy pursued an objective to "remake" Iraq in order to demonstrate US global military dominance at its "unipolar moment." The grand objective was the commitment that American global superiority, realized with the collapse of the Soviet Union, would never be surrendered.

America had the unmatched and unprecedented power to assure that its dominance would be made a permanent international reality. The strategically important Middle East would be remade in the American image. To that end, the invasion of Iraq would display America's crushing military power to a world reduced to the status of spectators in a spectacle of a state's destruction, marked by massive civilian casualties, cultural devastation, and the pauperization of its people. In the wake of state-ending, the Americans and their British allies would create a massive regional base in the very heart of the Arab Islamic world to guarantee that Western hegemony in this crucial region would be permanent and unchallengeable. There would of course be permanent military bases. Iraq would be held up as a bastion of the American example and a model for the transformation of the entire area. For its substantial contributions to the effort to subdue and destroy the old Iraq, America's most important regional ally, Israel, would be freed of the one Arab power that had supported the Palestinian resistance in a regional context of ever increasing accommodation and defeatism. Finally, Western corporations, with American companies in the lead, would be in a position to dictate the terms of favorable deals with the Iraqi occupation regime to gain Western control of the nation's oil.

Whatever the ultimate measure of their success or failure, these three ideological forces drove the comprehensive policy of state-ending in Iraq. In any event, all of these ideological motivations proved unrealistic in their maximalist aspirations but not before Iraqis died by the hundreds of thousands, Iraqi intellectuals were singled out in the hundreds for targeted assassination, Iraqi institutions were looted and destroyed, and Iraq's glorious culture, the pride of all Iraqis – and a treasure of world history – was irreparably wounded.

The Neo-Conservative Movement

President George W. Bush was surrounded by a neo-conservative and hyper-nationalist coterie that strove to establish a link between September 11 and Saddam Hussein's regime, whatever the actual facts of the matter. Secretary of Defense Donald Rumsfeld pushed the case for war with Iraq, even suggesting that the US forgo attacks on al-Qaeda and Afghanistan in favor of toppling Saddam Hussein's regime, which presented the US with better targets and the opportunity for a superior demonstration effect.[3]

Leading neo-conservative intellectuals and policy makers had long advanced the objective of eliminating the Iraq regime as the first step of an even more ambitious project of re-visioning the Middle East as a whole. After President George H.W. Bush had spared the Hussein regime following the 1991 Gulf War, Paul Wolfowitz, then the Undersecretary of Defense for Policy, along with similarly staunch-minded neo-conservatives, argued that the US had missed a vital opportunity to enact sweeping change throughout the Middle East. Wolfowitz and Zalmay Khalilzad responded by elaborating a new vision to achieve long-term US dominance in world affairs, starting with securing the Middle East.

This new thinking was articulated in a secret draft document written by Paul Wolfowitz and the later-incarcerated Lewis "Scooter" Libby, drawn up in 1992 and subsequently leaked to the *Washington Post*. The document, which was re-written by then Defense Secretary Dick Cheney and entitled "Defense Planning Guidance" (DPG) argued that the primary objective of US post-Cold War strategy should be preventing the emergence of any rival superpowers by safeguarding American hegemony over vital resources.[4] Iraq, of course, sat on the second largest pool of oil in the region and the Iraqi regime posed what was judged to be a serious challenge as well as a great opportunity for the sole superpower to act. The imperative of American dominance was tied rhetorically to efforts to "increase respect for international law, limit international violence, and encourage the spread of democratic forms of government and open economic systems."[5] In practice, it is not international law but American dominance that is to be preserved, just as the concern for democracy and free markets is always tempered by attention to US interests. US dominance, seen as a "guarantor of international order," was in neo-conservative polemics and policy papers, made a moral imperative, making it possible to associate any challenge to American dominance as a challenge to sacrosanct international values. Among the challengers to the "moral imperative" of US dominance, Iraq figured prominently. Iraq not only supported Palestinian resistance in the occupied territories but also created obstacles to US "access to vital raw materials, primarily Persian Gulf oil" and was also responsible for "[proliferating] weapons of mass destruction and ballistic missiles," and "threat[ening] U.S. citizens [with] terrorism...."[6]

The draft DPG served as the first major post-Cold War manifesto of the neo-conservative bloc that continued to strategize and create think tanks and press outlets to advance the vision of American dominance. Two major initiatives of the neo-conservatives were the reinvigoration of the American Enterprise Institute and the founding of the Project for a New American Century (PNAC), which both included Dick Cheney as an active member. These organizations played an especially influential role in designing a more aggressive posture for America in a post-Cold War world, most notably in the Middle East.

A bold example of this new assertive thinking was seen in a policy paper drafted in 2000 by PNAC entitled *Rebuilding America's Defenses: Strategy, Forces and Resources for a New Century*, endorsed by Paul Wolfowitz, I. Lewis Libby and a cadre of leading neo-conservative intellectuals. It reiterated the major themes of the DPG, citing that document as a major foundation for the updated analysis.[7] The PNAC protocol emphatically reiterated the importance of the Persian Gulf as a region of vital importance, with voluminous references to America's "special interests" in the region.[8] Additionally, the document called for an "enduring" US presence in this region of strategic and commercial interests.[9] In this assessment, the character of the Ba'ath regime in Iraq and its actual domestic and foreign policies were largely irrelevant, though they later figured largely in anti-Iraqi propaganda. What mattered was a pro-US presence in its place. "Indeed, the United States has for decades sought to play a more permanent role in Gulf regional security... the need for a substantial American force presence in the Gulf transcends the issue of the regime of Saddam

Hussein."[10] Shortly before September 11, Donald Rumsfeld had once again articulated this commitment to ending Iraq, arguing that the toppling of the Ba'ath regime and its replacement by a pro-American state, "would change everything in the region and beyond it. It would demonstrate what US policy is all about."[11] Iraq remade by force would be the exemplar of American aspirations for the region.

Given the fixation with US domination in the Persian Gulf, Iraq inevitably became a central component and major target of Bush's foreign policy. An important element of that policy entailed a rethinking of the US relationship with Israel and more aggressive support for Israeli expansionism. America would dominate the world, while Israel would exercise unchallenged hegemony in the Middle East. The moment was right, the neo-conservatives argued, for Israel to consolidate by force its maximalist claims against Palestinian nationalism. Iraq figured in a large way in these calculations as representing the single most powerful restraint on Israel's rightful ambitions, as neo-conservatives understood them. Within this framework, the removal of the Ba'athist state on which Saddam's regime rested was a priority well before the September 11 attacks.

A Clean Break: A New Strategy for Securing the Realm (1996), authored by prominent figures of the US neo-conservative movement and pro-Israel lobby, illustrates quite clearly how consistently Iraq loomed large in neo-conservative thinking about Israel's prospects. This influential position paper identified Iraq as a primary strategic threat to Israel's dominance in the region and the overthrow of Iraq was heralded as an opportunity to alter "the strategic balance in the Middle East profoundly."[12] This neo-conservative call for the destruction of Iraq included the fantasy proposal of restoring "Hashemite" control over Iraq, which was imagined as a lever to pull the country's Shi'ite majority away from Iranian influence. The idea of restoring the pre-revolutionary monarchy had little to no support in Iraq. This ideologically-driven misinformation in a document taken so seriously does help explain why US officials were so credulous when told that Iraq's

Shi'ites would be pro-American and quite prepared to turn away from their Iranian co-religionists.

In the light of the well-documented and longstanding emphasis on toppling Iraq by key figures in the Bush administration, there is little doubt that the September 11 attacks were seized upon as the enabling moment to enact a wide-ranging program in the Persian Gulf region. The imperative to invade Iraq and remodel the Middle East were parts of a larger strategic goal that considered a long-term presence in Iraq to be necessary for the extension of "US values" throughout the rest of the region. A reengineered Iraq would play a critical role as a staging ground to alter the behavior of recalcitrant states across the region. The consistent, underlying objective was the building of an unchallengeable American global hegemony, Israeli regional dominance as an extension of American power, and the assertion of unquestioned control over the enormous energy resources of the Persian Gulf. All of these objectives would contribute to the larger strategic task of blocking the ascent of any other would-be superpower.

Theory to Practice: The Modalities of State-Ending in Iraq

The policy of ending states, announced by Wolfowitz, was enacted with a vengeance in Iraq. Under occupation, Iraq has been stripped of its historical national project of state-building and turned into a shell state with little to no control over its national affairs. The modalities of this state-ending policy deserve close attention for what they reveal about the larger question of American–Israeli regional and global ambition and the engineering of chaos and violence to achieve those objectives. As we have seen, part of the difficulty in coming to terms with the dismantling of the Iraqi state has been a mainstream failure to acknowledge that the violence of state destruction in Iraq was deliberate. In fact, such purposive violence of terrible proportions has antecedents in the chronicles of US and Israeli foreign policy. The levels of violence and the forms that violence took are foreshadowed by the US record in confronting challenges to US dominance in the Americas. In parallel fashion, the Israeli pattern of unrestrained, deliberate violence against the occupied Palestinians regularly targeted both state and civil society institutions that expressed in pacific ways the Palestinian aspiration for statehood. Israel openly defended the necessity of not only torture but of kidnapping and targeted assassination to contain the threat of Palestinian nationalism.

It is important to bring just enough of this history into view to facilitate coming to terms with the appalling levels of violence suffered in post-invasion Iraq. American-trained and -supported death squads wrought havoc in Latin and Central America, matched by the fairly routine Israeli targeted assassinations of Palestinian resistance leaders. The Israeli use of the overwhelming force of one of the world's most advanced military machines against Gaza and its captive and essentially defenseless civilian population in 2008 makes it clear that whatever we can learn of state destruction in Iraq will have continuing relevance.[13] Such understanding, based on careful review of the consequences of state destruction in Iraq, can also assist in breaking through the obscurantist spell cast by the war on terror. The means and methods of state destruction were already part of the arsenal of the dominant superpower's arsenal as well as that of its regional junior partner, though the war on terror rationalized their use with great effectiveness.

Death Squads as Foreign Policy Tool

For the theorists of state-ending, there is a long and ignoble history on which they can draw of counterinsurgency efforts based on roving "death squads" to suppress indigenous resistance.[14] The apex of this policy was in the anti-Communist campaigns in 1980s Central America, whose emblem was the Nicaraguan "Contra" forces. Following the Boland Amendment of 1982 and its extension in 1984, formal US funding for the Contra forces was discontinued. This curtailment in the end led to surreptitious and unofficial forms of funding. Best known is the infamous Iran–Contra affair, where arms-for-hostage revenues were diverted to fund the Contras. Less discussed was the development of ties between the Contra army and South American drug traffickers as means of financial support. Suspicions of CIA participation in the Contra–cocaine nexus have been variously investigated, suggesting a shadowy and hard to document network.[15] At minimum, however, the Kerry Commission (Senate Committee Report on Drugs, Law Enforcement and Foreign Policy chaired by Senator John F. Kerry) revealed that the US State Department had paid $806,000 to known drug fronts in order to provide assistance to the Nicaraguan Contras. Allegations of direct CIA participation in drug dealings are frequent, though they were officially denied by the CIA in a 1997 internal investigation.

Death-squad activity is inherently murky and therefore it will come as no surprise that the rise of death squads in Iraq is shrouded in secrecy. However, available reportage does provide some illumination into this affair. Organized violence in Iraq falls into three broad categories. The first is the general criminality and gangsterism that exploded following the 2003 invasion. The second comprises various forms of anti-occupation violence and originates from the constellation of groups that target occupation forces and the official Iraqi security forces. The third form, with the clearest relevance to death squads, is the violence of organized paramilitary groups involved in sectarian killings and conflict with the resistance. Frequent claims tie such violence to the Iraqi Interior Ministry, though the evidence is never conclusive. In a similar way, the Kurkish *peshmerga* forces, particularly those alleged to have been trained by Israel, are widely believed to be involved in the targeting of elements of the Shi'i "insurgency." Circumstantial evidence points to death-squad activities, though their violent actions reflect the unique Kurdish circumstance and aspirations.

A direct and clear connection can be established between high American officials involved in "counterinsurgency" projects of Central America and those involved in contemporary Iraq. The most prominent of these figures is James Steele, who in the 1980s "honed his tactics leading a Special Forces mission in El Salvador during the country's brutal civil war." That bloody conflict resulted in 70,000 deaths. A UN truth commission found that as many as

85 percent of those deaths were attributable to US-backed forces.[16] Steele reemerged in occupied Iraq as an advisor to the Iraqi Interior Ministry, the Iraqi institution most associated with death-squad activity. He also played an advisory role to the Iraqi counterinsurgency force, the Special Police Commandos. The Commandos were formed by Falah al-Naqib, interior minister under the interim government of Ayad Allawi. The Commando forces were drawn from "veterans of [Saddam] Hussein's special forces and the Republican Guard."[17] By 2006 the paramilitary forces of the Interior Ministry were widely believed to be heavily involved in death-squad activity. The Badr Organization, the armed wing of the Supreme Council of Islamic Revolution in Iraq, played a lead role.[18] In July 2005 the "Wolf Brigade," a subset of the Interior Ministry Commandos, was implicated in a series of sectarian killings and, in November 2005, US soldiers stumbled upon a "torture chamber" of 170 "half starved and...seriously beaten" prisoners, again operated by the Interior Ministry. In any case, General Petraeus in 2005 "decided the commandos would receive whatever arms, ammunition and supplies they required."[19]

The cooption of indigenous forces into the occupation forces extended with the Petraeus-led "military surge" of 2007 onward, where the so-called "Awakening Councils" of *al-Anbar*, a network of Sunni-based tribes, were armed by the US occupation authorities. They formed a force numbering over 80,000 "Iraqi Security Volunteers" (ISVs). In the estimation of Chas Freeman, former ambassador to Saudi Arabia, the policy of "surge" served to

> essentially support a quasi-feudal devolution of authority to armed enclaves, which exist at the expense of central government authority... Those we are arming and training are arming and training themselves not to facilitate our objectives but to pursue their own objectives vis-à-vis other Iraqis. It means that the sectarian and ethnic conflicts that are now suppressed are likely to burst out with even greater ferocity in the future.[20]

In this way, a policy ostensibly designed to curb sectarian violence provided grounds for the escalation of future sectarianism. Indeed, according to research conducted by the University of California, the "surge" owes much of its putative success to ethnic violence.

The "cleansing" of Iraq's formerly mixed neighborhoods reduced available targets and thus the death tolls fell. This measure of success is dubious, to say the least. "If the surge had truly 'worked' we would expect to see a steady increase in night-light output over time," says Thomas Gillespie, one of the study co-authors, in a press release. "Instead, we found that the night-light signature diminished in only certain neighborhoods, and the pattern appears to be associated with ethno-sectarian violence and neighborhood ethnic cleansing."[21]

The Israeli Example: State Destruction in Palestine

Israel has a long record of attacking Palestinian government and civil society institutions to prevent the emergence of the infrastructure for a viable Palestinian state and civil society. The modalities of this Israeli pattern were recently put on more public display than has usually been the case. In late 2008, the Israelis launched an intensive ground-and-air offensive against Palestinian society, nominally to end the primitive rocket-attacks from Gaza, but in reality to undermine Hamas as an operational entity and bolster the compliant Fatah movement. In the end, over 1,300 Palestinians were killed, civilians representing at least a third, versus 13 Israeli fatalities. Physical damage was initially estimated at over $2 billion.[22] Moreover, Palestinian unity – already fragile – was further undermined in light of a widespread belief in Fatah collaboration in the Israeli assault. Accusations of this sort, and the round of anti-Fatah recriminations that followed the Israeli assault, undoubtedly are partly Hamas propaganda. However, they do contain more than a kernel of truth.

Hamas today faces attacks on two fronts, from IDF/IAF assaults as well as US-backed Fatah forces. A 2008 investigation revealed that the US had funded and backed an armed force under Fatah strongman Mohammad Dahlan. Beginning in late 2006, the US State Department solicited its Arab allies to bolster Fatah by providing military training and armaments. In conjunction with this fundraising, the US drafted a document titled "An Action Plan for the Palestinian Presidency," otherwise known as "Plan B," calling for

> ...Abbas to "collapse the government" if HAMAS refused to alter its attitude towards Israel... Security concerns were paramount... it was essential for Abbas to maintain "independent control of the security forces"... [The Plan] called for increasing the "level and capacity of 15,000 of Fatah's existing security personnel" while adding 4,700 troops in seven new highly trained battalions....[23]

Ultimately, the particulars of this plot became public knowledge and contributed to the outbreak of a civil war between Hamas and Fatah forces, to the great detriment of the Palestinian people and the project of Palestinian national unity.

The methods of the United States in Iraq and the methods of Israel in the Palestinian territories represent similar modalities of "counterinsurgency": overwhelming violence against civilian populations – keeping them in a state of sociopolitical catatonia; the suppression of all forms of resistance – military, political, or social; and a policy of divide-and-rule, which is to say the cooption of compliant groups in order to sow division and undermine national unity. In the case of Iraq, Shi'i-dominated "death squads" appeared to operate with impunity out of the Iraqi Interior Ministry, and thereafter, the United States directly coopted the former resistance of the *Anbar* province, creating a heavily armed force that counterbalanced the Shi'i armed-parties. These conflicting policies did create a temporary state of equilibrium between warring Shi'i and Sunni armed groupings. However, they also helped create the conditions of future civil war. Israel likewise has vacillated in its cooption of Palestinian groups, first the Islamic movements during the 1980s, and later the corrupt Fatah in order to undermine Hamas. The end result in both cases is engineered fracturing of national unity.

The Question of Oil

The thinking behind the invasion of Iraq did not neglect oil, no matter how often the denials of its role as a motivating consideration. In simple and direct terms, General John Abizaid, the former chief of US Central Command, terminated official pretense that oil was not a factor in the invasion of Iraq. "Of course it's about oil," he said bluntly, "we can't really deny that...."[24] Despite the calculated mists that clouded public discussion of the oil factor, there was already a public record of such acknowledgements of the centrality of oil. In 1999 Dick Cheney, then acting CEO of Halliburton, gave a speech at the Institute of Petroleum highlighting his vision of the critical role of oil in general and Middle Eastern oil in particular. He said:

> ...by 2010 we will need on the order of an additional fifty million barrels a day. So where is the oil going to come from? Governments and the national oil companies are obviously controlling about ninety per cent of the assets. Oil remains fundamentally a government business. While many regions of the world offer great oil opportunities, the Middle East with two thirds of the world's oil and the lowest cost, is still where the prize ultimately lies, even though companies are anxious for greater access there, progress continues to be slow.[25]

Consistent with the neo-conservative vision, Cheney as Vice President advanced the argument that control of Iraqi oil was key to dominance over the incomparable oil reserves of the entire Middle East. Cheney created the National Energy Policy Development Group on January 29, 2001. The group, commonly known as the "Cheney Energy Task Force" included many of the Chief Executive Officers of the major energy corporations. It produced a National Energy Policy report in May of its first year of activity. In its recommendations, the group urged the US administration to take the initiative in pressing the governments of the Middle Eastern countries to open their economies for foreign investments.

Earlier, in 1993, six giant oil companies, Royal Dutch Shell, British Petroleum, Conoco Phillips, Exxon Mobil, Halliburton and Chevron, sponsored the International Tax and Investment Center (ITIC) which eventually included 110 corporations. Documents obtained through the Freedom of Information Act reveal that in late 1990s Anglo-American representations were made on behalf of oil companies to secure Iraqi oil contracts. ITIC was advised to write a report emphasizing Production Sharing Agreements (PSA) to ensure the success of long-term control over oil. By April 2002 the State Department had already organized 17 working groups, made up of over 200 Iraqi engineers, lawyers, businesspeople, doctors and other non-Iraqi experts, to strategize on post-Saddam Iraq. This initiative came to be known as the Future of Iraq Project. The group on "Oil and Energy" envisioned a de-monopolized Iraqi National Oil Company, where private investors in upstream oil production would have a free hand, calling for "...production sharing agreements (PSA) structured to facilitate participation in Iraq's upstream oil industry of the best international oil and gas companies."[26] On May 12, 2003, Gal Luft, co-director of the Institute for the Analysis of Global Security, in an article entitled "How Much Oil Does Iraq Have?" wrote:

> Over the past several months, news organizations and experts have regularly cited Department of Energy (DOE) Energy Information Administration (EIA) figures claiming that the territory of Iraq contains over 112 billion barrels (bbl) of proven reserves – oil that has been definitively discovered and is expected to be economically producible. In addition, since Iraq is the least explored of the oil-rich countries, there have been numerous claims of huge undiscovered reserves there as well – oil thought to exist, and expected to become economically recoverable – to the tune of hundreds of billions of barrels. The respected Petroleum Economist Magazine estimates that there may be as many as 200 bbl of oil in Iraq; the Federation of American Scientists estimates 215 bbl; a study by the Council on Foreign Relations and the James A. Baker III Institute at Rice University claimed that Iraq has 220 bbl of undiscovered oil; and another study by the Center for Global Energy Studies and Petrolog & Associates offered an even more optimistic estimate of 300 bbl.[27]

In December 2002, *Oil and Gas Journal* published a study to the effect that "Western oil companies estimate that they can produce a barrel of Iraqi oil for less than $US 1.50 and possibly as little as $US 1, including all exploration, oilfield development and production costs and including a 15% return. This production cost is similar to Saudi Arabia and lower than virtually any other country." Iraqi oil, henceforth, was envisioned as the petrochemical prize of the Persian Gulf, particularly if de-nationalized and in the hands of American or American-friendly multinational entities.

Under occupation, the oil factor imposed itself in an entirely predictable fashion. Iraq's oil industry, which had been the fulcrum of its national development, was slated for repossession by the forces of corporate capitalism. The US attempted to bully through a comprehensive oil law. If passed that law would have granted Western oil conglomerates 25–30 year contracts, awarded on a non-competitive basis, over the production of oil. By such arrangements, the bulk of revenues would return to the corporate giants rather than the Iraqi nation, on the model of the "glory days" of British domination over the oil-producing Gulf region. Iraq's national oil industry, which for decades had served as a unifying source of pride and the lever of Iraq's socioeconomic development, risked falling into the hands of occupying forces. The bulk of Iraqi society stands opposed to any such outcomes. The Iraq Federation of Oil Unions, which represents over half of the industry workers in southern Iraq, consistently opposed the law. The Federation saw it as an imperial grab by multinational corporations that would mean the surrendering of Iraq's national sovereignty. In spite of this opposition, even from the pro-US parliamentarians who nominally govern the country, the push for a multinational oil grab continued.

A first round in the contest ended in June 2008 when the *New York Times* on June 19 reported that "deals with Iraq are set to bring the oil giants back." In its subtitle the *NYT* summed up the outcome of the negotiations by commenting on "Rare No-bid Contracts, A Foothold for Western Companies Seeking Future Rewards." It is worth noting that the four companies involved, were precisely those that lost their concessions in 1972. The agreements fell short of the production sharing arrangements that the four oil giants – Exxon Mobil, Royal Dutch Shell, the French company Total, and BP, formerly British Petroleum – initially sought. The companies did not get quite the level of control they sought, although the agreements did provide a foot in the door and an opportunity to reap huge profits from the rise in oil prices. Iraq, indeed, has been remade economically with the transformation of the oil industry, though not completely and not without significant resistance.

The Israeli Role in Iraq

The Israeli role vis-à-vis Iraq has deep and complex roots that go beyond the demonstration effect of its own role in the occupied Palestinian territories, considered earlier. It requires more detailed consideration here as one of the three major drivers behind the invasion. Since the consolidation of the Israeli state, though particularly following Israel's victory in the 1967 war, the United States has relied upon the state of Israel as its junior partner *contra* Arab nationalist movements. Israel, to be sure, was not the only regional power to play this role. Saudi Arabia was the crucial Arab ally in sponsoring reactionary Islamic movements to oppose both assertive Arab nationalist regimes and their Soviet allies.

Within occupied Palestine, Israel also looked in the Islamic direction for allies against the secular nationalism represented by the PLO. According to Zeev Sternell, historian at the Hebrew University of Jerusalem, Israel's tilt to the Islamists included authorizing Islamic forces "to receive money payments from abroad."[28] The policy worked in the short run and secular-nationalist forces in Palestine were indeed weakened by the rise of Islamic movements. However, the success had its costs. Nurtured by Israel, the Islamic embryo later emerged as Hamas, Israel's contemporary nemesis.

Beyond the sponsorship of Islamic and traditionalist forces to counter Arab nationalism, regional American–Israeli strategy has aimed, when opportunities arise, for the marginalization or even cooption of nationalist regimes. Under American auspices, Egypt signed the Camp David Accords in 1978, leading to an Egyptian–Israeli peace treaty and normal diplomatic relations.[29] Egypt, having broken the regional taboo against accommodation with Israel, sacrificed its pretensions of regional leadership in confronting the assertive Zionist state. Iraq attempted to pick up that mantle with overt support for the Palestinian resistance. As a result Iraq, previously a tangential participant in Arab–Israel wars, saw itself attacked by Israel in 1981 when the Osirak nuclear facilities were bombed. That attack had as much to do with undercutting Iraq's pro-Palestinian stance as with any nuclear threat to Israel. Both were viewed as challenges to unquestioned Israeli regional hegemony. As a matter of doctrine, Israel asserts a unilateral right to nuclear weaponry within the region, a posture that today teases possible strikes against Iran.

As with Egypt, there have been Israeli attempts to co-opt Iraq with the hope of converting it from a rejectionist to accommodationist regime. In 1984, Donald Rumsfeld presented Iraqi Foreign Minister Tariq Aziz with a proposal from Yitzhak Shamir to reopen the trans-Arabian oil pipeline, according to Nigel Ashton in *Hussein: A Political Life*. Ashton tells us that when the offer was presented by Rumsfeld, "Aziz turned pale and begged Rumsfeld to take back his message."[30] An apparent follow-up was attempted in 1995, where Israel sought improved relations with Iraq as part of an attempt to marginalize Assad's Syria and the growing Iranian presence. This secret diplomacy, undertaken through King Hussein's Jordan, apparently saw Saddam "not rul[ing] out direct contacts with [Prime Minister] Rabin." In any event, this secret diplomacy ended with the deterioration of Israeli–Jordanian relations.[31]

Israel in Occupied Iraq

The US has found it politically necessary to disavow any level of Israeli–US cooperation in the invasion and occupation of Iraq, making the unlikely claim that Israel took no position on the matter of invading Iraq.[32] Investigative journalism suggests an entirely different and far more plausible picture. In fact, given Israel's deep resentment of Iraq as the erstwhile champion of Arab nationalism and the Palestinian cause, Israel clearly had a stake in weakening or eliminating the Iraqi state. It is no surprise to learn, therefore, that the Office of Special Plans, an unofficial intelligence cadre answerable to Vice President Dick Cheney, "forged close ties to a parallel, *ad hoc*, intelligence operation inside Ariel Sharon's office in Israel. This channel aimed specifically to bypass the Mossad and provide the Bush administration with more alarmist reports of Saddam's Iraq than the Mossad was prepared to authorize."[33]

As Iraq was in the thrall of occupation and domination by Anglo-American forces, available reports suggest anything but Israeli passivity. In late 2003 Seymour Hersh wrote:

> Israeli commandos and intelligence units have been working closely with their American counterparts at the Special Forces training base at Fort Bragg, North Carolina, and in Israel to help them prepare for operations in Iraq. Israeli commandos are expected to serve as ad-hoc advisers – again, in secret – when full-field operations begin.[34]

Israel took an even more direct role in Iraq in 2003, providing materiel support and training for Kurdish *peshmerga* forces in order first to "penetrate, gather intelligence on, and then kill off the leadership of the Shiite and Sunni insurgencies in Iraq," and finally to aid in Israeli efforts "to install sensors and other sensitive devices that primarily target suspected Iranian nuclear facilities."[35] In the context of intensified sectarian conflict and Arab–Kurdish wrangling over the fate of oil-rich Kirkuk, such actions had a highly incendiary effect.

Israeli involvement in Iraqi national affairs extends to political and diplomatic affairs. Israel has always drawn attention to the ethno-religious diversity of Iraq and has consistently sought to exploit those differences Again, the Kurdish connection stands out. Relations between the Zionist movement and the Kurds predate the founding of Israel. As early as the 1930s Ruvin Shiloh, a delegate of the Jewish national agency met with members of the Barzani clan as part of efforts to forge relations with the various Kurdish factions within Iraq. Israel has maintained sporadic ties to the Kurdish factions ever since, with the notable exception of the PKK, given their leftism and vigorous support for the Palestinian cause. These relations allegedly extended as far as Mossad participation in the creation of the *Paristan* – the Kurdish Intelligence Agency – working with Massoud al-Barzani, head of the organization, who underwent a concentrated training program in Kurdistan and Israel. According to Obaidullah al-Barzani, son of Mulla Barzani, Israelis were permanently accompanying my father, were always calling Israel by a wireless device and performed espionage acts in Iraq.[36]

In 1980 Israel's Prime Minister Menachem Begin acknowledged that his country had been providing the Kurds with military and humanitarian aid for years.[37]

Israel today continues to make overtures to the Kurds, even though at present diplomatic contacts between Israel and Iraq are limited. During an official visit to Kuwait in 2006 Massoud commented pointedly that, in principle, "it is not a crime to have relations with Israel." Noting that such important Arab countries as Egypt and Jordan already had such relations, Massoud announced that "should Baghdad establish diplomatic relations with Israel, we could open a consulate in Irbil."[38] Massoud was clearly signaling interest in open accommodation of the Israeli regime with the inevitable consequence of compromise on support for Palestinian nationalism.

Similar possibilities were suggested on July 1, 2008, with a brief meeting and public handshake between Jalal Talabani, head of the Patriotic Union of Kurdistan (PUK) and President of Iraq, and then Israeli Defense Minister Ehud Barak. The meeting occurred during the 23rd congress of the Socialist International (of which Israel's Labour Party and the PUK are members).[39]

America in Iraq and Israel in the occupied territories share the goal of undermining and de-legitimating national-minded resistance movements and independent-minded regimes. At the same time, they aim to bolster the power of regional clients to the frequent detriment of the societies they claim to represent. These objectives fit into a larger pattern of interests shaped by the American vision of global dominance, the Israeli goals of a greater Israel, and the aspirations of the multinational oil companies to regain more effective control of Middle East oil. The coming together of these powerful ideological forces produced the invasion of Iraq with its objective of state-ending and with all the disastrous consequences that have followed from it, most of all for Iraqis.

The Contours of Cultural Destruction

With an understanding of the ideologically-driven goal of dismantling the Iraqi state, we can now turn to an overview of the cultural and human costs of the policy as they are reflected in the facts on the ground. The magnitude of the destruction and its systematic character cannot possibly be explained as a series of unforeseen, unrelated, and/or tragic mishaps. In our collective view, the killings and destruction flowed from the inherently violent policy objective of remaking rather than reforming Iraq. To make this case, the devil is in the details, and those details are provided in the case study chapters that follow. Readers will find in these chapters a pattern of available, protective actions not taken. Even more striking in the record are the documented cases where the occupiers themselves fostered, facilitated, or directly engaged in the calculated destruction of Iraq's culture and the degrading of the intelligentsia who embodied it. In all cases readers will note the failure to judge these crimes worthy of serious investigation. This calculated neglect has left crimes against culture unreported, the dead unnamed, and all the crimes of cultural cleansing uninvestigated. In short, we believe that a close look at the evidence makes the case that state-ending in Iraq did entail willful cultural cleansing. The counter arguments of accidents of chance or poor planning must be examined and laid to rest. They simply do not make reasonable sense of the facts on the ground as those facts are recorded and evaluated in the chapters that follow.

According to Lebanese archaeologist, Joanne Farchakh, who assisted in the investigation of the stolen historical wealth from Iraq after the invasion, "Iraq may soon end up with no history."[40] With the protective shield of the state and the educated elite removed, Iraq's incomparable cultural riches were an easy target. The military onslaught of US-led forces against the Iraqi state and society already weakened by twelve years of economic sanctions coincided with a multi-dimensional pattern of cultural cleansing.

Such cleansing began in the very early days of the invasion, with the wide-scale looting of all of the symbols of Iraqi historical and cultural identity. Museums, archaeological sites, palaces, monuments, mosques, libraries and social centers all suffered looting and devastation. They did so under the very watchful eyes of the occupation troops. American forces in Baghdad guarded only, and very carefully, the Iraqi Oil Ministry, which securely kept all oil data, as well as the Ministry of the Interior, where the potentially compromising files of Saddam's security apparatus were housed.

On America's watch we now know that thousands of cultural artifacts disappeared during "Operation Iraqi Freedom." These objects included, no less than 15,000 invaluable Mesopotamian artifacts from the National Museum in Baghdad, and many others from the 12,000 archaeological sites that the occupation forces, unlike even Saddam's despotic regime, left unguarded.[41] While the Museum was robbed of its historical collection, the National Library that preserved the continuity and pride of Iraqi history was destroyed by deliberate arson. As Nabil al-Takriti points out in Chapter 5, Iraqi and international cultural specialists knew the exact location of the most important cultural sites and so informed the occupiers. However, once the looting began, occupation authorities took no effective measures to protect them.

Some 4,000 historical artifacts have been recovered, at times in inventive ways as when some Shi'ite clerics exhorted women "not to sleep with their husbands if looted objects were not returned."[42] However, many treasures were smuggled out of Iraq and auctioned abroad. These thefts often occurred with the help of foreigners who arrived with the occupation forces, like journalist and Middle East expert, Joseph Braude,[43] who was arrested at New York JFK International Airport with ancient Mesopotamian antiquities. Braude was sentenced to six months of house arrest and two years of probation. Priceless artifacts may have also been auctioned off on the Internet as forewarned by professor of anthropology at Arizona State University, Michael E. Smith.[44] On December 18, 2007, the BBC reported that a German archaeologist spotted stolen Iraqi antiquities on a Swiss eBay site.

These priceless antiquities were auctioned at a starting bid of $US 360.[45] According to a recent update on the number of stolen artifacts by an expert archaeologist on Iraq, Francis Deblauwe, it appears that no less than 8,500 objects are still truly missing, in addition to 4,000 artifacts said to be recovered abroad but not yet returned to Iraq.[46]

During the Iran–Iraq war that raged for eight years neither side deliberately targeted the archaeological sites or the cultural resources of the other. There is no comparison between the impact of that war on Iraq's cultural treasures and the subsequent American-led invasion and the terrible destruction that followed. Consistent American failure to protect the Iraq's cultural treasures directly contravened the Geneva Convention stipulation that an occupation army should use all means within its power to guard the cultural heritage of the defeated state.[47] As a result, "legions of antiquities looters" emerged, and established mass-smuggling networks of armed cars, trucks, planes and boats to ship Iraq's plundered historical patrimony to the US, Europe and the Gulf region.[48]

The attitude of the US-led forces to this pillage was, at best, indifference. In 2003 Defense Secretary Donald Rumsfeld sneered at reports of widespread looting, glibly commenting that "stuff happens" during war while dismissing the looting as the understandable targeting of the hated symbols of the ousted regime.[49] Answering journalists' questions about the destructive chaos with disdain, Rumsfeld responded that

> very often the pictures are pictures of people going into the symbols of the regime, into the palaces, into the boats and into the Baath Party headquarters and into the places that have been part of that repression.... And while no one condones looting, on the other hand one can understand the pent-up feelings that may result from decades of repression and people who've had members of their family killed by that regime, for them to be taking their feelings out on that regime.[50]

Representing the looting, arson and destruction of Iraq's heritage as "understandable" and almost "natural" and unavoidable under the "circumstances," as Rumsfeld does, contradicts the fact that

> For several months before the start of the Iraq war, scholars of the ancient history of Iraq repeatedly spoke to various arms of the US government about this risk. Individual archeologists as well as representatives of the Archaeological Institute of America met with members of the State Department, the Defense Department and the Pentagon. We provided comprehensive lists of archeological sites and museums throughout Iraq, including their map coordinates. We put up a website providing this same information. All of us said the top priority was the immediate placement of security guards at all museums and archeological sites. US government officials claimed that they were gravely concerned about the protection of cultural heritage, yet they chose not to follow our advice... and the US troops abused [archeological] sites themselves.[51]

In 2006 the American-sponsored Iraqi government, despite reports of a budget surplus in 2006 and a problem with unspent funds, cut the budget of the Antiquities Department. Its small task force was deprived of the necessary funds to pay for patrol-car fuel. This cut meant, for example, that the Antiquities Task Force sat in its offices attempting to fight looting that was taking place dozens of miles away at 800 archaeological sites in the province of Dhi Qar.[52] When outraged Iraqis, desperate to prod the Americans to action, told US forces that the Saddam regime had made looting of the heritage a capital offense, the occupation force declared irrelevantly that "we weren't going to fly helicopters over the sites and start shooting people."[53] The demand was not that the Americans adopt Saddam's methods but rather that they assume responsibility as international law required for protecting Iraq's incomparable treasures. Consistently, such exhortations fell on deaf ears.

In the summer of 2004 world outrage over the pillaging of Iraq's cultural treasures seriously affected the international image of the Bush administration. At that point, USAID finally arranged a program, headed by Professor Elizabeth Stone, from Stony Brook University, to furnish Iraqi graduate students in archaeological studies with state of the art equipment. The aim was also to train

Iraqi specialists in the most recent methods of the field from which they had been isolated when for the last two decades Iraq under Saddam was cut off from the rest of the world by the Anglo-American imposed sanctions. Several Iraqi students went to study in the US. However, one year later, the program was suddenly stopped.[54] While the US could afford to spend $US 1 billion per day on its military machine in Iraq, the administration declined to spare few millions to enhance the training of Iraqi archaeological students and teachers who could help repair the Iraqi cultural patrimony.

The failure of the US to carry out its responsibilities under international law to take positive and protective actions was compounded by egregious direct actions taken that severely damaged the Iraqi cultural heritage. Since the invasion in March 2003, the US-led forces have transformed at least seven historical sites into bases or camps for the military. These desecrated sites include Ur, one of the most ancient cities in the world, which is said to be the birthplace of Abraham, father of the three great monotheistic religions (Judaism, Christianity, and Islam). The brickwork of the Temple Ziggurat at the site of Ur, which Iraqis have preserved and maintained with national pride, are being damaged under the weight of American military equipment and the callous treatment of military forces. When Abbas al-Hussaini, then head of the Iraqi Board of Antiquities and Heritage and the author of Chapter 4 in this book, attempted to inspect the site of Ur in early 2007, the US military refused him access. Such has also been the fate of Babylon where a US military camp has irreparably damaged the ancient city. Such ancient sites are not Sunni, Shi'ite, Yazidi, or Christian, nor are they Turkoman, Kurdish or Arab – these historical sities are the Mesopotamian historical patrimony of all Iraqis.[55]

Such massive cultural destruction has a devastating impact on two distinct levels. The first pertains to all humanity because of Iraq's unique provenance of artifacts and monuments that record in a well documented, material way an unmatched sense of the continuity of human civilizations in this unique site. The second level is crucial to the Iraqi people and their distinctive historical identity, shaped by the way they understand their own history. Memory in all its forms, personal, cognitive, and social, provides the imaginative infrastructure of identity, whether of the individual or group, national or sub-national.[56] Memory evokes emotionally charged images as well as desires, which link one's past to the future through the present interpreted in light of recollection. However, memory is mortal in two senses: first it dies with the body; second, it changes through forgetfulness. Hence, memory, particularly people's or social memory, needs to be preserved actively to supply the continuity of social meaning from the past to the future. The preservation of memory is the function of museums and historical monuments. Museums are the storehouses of historical relics that nurture social memories, that is to say the imaginative recollection of past events. Monuments are the eyewitnesses to historical events. In all these ways, the Baghdad Museum was memory-objectified, not only of the Mesopotamian cradle of civilization but also for the Iraqi people. By selecting what to keep, display, and remember, the Baghdad Museum enacted the permanence and continuity of a culture and a nation since time immemorial, to which archaeological sites and monuments bear witness. The objects and artifacts were staged to trigger "memories in, and for multiple, diverse collectives," and "the memories become components of identity."[57] Without a framework of collective memory, there is no mode of articulation for individual memory. Individual memory requires the context of group identity which is inseparable from the history and cultural artifacts[58] that the Baghdad Museum, the Central Library in Baghdad and the monument sites once preserved. However questions of intent on the part of the occupiers are eventually resolved, the actual consequences of policies pursued in post-invasion Iraq, as Nabil al-Takriti argues in Chapter 5, can fairly be characterized as the destruction of cultural memory.

This desecration of the past and undermining of contemporary social gains is now giving way in occupied Iraq to the destruction of a meaningful future. Iraq is being handed over to the disintegrative forces of sectarianism and regionalism. Iraqis, stripped of their shared heritage and living today in the ruins of contemporary social institutions that sustained a coherent and unified society, are now bombarded by the forces of civil war, social and religious atavism, and widespread criminality. Iraqi nationalism that had emerged through a prolonged process of state-building and social interaction is now routinely disparaged. Dominant narratives now falsely claim that sectarianism and ethnic chauvinism have always been the basis of Iraqi society, recycling yet again the persistent and destructive myth of age-old conflicts with no resolution and for which the conquerors bear no responsibility.

Destruction of Social Institutions

Concomitant with the ruination of so many of Iraq's historical treasures has been the rampant destruction of Iraq's social and cultural institutions. Iraq's education system, once vaunted as the most advanced in the region, has suffered a patterned process of degradation and dismantling. Under the occupation, according to a report by the United Nations University (UNU) International Leadership Institute in Jordan:

> The devastation of the Iraqi system of higher education has been overlooked amid other cataclysmic war results but represents an important consequence of the conflicts, economic sanctions, and ongoing turmoil in Iraq.... The Iraqi Academy of Sciences, founded in 1948 to promote the Arabic language and heritage, saw its digital and traditional library partially looted during the war and it alone needs almost one million dollars in infrastructure repairs to re-establish itself as a leading research centre.[59]

According to Jairam Reddy, director of the UNU, "some 84 percent of Iraq's institutions of higher education have been burnt, looted, or destroyed. Some 2,000 laboratories need to be re-equipped and 30,000 computers need to be procured and installed nationwide."[60]

Immediately after the occupation of Iraq, the American authorities also imposed a new curriculum that removed any criticism of the US policy in the Middle East, as well as any reference to either the 1991 war or to Israeli policy in the occupied territories. An estimated $US 62 billion was awarded to Creative

Associates Int. and $US 1.8 billion to Bechtel by USAID in April 2003 to re-build Iraq's infrastructure, including schools and higher education institutions. However, these efforts have been plagued by shoddy construction, signaled by the frequent flooding of schools with sewage, by inadequate infrastructure, and the failure to replace outdated equipment and teaching materials. The rapidly deteriorating conditions and a complete failure to establish a functioning education system has produced a spiraling dropout rate of almost 50 percent.[61] Iraqi academic institutions, once leaders among universities and research centers in the rest of the Arab world, were instrumental in creating a strong Iraqi national identity after years of foreign colonization. The virtual collapse of Iraq's educational infrastructure has gutted the vehicle that had served to cement a unifying history in the public mind.

Massive out-migration in the wake of the foreign invasion has undermined national coherence in even more direct and devastating ways. Between January and October 2007, the war in Iraq has displaced nearly 1 million Iraqis to Syria, in addition to the nearly 450,000 that had fled Iraq in 2006. The refugees come disproportionally from the educated middle class, who embodied this hard-won sense of national coherence. The literacy of refugee children is falling precipitously, which bodes ill for the next generation. Iraqi young women and girls are being forced by the destitution of their families into survival sex and organized prostitution.[62]

From the outset, something more ominous than displacement by the chaos of war was at work in Iraq. The mind of a unified nation is being killed in what Max Fuller and Dirk Adriaesens conclude in Chapter 7 has all the earmarks of a systematic campaign of targeted assassinations. While their work focuses on academics, they emphasize that the decimation of professorial ranks took place in the context of a generalized assault on Iraq's professional middle class, including doctors, lawyers, judges as well as political and religious leaders. The killings of over 400 university professors took place at the hands of professional and able killers as the means and timing of the murders makes clear. By 2006, they report, some 2,500 faculty members had been killed, kidnapped, or intimidated into leaving the country or face assassination. To this date, there has been no systematic investigation of this phenomenon by the occupation authorities. Not a single arrest has been reported in regard to this terrorization of the intellectuals, as Dirk Adriaensens reports in Chapter 6. The inclination to treat this systematic assault on Iraqi professionals as somehow inconsequential is consistent with the occupation powers' more general role in the decapitation of Iraqi society. That aspect of post-invasion Iraq is best exemplified by the Bremer de-Ba'athification policy that had the effect of removing professional leadership cadres in the political, economic, and military spheres. It is less often remembered that this bureaucratic purging extended to the educational and cultural spheres with alarming consequences. As Dahr Jamail reports in Chapter 8, the end result of the purge of Ba'athists has been the almost complete and quite clearly deliberate destruction of Iraq's human capital. With a parallel argument, Philip Marfleet in Chapter 9 examines the patterns of emigration from Iraq and concludes that they emerge as strong indicators of a purposive assault on the institutions and ideological resources of Iraq as a national society. This loss of intellectual capital will deprive Iraq of the professional cadres that reconstruction will require.

It is simply untrue that the war planners could not have gauged the scale of responsibilities that occupation would entail or the resources that would be required to maintain order and protect human and cultural resources. Military sources had made it abundantly clear that the troop levels committed to maintaining responsible governance in post-invasion Iraq were completely inadequate. General Eric Shinseki was most explicit and precise in detailing the responsibilities the occupiers would assume by the invasion. What attracted most attention in Shinseki's remarks to congressional committees was his firm judgment that troop levels provided for post-invasion Iraq could not possibly fulfill the role they were assigned. "Beware a 12-division strategy for a 10-division Army," Shinseki cautioned with memorable succinctness. In comments to Senator Carl Levin in February 2003 Shinseki said clearly that "something on the order of several hundred thousand soldiers" would be needed as an occupation force. Shinseki provided a prescient warning that ethnic tension might well spill over into civil war and that the task of providing basic security and services for the Iraqi people should not be underestimated. In less than 48 hours Shinseki's 38 years of military experience and two purple hearts were vaporized in the ridiculing reaction of Wolfowitz, himself innocent of any military background at all. The Deputy Defense Secretary pronounced that Shinseki's figures were "wildly off the mark." Shinseki was removed and his career sidelined until his appointment by President Barack Obama to the honorable, but low-profile, post of Secretary of Veterans Affairs.[63]

Nor is it true that the policy makers had no more reasonable and humane alternatives to the disastrous course taken. It is too often forgotten now that Paul Bremer was not the first American pro-consul. Nor were the destructive policies he pursued the first put on the table. There were alternatives to the engineered chaos, structural dismantling, and cultural cleansing over which Bremer presided. In early April 2003, the Pentagon appointed retired general Jay Garner as Head of the Office of Reconstruction and Human Assistance in Iraq (ORHA). He arrived in Baghdad on April 20, 2003, and drafted his "Unified Mission Plan" that aimed to minimize American intrusions. The basic foundation of his plan rested on a firm commitment to create and maintain a secure and stable environment of law and order from day one. Garner set the immediate goal of providing that provisions did reach the 60 percent of Iraqis who depended on the Oil-for-Food Program that provided minimal support for Iraqis for whom that support was a life line. More generally, the Garner plan provided, among other things, that oil would remain in Iraqi hands, lower rank police officers would remain on paid, active duty, and the major bureaucratic, technocratic and judiciary institutions would be kept in place to carry out basic government functions.[64] In short, Garner proposed to use state institutions and Iraqi oil wealth to provide security for the people. He too was removed.

Paul Bremer arrived in Iraq in early May to replace Garner. Bremer quite deliberately rejected and reversed Garner's stabilizing orientation. On May 10, 2003, Bremer drafted a memorandum to dissolve eleven key state institutions, including the National Assembly, as well as their affiliated offices, all military organizations, and the major military industries. With explicit blessings from the Pentagon,[65] the dissolution of these critical state structures was achieved by his first two orders issued on May 16 and May 23. Order number one provided for de-Ba'athification, which meant the removal of all Ba'ath Party members, and not just the top leadership figures, from their positions. In practice, this order meant that the majority of the Iraqi work force was laid off without pay. In Saddam's Iraq, the state was the primary employer. One had to join the ruling Ba'ath Party to be eligible for positions. Membership in the party had less to do with ideological commitment or support for Saddam than with the necessity of earning a living. For the regime, the party was above all an instrument of absolute control. Bremer's de-Ba'athification stripped the professions, industry, and social projects of experienced and skilled personnel. Many simply collapsed while others limped along with greatly diminished competence. Bremer's order number two disbanded the army and its civil affiliates, also without pay. In both cases, pensioners as well were deprived of their income. What is clear in terms of stated intent and observable outcomes is that Bremer's policies quite consciously decapitated the country's governing elite and dismantled the major state institutions. Bremer's raft of 97 edicts in total disemboweled the middle class that cemented Iraqi society, and thrust some 15,500 researchers, scientists, teachers and professors into unemployment. The order to disband the army created approximately 500,000 jobless people with military experience.

Predictably, a huge human pool of angry, pauperized Iraqis turned to the rising insurgency for redress. The occupation forces dampened down the emerging resistance with indiscriminate collective punishment that took on the character of yet another "shock and awe" that overwhelmed Iraqis and left them helpless and desperate. With the protective shield of the state removed, criminal elements of all descriptions moved to prey on the defenseless and disorientated population. The Iraqi people and their extraordinary cultural heritage were left unprotected and vulnerable. This policy of state-ending led to the fully predictable and willful cultural cleansing of Iraq.

* * *

In the chapters that follow on the cultural destruction and targeted assassinations that have taken place in post-invasion Iraq the authors carefully weigh the record of conscious choices made that created precipitating conditions of chaos and lawlessness, of inaction in the face of attacks on cultural monuments and intellectuals when action was possible, and of documented direct actions by the occupying powers that had dire human and cultural consequences. In many cases our work first required simple and straightforward documentation of cultural artifacts destroyed, archaeological sites damaged, and intellectuals murdered. The occupying powers and the post-invasion governments that they installed have consistently shown no interest at all in keeping these records. They have shown even less inclination to investigate the crimes and to bring the perpetrators to justice. This calculated disinterest, carefully documented in the chapters that follow, is itself revealing.

We also report in these detailed case studies those occasions when official spokespersons or agents give overt expression to the pervasive inclination of the occupiers to view chaos and lawlessness as "creative" in the sense of providing opportunities to wipe the slate clean, to create new beginnings, or start over from scratch. This permissive attitude to destruction was justified by the vision of a new Iraq that would arise under American and British tutelage from the ruins of the old Iraq. Looting becomes privatization by direct, mass means in such an ideological framework. The destruction of cultural monuments is taken to represent constructive cleansing that prepares the ground for new building. There is even a silver lining to the demise of the old intelligentsia whose disappearance opens opportunities for a new generation of Iraqis with the "right" values and social commitments.

In the context of engineered chaos, the wanton degradation of Iraq's once vaunted educational and health systems represents an opportunity to begin again, unencumbered by the attachments to the old order that had generated those social services. As a result, the occupying authorities, as Nabil al-Takriti documents in Chapter 5, displayed a remarkably cavalier attitude to this deliberate destruction of Iraq's public infrastructure and its reserves of educated human resources to staff it. In the wake of sweeping privatization measures, Peter McPherson, senior economic advisor to the proconsul Paul Bremer, characterized the dismantling of the public sector as "shrinkage."[66] John Agresto, then director of higher education reconstruction for the occupation, described the devastation of Iraq's schools and universities as an "opportunity for a clean start."[67]

To make the case for cultural cleansing we cannot point to one single directive or policy statement, like Bremer's de-Ba'athification order for dismantling state structures or the new laws to remake the economy. For the cultural cleansing dimension of state-ending what we have instead is the painstaking accumulation of documented incident after incident. They add up, in our collective view, to a clear pattern that allows for a clear and reasoned judgment. We show how conditions of chaos resulted from actions taken or abstained from. We document how those conditions and the lawlessness they engendered were welcomed and rationalized in the interest of the Iraq yet to be made. Chaos, we show, released violent forces and impulses. Once released, those forces could not really be directed and kept purposeful so destructive behaviors became more and more erratic. The creativity in chaos is revealed to reside not so much in purposive destruction but rather in the removal of all obstacles – political, economic, cultural, and human – to ending the Iraqi state and beginning anew.

Successive Iraqi states and regimes, whatever their shortcomings and at times terrible limitations, had nevertheless held together a layered and culturally rich nation. Iraq, as Mokhtar Lamani explains in Chapter 10, was an incredibly complex but fragile mosaic. It was formed not only of the three major ethnic and sectarian groupings on which the occupation forces concentrated but also of countless minority communities. In conditions of engineered chaos that intricate fabric that had persisted for thousands of years in embracing astonishing diversity was rent and perhaps destroyed forever. The major ethno-religious groups were deliberately separated out. With the bonds of national unity weakened, they were played one against the other. The small and vulnerable minorities were more often than not simply swallowed up in the turmoil.

To refashion Iraq into the neo-liberal model for the Middle East it was first necessary to destroy in these ways Iraqi national identity and those social forces and cultural productions that expressed it. The occupiers acted in ways that clearly signaled that weakening of collective identity and the decimation of an intelligentsia with ties and mentalities linked to the old Iraq was not a loss at all. Rather, in the eyes of the occupiers it was an opportunity. It helped enormously that those placed in charge of Iraq's fate had little or no experience or knowledge of the country. Ignorance of the past and of the layered complexity of contemporary Iraqi society made it easy to look forward to turning the page. Iraq, after all, was a terrorist state and, somehow this small and battered country with its glorious cultural heritage was transformed into an existential threat to the West and to civilization itself. In such a climate, Iraq's culture was ravaged and its intellectual class decimated. In our considered view it is impossible for reasonable people to see it any other way, once they have reviewed the evidence laid out in the chapters to come. The pattern of cultural cleansing is etched in the facts on the ground of museums looted, libraries burned, and the most prominent and productive intellectuals systematically eliminated. The occupiers showed no inclination at all to protect those cultural and human resources and they failed to do so, in violation of international and humanitarian law. Worse, at critical moments they contributed in substantial ways to the destruction, as for example, by the stationing of occupation troops in the midst of some of the nation's most important archaeological sites, thereby doing them great damage, as Abbas al-Hussainy documents in Chapter 4. These outcomes, we are persuaded, were not tragic, unintended consequences. The culture that was ravaged, as Zainab Bahrani explains in Chapter 3, was an Iraqi cultural patrimony in the first instance, destroyed in an occupied country on the watch of the occupiers, notably the United States and Britain. The intellectuals who were murdered and whose killings have not been investigated to this day represented some of the most productive and creative of the Iraqi intelligentsia who were educated, trained, and employed by the Iraqi state, as Dirk Adriaensens, Max Fuller and Dahr Jamail document in exacting detail in Chapters 6, 7 and 8. They were the human embodiment of the Iraqi state and thus fair targets for ending. They were killed not primarily for sectarian reasons, though such incidents did occur, but simply because they were the best of Iraqi brains as a careful review of the statistical evidence makes clear. These cultural erasures and eliminations represent a concerted effort to shatter Iraqi collective memory as an essential condition for state-ending. It seems clear to us from the evidence presented and weighed in the chapters that follow that these devastating outcomes represent the consequences, both direct and indirect, of an ideological, totalizing vision. That vision of state-ending required the dismantling not just of the old political and economic structures. It demanded as well the destruction of the cultural and human reserves of the Iraqi state, all in the interest of an imagined remaking.

The war planners have told us that the violence of shock and awe was a gift to Iraqis. The putative aim was to end dictatorship and open the way to the dismantling of the tyrannical state that had terrorized the people of Iraq. From the beginning, critics have debunked these explanations and argued forcefully that the invasion aimed for domination. It is important to note, however, that all sides in that debate took for granted that the aim of the invasion was the violent remaking of the Iraqi state, whether for liberation or for domination. Today, in the United States and Britain, a self-referential debate centers on these issues of the motivations of American and British policy makers for the remaking of Iraq. Did the invasion aim to remake Iraq in order to bring freedom to Iraq and the Middle East beyond, as the neoconservatives would claim, or was the aim imperial domination, as the critics forcefully argue? Regrettably, with attention riveted on the ideological rationale for the invasion, the depredations suffered by Iraqis recede into the background, no matter which position is taken. What emerges out of this insular debate are questions of Anglo-American motives rather than a consideration of the actual consequences for Iraqi culture and humanity. Eyes glaze over when figures on Iraqi civilian casualties are debated. When the museums in Baghdad were looted and libraries burned, the world did pay attention, but not for long. The pillage in Baghdad was only the tip of the iceberg. Abbas al-Hussainy surveys the richness of the Iraqi cultural legacy in Chapter 4, noting that there are some 12,000 registered archaeological treasures within Iraq's borders. Tragically, as Abbas al-Hussainy concludes, no other nation in modern terms has ever suffered destruction of its cultural legacy comparable to what Iraq endured under occupation. But the occupiers and their publics at home found it hard to focus on the fate of Iraqi culture. As Zainab Bahrani explains in Chapter 3, the really catastrophic cultural devastation took place in the five years following the initial destruction in Baghdad. It eventually engulfed the whole country, though these prolonged acts of pillage have met with a remarkable silence and culpable inaction. Had there been any inclination to do so, there was ample time to put protective measures in place. This course of action was simply not taken and very few even noticed.

Across the board, Iraq's unprotected cultural and social institutions were wantonly looted and in many cases irreparably damaged or destroyed. In these ways contemporary Iraq has been stripped both of its impressive historic past as well as its more recent social attainments. Iraq's modern institutions, in particular its once vaunted health and education infrastructure funded by the national oil industry, were degraded by initial bombardment and subsequent civil disorder. Dahr Jamail documents in Chapter 8 the devastating consequences, pointing out that many medical and educational facilities in Iraq are barely operating with skeletal staffing and little supplies. Hard-won social gains, among the most advanced of Arab states, were then further undermined by the haphazard privatization and reform schemes of Iraq's self-appointed rulers. Iraq's human resources, notably its educated and technocratic classes, have also been seriously depleted, either by flight, forced exile, or assassination. Readers will find in Chapters 6, 7 and 8, by Dirk Adriaensens, Max Fuller and Dahr Jamail, the most comprehensive and painstaking record and analysis of these human tragedies yet assembled. They provide as well a careful evaluation of the evidence for placing responsibility for this outcome on the shoulders of the occupiers.

Those human and cultural outcomes on the ground in Iraq do matter, in the first instance for Iraqis and their prospects for the future. They also matter for American and British citizens who want to understand how and why power was exercised in their name and what responsibility they bear for its outcomes. The focus on the liberation versus domination debate obscures the fact that, whatever the motive, a totalitarian and inherently violent aim of state-ending was pursued. That deliberate policy had particularly devastating cultural and human consequences. Ending and remaking are inherently violent processes. Nation-building, as Glenn Perry points out in Chapter 2, implies a prior process of nation-destroying that we are inclined to overlook, even when considering our own Western history. Cultural identity is everywhere a component of state power and empires have always known that to weaken the collective identity of a people is to make them available for occupation, colonization, and worse. The destruction of archives and historical monuments, so wanton in Iraq, has always been part of the wars of empires, as Zainab Bahrani explains in Chapter 3. Everywhere in the modern world there is a strong and complex linkage between the intelligentsia and the state. Philip Marfleet explains in Chapter 9 that attenuating or breaking that connection and clearing out the old intelligentsia facilitates the pathway to a new Iraqi state of imperial design. Only when these implications of a totalizing war objective are ignored is it possible to entertain the facile explanations for the terrible destruction that has taken place in Iraq as the product of chance and lack of foresight.

Conclusion

The invasion and occupation of Iraq with its destructive assault on Iraq's cultural integrity, political unity, and economic capacity did destroy a state that claimed to represent Arab nationalism and opposition to Israeli expansionism. Yet today it is far less clear that the new realities that will emerge from the willed chaos that is Iraq today will in fact be as amenable to American and Israeli interests as the neo-conservatives and their Israeli allies dreamed. To be sure, they have removed Iraq as an Arab power able to mount a plausible Arab challenge to Israeli dominance, though not one that could seriously threaten Israel itself. However, in doing so they have released sub-national forces that are proving to be far less amenable to control from a distance than the ideologues imagined. Meanwhile, Iraq has been shattered and humanity diminished by that terrible spectacle of willed destruction.

Iraq's national project has suffered the loss of its historical, intellectual, and cultural foundations. Once proud Iraq now risks becoming little more than a conglomerate of ethno-sectarian fiefdoms, vulnerable to all kinds of foreign exactions and intrusions. War and occupation has ended for the foreseeable future any Iraqi aspirations of achieving an autonomous leadership role in the Arab world.

In November 2007, the US administration and the dependent regime in Iraq signed a "Declaration of Principles," establishing an open-ended US military involvement in Iraq, and thus, the Persian Gulf. Key Bush administration officials, notably Vice President Dick Cheney and Deputy Defense Secretary Paul Wolfowitz, had from the outset aimed at permanent military bases in Iraq. However, the Iraqis proved far more resistant to these infringements on national sovereignty than anticipated. A year later, on November 17, 2008, Iraqi Foreign Minister Hoshyar Zebari and US Ambassador Ryan Crocker signed a Status of Forces (SOF) agreement that stipulates in article 24 that all United States combat forces will withdraw from "Iraqi cities, villages and localities" no later than June 30, 2009. Article 24 of the agreement explicitly provides that "all the United States Forces shall withdraw from all Iraqi territory no later than December 31, 2011." This provision seems to preclude US retention of long-term bases. However, at the time of writing there remains some ambiguity and a need for caution in drawing this conclusion in too definitive a way. The preamble to the SOF agreement does suggest that not all loopholes have been closed. The preamble, it should be noted, speaks of the United States and Iraq "strengthening their joint security... combating terrorism in Iraq, and cooperating in the security and defense spheres...." It will be up to the Obama administration to define with the Iraqis exactly what will be the nature of any longer-term security relationship between the US and Iraq.[68]

Meanwhile, it is already clear that the American mission in Iraq, designed to create a pro-American model for the region and a bulwark against anti-American militancy, has achieved precisely the opposite. The defeat of Iraq was supposed to illustrate how instructional violence could intimidate and de-legitimate the region's so-called "rogue states." Instead, the policies driven by neo-conservatism, Israel, and the oil conglomerates ironically served to empower Iran, the one regional power best positioned to resist all of those pressures and now the "rogue state" of choice. Iran's regional status has risen in ways unimaginable without this backdrop of failed imperial policies. The Iranian threat is now on the table and the pro-American authoritarian regimes in Egypt, Saudi Arabia, and Jordan have helped put it there. Predictably, however, Israelis lead the chorus for regime change in Tehran. The Obama administration has been ambivalent in its statements on Iran, though there have been positive initiatives. Most recently, on March 19, 2009 – in commemoration of the Persian *Nowruz* festival – President Obama called for "diplomacy that addresses the full range of issues before us, and to pursue constructive ties among the United States, Iran and the international community." However the relationship with Iran develops, the debacle in Iraq has permanently stained US democracy-promotion as simply a cover for a particularly violent and destructive ambition for empire. Meanwhile, in the deplorable reaction to the legitimate election of Hamas in Palestine, American and Israeli dedication to the principles of democracy in the region have been exposed once again as a cruel chimera. It would be premature to believe that the policy of ending states has itself ended with the passing of the Bush administration. Our need to understand fully the meaning and implications of that policy of state-ending, as enacted in Iraq, is unfortunately as compelling as ever.

Notes

1. For an assessment of the various estimates, see Chapters 6, 7 and 8.
2. For discussion of cultural cleansing as a dimension of domination in comparative perspective see Chapter 2 by Glenn Perry.
3. Tina Susman, "Poll: Civilian Toll in Iraq may top 1M," *Los Angeles Times*, September 14, 2007, http://www.latimes.com/news/nationworld/world/la-fg-iraq14sep14,0,6134240.story, accessed December 2008.
4. "The War Behind Closed Doors: Excerpts from 1992 Draft 'Defense Planning Guidance'," *PBS: Frontline*, http://www.pbs.org/wgbh/pages/frontline/shows/iraq/etc/wolf.html, accessed December 2008.
5. Ibid.
6. Ibid.
7. Thomas Donnelly, *Rebuilding America's Defenses: Strategy, Forces and Resources for a New Century*, Washington: Project for a New American Century, September 2000, p. ii.
8. Ibid., pp. 16, 21, 23, 26, 47, 86, 88.
9. Ibid., p. 16.
10. Ibid., p. 26.
11. Ron Suskind, *The Price of Loyalty: George W. Bush, the White House, and the Education of Paul O'Neill*, New York: Simon & Schuster, 2004, p. 85.
12. Richard Perle (Study Group Lead), *A Clean Break: A New Strategy for Securing the Realm*, The Institute for Advanced Strategic and Political Studies' "Study Group on a New Israeli Strategy Toward 2000," http://www.iasps.org/strat1.htm, accessed December 2008.
13. See Richard Falk, "Israeli War Crimes," Agence Globale, March 14, 2009.
14. The background on death squads and the evidence for their role in Iraq is discussed and evaluated in Chapters 6, 7 and 8.
15. See the 1996 Gary Webb "Dark Alliance" articles in the *San Jose Mercury News*, later compiled in Gary Webb, *Dark Alliance: The*

CIA, the Contras, and the Crack Cocaine Explosion (Seven Stories Press, 1999).

16. David Corn, "From Iran-Contra to Iraq," *The Nation*, May 7, 2005, http://www.commondreams.org/views05/0507-26.htm, accessed March 2009.

17. Pater Maass, "The Way of the Commandos," *New York Times*, May 1, 2005, http://www.nytimes.com/2005/05/01/magazine/ 01ARMY.html, accessed March 2009.

18. "Iraq 'Death Squad Caught in Act'," BBC News, February 16, 2006, http://news.bbc.co.uk/2/hi/middle_east/4719252.stm, accessed March 2009.

19. Maass, "The Way of the Commandos."

20. Nir Rosen, "The Myth of the Surge," *Rolling Stone*, May 6, 2008, http://www.rollingstone.com/politics/story/18722376/the_myth_ of_the_surge/print, accessed March 2008.

21. Foreign Policy, "Study: Surge of Violence Led to Peace in Iraq," *Foreign Policy: Passport*, September 18, 2008, http://blog. foreignpolicy.com/posts/2008/09/19/study_surge_of_violence_led_ to_peace_in_iraq, accessed March 2008.

22. Sue Pleming, "US Plans 'Substantial' Pledge at Gaza Meeting," Reuters, February 23, 2009, http://news.yahoo.com/s/nm/ 20090223/pl_nm/us_palestinians_clinton_4, accessed March 2009.

23. David Rose, "The Gaza Bombshell," *Vanity Fair*, April 2008, http://www.vanityfair.com/politics/features/2008/04/gaza200804, accessed March 2008.

24. Gerry Shih and Susana Montes, "Roundtable Debates Energy Issues: All-star panel calls for climate change research, market solutions," *The Stanford Daily*, October 15, 2007.

25. Dick Cheney, "Full text of Dick Cheney's speech at the Institute of Petroleum Autumn lunch 1999," London Institute of Petroleum, June 8, 2004, http://www.energybulletin.net/559.html, accessed December 2008.

26. United States Department of Iraq, "Oil and Energy Working Group," *Future of Iraq Project*, http://www.gwu.edu/~nsarchiv/ NSAEBB/NSAEBB198/FOI%20Oil.pdf, accessed December 2008.

27. Gal Luft, "How Much Oil Does Iraq Have?" Brookings Institute, May 12, 2003, http://www.brookings.edu/papers/2003/ 0512globalenvironment_luft.aspx, accessed December 2008.

28. "Hamas Is a Creation of Mossad," *L'Humanité*, Summer 2002, http://globalresearch.ca/articles/ZER403A.html, accessed March 2008.

29. Notwithstanding formal peace between Israel and Egypt, a poll conducted in 2006 found that 92 percent of Egyptians saw Israel as a "hostile" nation. See: http://news.bbc.co.uk/2/hi/middle_east/6107160.stm.

30. Amir Oren, "British Author: Rabin asked Jordan to arrange secret visit with Saddam," *Haaretz*, February 27, 2009, http://www.haaretz.com/hasen/spages/1067306.html, accessed March 2009.

31. Ibid.

32. Yitzhak Benhorin, "Doug Feith: Israel didn't push for Iraq war," *Ynet*, May 13, 2008, http://www.ynetnews.com/Ext/Comp/ArticleLayout/CdaArticlePrintPreview/1,2506,L-3542925,00.html, accessed March 2008.

33. Julian Borger, "The Spies who Pushed for War," *Guardian*, July 17, 2003, http://www.guardian.co.uk/world/2003/jul/17/iraq.usa, accessed March 2009.

34. Seymour Hersh, "Moving Targets," *The New Yorker*, December 15, 2003, http://www.newyorker.com/archive/2003/12/15/031215fa_fact, accessed March 2009.

35. Seymour Hersh, "Plan B," *The New Yorker*, June 28, 2004, http://www.newyorker.com/archive/2004/06/28/040628fa_fact, accessed March 2009.

36. Hoshnag Ose, "A Secret Relationship," *Niqash*, September 8, 2008. http://www.niqash.org/content.php?contentTypeID=75&id=2285&lang=0, accessed March 2009.

37. Ibid.

38. Institut Kurde de Paris, "Iraqi Kurdistan Unifies its Administration with a Single Government," *Institut Kurde de Paris 254*, May 2006, p. 2, http://www.institutkurde.org/en/publications/bulletins/254.html, accessed March 2009.

39. Associated Press, "Historic Handshake: Barak Meets Iraq's President in Athens," *Haaretz*, July 1, 2008, http://www.haaretz.com/hasen/spages/997941.html, accessed March 2009; for a critical assessment, see Ramzy Baroud, "The Not-so-Historic Barak–Talabani Handshake," *Counterpunch*, July 11, 2008, http://www.counterpunch.org/baroud07112008.html, accessed March 2009.

40. Robert Fisk, "It is the Death of History," *Independent*, September 17, 2007, http://www.independent.co.uk/opinion/commentators/fisk/robert-fisk-it-is-the-death-of-history-402571.html, accessed March 2008.

41. Cara Buckley, "Rare Look Inside Baghdad Museum," *New York Times*, December 12, 2007, http://www.nytimes.com/2007/12/12/world/middleeast/12iraq.html?em&ex=1197522000&en=30bbb59d472df2fb&ei=5087%0A, accessed December 2008.

42. Simon Jenkins, "In Iraq's four-year looting frenzy, the allies have become the vandals," *Guardian*, June 8, 2007, http://www.guardian.co.uk/Iraq/Story/0,2098273,00.html, accessed December 2008.

43. Guy Gugliotta, "Looted Iraqi Relics Slow to Resurface; Some Famous Pieces Unlikely to Re-appear," *Washington Post*, November 8, 2005, http://www.washingtonpost.com/wp-dyn/content/article/2005/11/07/AR2005110701479.html, accessed December 2008.

44. Dr. Michael E. Smith, "This is not the 'Antiques Roadshow'," http://www.public.asu.edu/~mesmith9/Antiquities.html, accessed December 2008.

45. "eBay Iraq Relic Auction Stopped," BBC News, December 18, 2007, http://news.bbc.co.uk/2/hi/europe/7150622.stm, accessed December 2008.

46. Dr. Francis Deblauwe, "The Iraq War and Archaeology," Institute of Oriental Studies, University of Vienna, Austria, http://iwa.univie.ac.at/site.html, accessed December 2008.

47. Jenkins, "In Iraq's four-year looting frenzy, the allies have become the vandals."

48. Fisk, "It is the Death of History."

49. Sean Loughlin, "Rumsfeld on looting in Iraq: 'stuff happens' – Administration asking countries for help with security," CNN, April 12, 2003, http://www.cnn.com/2003/US/04/11/sprj.irq.pentagon/, accessed December 2008.

50. Ibid.

51. Zainab Bahrani, "Looting and Conquest," *The Nation*, May 14, 2003, http://www.thenation.com/doc/20030526/bahrani, accessed December 2008.

52. Robert Fisk, "Another Crime of Occupation Iraq: Cultural Heritage Looted, Pillaged," *Independent*, September 17, 2007, http://www.alternet.org/waroniraq/62810/, accessed December 2008.

53. Gugliotta, "Looted Iraqi Relics Slow to Resurface."

54. Francis Deblauwe, "Mesopotamian Ruins and American Scholars," August 2005, http://www.bibleinterp.com/articles/Deblauwe_Mesopotamian_Scholars.htm, accessed December 2008.

55. Felicity Arbuthnot, "Iraq: Erasing History," *Global Research*, April 14, 2007, http://www.globalresearch.ca/index.php?context=viewArticle&code=20070414&articleId=5384, accessed December 2008.

56. All of the case study chapters that follow deal with the destruction of memory in post-invasion Iraq as a feature of willful cultural cleansing that aims to weaken or destroy collective identity. The

evidence for such destruction as conscious policy is carefully evaluated in these detailed studies.

57. Susan A. Crane (ed.), *Museums and Memory*, Stanford: Stanford University Press, 2000, p. 3.
58. Ibid., pp. 6, 12.
59. Quoted by Ghali Hassan, "The Destruction of Iraq's Educational System under US Occupation," May 11, 2005, http://www.globalresearch.ca/articles/HAS505B.html, accessed December 2008.
60. Ibid.
61. Ibid.
62. Juan Cole, "Informed Comment," December 20, 2007, http://www.juancole.com, accessed December 2008.
63. Mark Thompson, "Shinseki, a Prescient General, Re-Enlists as VA Chief," *Time*, December 8, 2008, http://www.time.com/time/politics/article/0,8599,1864915,00.html.
64. "A unified Mission Plan for post-hostilities Iraq," http://www.pbs.org/wgbh/pages/frontline/yeariniraq/documents/orha.html.
65. For details of Bremer's memo, see: http://www.pbs.org/wgbh/pages/frontline/yeariniraq/documents/bremermemo.pdf.
66. Naomi Klein, *The Shock Doctrine*, Alfred A. Knopf Canada, 2007, p. 406.
67. Ibid., p. 407.
68. See Patrick Seale, "Iraq's Rocky Future," Agence Globale, November 24, 2008.

2

CULTURAL CLEANSING IN COMPARATIVE PERSPECTIVE

Glenn E. Perry

The horrific destruction of Iraq's cultural heritage as the country came under foreign occupation in 2003, whether one attributes it to calculated policy or to reckless incompetence, ignorance, and contempt, reenacted experiences of those who have undergone subjugation throughout history. One can find many other examples of this phenomenon in recent memory. The destruction of such aspects of a people's culture as monuments, ancient manuscripts, languages, religions, historical narratives, and identities constitutes what a recent work on the subject of architecture in particular so aptly terms "the destruction of memory." Sometimes this destruction is the byproduct of achieving military objectives; mere "collateral damage." However, the destruction of buildings, sculptures, documents, artifacts and the like is connected to a people's memory and identity. Their erasure is intended as a means of dominating, terrorizing, dividing or eradicating. It has been suggested that this kind of "genocide by other means" should be included in the broader crime of genocide.[1]

In destroying memory, conquerors hope to stifle future resistance. With memory of the self gone, there may no longer be a desire to end subjugation. Even if the victims' memory survives, the subjugators may hope to remove evidence of their ties to the land and construct distorted historical narratives to the extent that their own people as well as outside observers will have difficulty even comprehending calls for redress.

The Cleansing of Civilizations

Cultures have come and gone throughout the course of human existence. This is true of the largest cultural units, which historians customarily have designated as "civilizations." Sometimes it is argued that each passes through the same kind of stages from birth to death much like an organism. At other times the fate of *civilizations* is presented as having an open-ended existence. In any case, history has been a graveyard for *civilizations*. A long-lived one such as that of ancient Egypt finally demonstrated its mortality although it bequeathed many of its genes to later ones in the Middle East and Europe. At least in Toynbee's classification, the ancient Syriac and Hellenic civilizations made way for new societies, the Islamic and the Western and Orthodox Christian respectively.

Today there is reason to believe that a variety of distinct civilizations are surviving, and some argue that healthy "modernization" does not require giving up civilizational identity – even that such attempts to Westernize are unhealthy.[2] It was not long ago that one such civilization, the "Western," was seen as replacing them, all of which were dead or in the process of dying as the "inevitable" process of Westernization took its course. There was a widespread assumption that Western imperialism, through its conquests and then by demonstrating that Westernization was the only option for those who wanted to get on in the world, had made such divisions obsolete. Or else, it was said that all past civilizations, including the Western and the Islamic, had now made way for a single "Modern Technological" one.[3] Quincy Wright wrote in his classic *Study of War* that there now "is only one civilization."[4] While giving credit to the contributions of other civilizations, Wright opined that "This civilization has gradually destroyed, or incorporated with some adaptations" all of the others, leaving "distinctive nationalities in their place" and that while "the ghosts of several old civilizations still mediate between the nations and the world-community, ...these ghosts are in the process of evaporation."

The Cleansing of Peoples

Cultures on national and sub-national levels are always fading away in large numbers. According to a recent report, nearly half of the world's 7,000 languages will probably become extinct, at a faster rate than that of living species, by the end of the twenty-first century. One such language ceases to be spoken during a typical fortnight.[5]

While much of this has been unplanned, it reflects the relative power of different groups. The languages of those who dominate the world militarily, politically, and economically have tended to spread, while those of weaker peoples die out. Their societies are flooded with colonial settlers, as states use other languages in administration and in education, and as the tongues of the dominant groups are heard on the radio and television. Many times, the dominant group consciously adopts assimilationist policies that penalize the use of minority languages precisely in order to promote the sort of homogeneity that will bolster a common identity and thus facilitate maintaining its own power and domination.

Sometimes assimilation comes about through the working of more subtle processes that nevertheless reflect the influence of those who wield military and commercial domination, as in the case of people gradually adopting the religion of their conquerors as way of enhancing their prospect of obtaining the patronage of their rulers and also in order to facilitate contact with those who have come to dominate trade.[6] Colonial policies varied. The French persistently had the goal of Gallicizing subject peoples. Some of the colonized peoples became more proficient in French than in their own indigenous tongues, and a French identity was pushed on them. Under French rule, history textbooks used by Algerian children famously started with the phrase, "Our ancestors, the Gauls..."[7]

Building and Destroying Nations

Insofar as some states are also nations, this is almost entirely the result of assimilationist policies that brought the cultural or even physical demise of different groups. As Walker Conner put the matter in his classic article on the subject, what many writers so glibly term "nation-building," if successful, might more meaningfully be dubbed "nation-destroying."[8] We often hear of the contrast between Western countries and the Developing World in terms of much greater heterogeneity in the latter. However, aside from those countries that resulted from the breakup of multinational entities along ethnic lines during the twentieth century, few countries in Europe were linguistically homogeneous when they came into being. Lucian W. Pye pointed out that "regional and linguistic differences had to be overcome" even in such cases as Britain and France that eventually developed "exceedingly high levels of national consciousness."[9] In some cases, particularly in the last century, ethnic homogeneity was helped along by ethnic cleansing. Where actual expulsion or extermination did not take place, the process of cultural cleansing extended over the course of several centuries.

Sometimes there were small holdouts. As Conner points out in distinguishing between cultural and psychological assimilation, a person "can shed all of the overt cultural manifestations customarily attributed to his ethnic group and yet maintain his fundamental identity."[10] The Celtic peoples of the British Isles lost their languages for the most part, although they retained some of their separate identities, leading in recent decades to the emergence of separatist nationalist parties in the cases of the Welsh and the Scots. With their identity marked by a sectarian distinction from their Protestant British rulers and by centuries of suffering from discrimination and Protestant settler colonialism, the Irish adopted a fierce nationalism that led to the independence of most of their island in 1920. They tried, but never really succeeded in the formidable task of reviving their old tongue. France looks like an almost pure ethnic, national state (aside from a few areas in which some people still speak their regional languages and, of course, recent immigrants). However, only a lack of knowledge of the history of the country would lead anyone to think that its boundaries emerged as a result of an early form of self-determination on the part of those who already spoke French.

It has been estimated that in 1861, when Italy was being united, "the Italian common tongue was used primarily in written and formal discourse" except in Rome and Tuscany and that "only 2.5 percent of the population employed it easily and habitually," increasing to about "40 percent by 1900."[11]

Whether in Europe or Africa, the process of linguistic and ethnic assimilation does not proceed so easily today. Anderson et al. point out that, "before the self-awareness of many cultural groups had become intense, this method was no doubt highly efficacious" but that after a group "has achieved self-awareness, assimilation is likely to encounter bitter resistance."[12] Contrary to the usual assumption of modernization theorists of the 1960s, perceptive analysts began to see that processes such an urbanization, increased literacy, and growth of mass media are likely to intensify ethnic and linguistic particularism rather than result in "nation-building."[13] While assimilation was widespread before the rise of nationalism in the nineteenth century among people who "were not aware of belonging to a separate culture-group with its own proud traditions and myths," there have been no recent examples of such on a large scale in recent times.[14] Indeed, while some governments have been committed to creating national homogeneity through banning the use of regional languages and cultural expressions, as in the case of the Kurds in Turkey, whose identity was long denied in favor of the euphemistic term "Mountain Turks," the bulk of the Kurds have resisted such attempts to cleanse their culture and identity. Although a few people of Kurdish origin have taken advantage of the opportunity to cleanse themselves of their ancestors' culture and gain full equality as Turks, even those who have migrated to places such as Istanbul or Ankara and, for that matter, Berlin and lost their ability to speak Kurdish have mostly clung to a Kurdish identity.

In some cases, cultural assimilation to the predominant "national" language and culture exists alongside a toleration of regional distinctiveness. Thus the Azeris, a Turkic-speaking people who make up a major portion of the population of Iran (sometimes estimated as one-third of the total), have historically been little affected by separatist nationalism.[15] There has been some speculation that this may change and that the independence of Azerbaijan next door may threaten Iranian unity. One reason for the ability of Iranian nationalism to transcend such linguistic diversity is that the Azeris, unlike some other Iranian ethnic minorities, share Shi'ism with the Persians. Indeed, modern Iran is the creation of a Turkic dynasty from Azerbaijan, the Safavids, who imposed Shi'ism on the Persians in the sixteenth century, and Turkish dynasties reigned in Iran until the coming of the Pahlavis in 1925. However, much of the explanation for the weakness of Azeri separatism can be attributed to the fact that the Azeris' embrace of the Persian *lingua franca* is matched by a willingness of the Iranian state to allow them to continue to use their provincial tongue too. It is reported that, notwithstanding their integration into the Iranian national identity, Azeris and also Gilanis and others whose vernaculars are distinct from Persian always use their own languages when no outsiders are present.[16] The cultural autonomy that Iraq allowed to its Kurds, in contrast to the Turkish case, might also have facilitated unity had outside powers not been so eager to cultivate separatism.

Crimes Against Culture: The Former Yugoslavia

As Yugoslavia came apart during the 1990s, the phrase "ethnic cleansing" gained fame throughout the world. Killing and expulsion were at the center of this terrible process. Cultural cleansing also played a key role. The destruction of the Stari Most bridge, dating back to Ottoman times and serving as a symbol of the long united community, has been described as "an attack on the very concept of multi-ethnicity." Thousands of Ottoman monuments in Bosnia were destroyed, for "libraries, museums, Islamic schools, tombs and fountains were the enemy."[17] While this aspect of ethnic cleansing understandably received less attention than did deaths, one Croatian writer expressed his feeling that while people are mortal, the great monuments to the past are expected to live forever:

Overlooking these attacks on cultural patrimony and failing to understand their direct links to the cultural survival of a people risks setting aside some of the very attributes that give meaning to a group identity. More than this, where a group is under physical attack, the destiny of its representative architecture is an excellent indicator of whether genocidal intent is present or incipient.[18]

Such cultural cleansing was intended to make ethnic cleansing "permanent and irreversible."[19] After destroying 20,000 to 40,000 Islamic monuments in Bosnia, Serbian nationalists were then able to argue that no such thing had ever existed in these places. Even Muslim cemeteries were destroyed as a form of "retroactive ethnic cleansing." "History was being rewritten; a new future and a new past were being invented in the service of a Greater Serbia and a Greater Croatia."[20] That was the main purpose of the destruction, little of which was carried out for "purely military reasons."[21]

Crimes Against Culture: Palestine

In many ways, Palestine in the twentieth century was unique, although the parallels between what happened in that country and in Bosnia are compelling.[22] In this case, a settler community claiming to be "returning" to its ancient homeland carried out an incredible sort of ethnic cleansing of most of the country's indigenous population, including all but a small minority within the frontiers of the new State of Israel established during 1948–49. In doing so, the settler state erased much of the evidence of the people they displaced, as though to make it seem that the new society had been established on a land that had been empty. Although in the additional territories that Israel occupied in 1967 the process of cleansing and settling faced the obstacle of "natives" who in most cases were difficult to uproot or extirpate, some successes for the colonial enterprise were registered there too. One such case was the replacement, immediately following the 1967 conquest, of the newly cleansed Palestinian village of Imwas, near Jerusalem, by a park. The "virginal appearance of the rocky hillside laced with narrow wadis" was noted in the Israeli press, evoking the sarcastic response of a writer in *Haaretz*, who opined that the park would be a great place for Jewish children to play and learn about how bad the Arabs who had "abandoned" it were. The same article warned that the children should not be allowed to dig lest they find "the remains of houses that had been destroyed... although if that happened it would always be possible to pass it off by explaining that they were in fact the remains of a 12th Century synagogue."[23] Although the Jewish National Fund, the organization that obtained control over confiscated Arab land, agreed in 2005 to put up signs noting the location of this and some other villages, they were soon removed. There was another agreement three years later to place commemorative markers for several such sites.[24]

Meron Benvenisti provides a remarkable account of the way the physical landscape of Palestine was destroyed as "the inevitable outcome of the eradication of the human landscape."[25] He predicts that soon "the vanished Arab landscape will be considered just a piece of Arab propaganda."[26]

All that is left of the dispossessed, replaced former population in many places is

> a few layers of withered stone, a half-buried arch, a broken millstone. In some places a few structures still remain – neglected mosques, school buildings, imposing houses renovated by Israelis–and seven villages completely escaped destruction because Israelis found them picturesque enough to preserve.[27]

In the case of one large house that recently was restored, publications made available to visitors relate its history and that of the village in which it was located, going back to ancient times, but conveniently skip "the period in which it was an Arab/Palestinian village, and what happened to its residents."[28] With cartography being used as a powerful instrument of cultural cleansing, even new place names were artificially devised to remove the memory of the former inhabitants. At times, sites were given biblical-sounding names to create a myth of continuity with the ancient Israelites.[29] Benvenisti suggests that this immense effort to eradicate the non-Hebrew heritage arose from a sense of the rootedness and power of the Arabic names, which, if not extirpated, were liable to imperil the new map. This was not a show of contempt for the Arabic heritage. On the contrary, it was a declaration of war on it. The effort the Zionists invested in this project is proof of their recognition that the Arabic shadow-map...would remain very much in existence as long as there were people living in this land who took care to preserve it.[30]

Benvenisti points out that many of the Arabic place names were ancient, often derived from Hebrew, and that the Zionists, who otherwise would not have known the location of places after two millennia, demonstrated "sheer ingratitude" by trying to wipe out the Arab heritage of the country.[31] He notes that this procedure represents a kind of "ethnic cleaning" by inventing totally artificial names from scratch and that he can find few parallels for "such radical alterations of the map" elsewhere in the world.[32]

As in Bosnia and elsewhere, "cleansing" in Palestine extends to the remains of the dead and the memory that they inhabited the land too. With regard to the destruction of Muslim graves in Jerusalem and the way "the protests of the Muslim clergy were ignored," Benvenisti noted that "Preservation of the dignity of the dead, like that of the living, is a matter of religious affiliation."[33] According to Benvenisti, "Of the hundreds of Muslim cemeteries extant before 1948 [in the area within what was to become the "green line"], vestiges of only about 40 are still discernible, while others made way for roads, homes, and the like, and still bulldozers leave shattered tombstones, open graves, and human bones rolling around."[34] A decision to relocate Jaffa's only remaining Muslim cemetery in 2008 shows the continuing nature of this process.[35] Shrines commemorating the graves of medieval Muslim saints were in many cases appropriated by the Zionists and reconsecrated as tombs of Old Testament figures.[36] In an act of perhaps unprecedented chutzpah, the Simon Wiesenthal Center chose a centuries-old Muslim cemetery in Jerusalem as the site of its Museum of Tolerance in 2008, a decision that the Supreme Court gave the green light for over Muslim protests.[37]

Thus facts increasingly are being destroyed to avoid reminding later generations that this was not a land without a people before the arrival of the Zionists and to create a fictional continuity between the modern state of Israel and the ancient Israelites.

Some Palestinians and other Muslims and Arabs fear the prospect of their holy places in Jerusalem being cleansed. Archaeological excavations have involved the use of bulldozers in close proximity to the Haram al-Sharif, the third holiest place for Muslims. If such actions were to lead to the destruction of Al-Aqsa Mosque, this would "crown the Israeli cleansing of the Palestinian cultural structure."[38]

The European Zionists who cleansed Palestine subsequently proceeded to bring in Jews from the non-Western countries too. These latter-day recruits to the Zionist project, who, at least until the large influx of immigrants from Russia in the 1990s, would eventually outnumber the original European settlers, also became victims of cultural cleansing. Such treatment has left a bitter legacy for many Mizrahi (Oriental) Jews that is shown in the way they revolted against the Mapai/Labour Party which dominated the state in its early decades and fueled the eventual rise to predominance of the rightist Likud bloc, but among a few at least, as shown by the emergence of the Black Panther movement in the 1970s, it created an aversion to Zionism and identification with the Arab world. Writing about her concern over the rise of a Mizrahi variant of the post-Zionist movement of Jewish Israelis who challenge the legitimacy of Israel as a Jewish state, a militant Israeli spokesperson, Meyrav Wurmser, tells us about one Sephardic Israeli poet, Sami Shalom Chetrit, who proclaims himself "a Palestinian" and "an Arab refugee."[39] According to Wurmser, the continuing Mizrahi "fury" results not just from the events of the mid twentieth century, when they were subjected to such indignities as having their heads shaved and their bodies sprayed with DDT when they entered the country, the "enforced secularization," the humiliation of "the patriarch" by reduced status, and "the state-sponsored kidnapping" of children (see below) but also from "the extent to which, in their view, the Zionist narrative denied, erased, and excluded their historical identity." She points to various Israeli writers who expressed utter contempt for such "primitive people" and about "genetic inferiority" and admits that David Ben-Gurion deemed them totally devoid of "the most elementary knowledge" and warned about the danger of his society being corrupted by Arabization and "the spirit of the Levant." The author explains that this occurred despite the fact that they were "largely literate," with "most men and even some women" able to "read the Torah."

In many cases involving children of Yemeni origin (and possibly others from Middle Eastern countries), the Zionists' enthusiasm for cleansing their non-Western co-religionists of what were deemed undesirable cultural attributes arguably crossed the line into the realm of genocide, which in Article II of the convention of 1948 that declared this a crime includes, *inter alia*, "Forcibly transferring children of the group to another group." Approximately 50,000 Yemeni Jews migrated to Israel during 1949–50, and at least several hundred – some put the figure in the thousands – of their babies, ironically paralleling a practice established in Yemen during the 1920s whereby the state raised Jewish orphans as Muslims,[40] were put in hospitals or nurseries from which they subsequently disappeared. With their desperate parents told that they had died, the babies were turned over for adoption by Jews of European origin, including Holocaust survivors. Parents were shown "graves" of the missing children almost half a century later, but when the "graves" were opened, it was found that no bodies were buried there. Some of the Yemeni Israelis argue that this was part of a deliberate policy, with "perfectly healthy" children forcibly hospitalized as part of the plan. Israeli apologists deny the existence of "an organized conspiracy" but admit that "there was a condescending attitude toward" the Yemenis that stressed the need for "absorption through modernization, by inculcating the values of Western society" in which "The parents were treated like primitive people who didn't know what was good for them, who aren't capable of taking care of their own kids."[41] One Israeli, writing in *Haaretz* and later quoted by William Pfaff, explained that the Yemeni Jews' "primitivism touches the limits" and that "They are hardly superior to Arabs, or Blacks, or other barbarians."[42]

According to one interpretation, the European Zionists themselves were victims of their own cultural cleansing. Michael Selzer traces the origins of Zionism back to the eighteenth century Eastern European Haskalah movement, which "denounced what was regarded as the traditionalism, obscurantism and backwardness" of the Jewish people and insisted that Jews must "renounce all that was unique about them" and recreate themselves in the image of other Europeans.[43] Zionist settlers in Palestine typically rejected their old Jewish names, such as Rosenthal and Silberberg, in favor of romantic Hebrew ones that had not previously been used.[44] Selzer argues that this movement had "contempt" for its own people and required the future founders of the Jewish state "to mold themselves in the image of those who hated them most" in order to "ensure the approval of the anti-Semites."[45] In this way, they ensured "the 'Aryanization' of the Jew" and the end of the Jews' condition, as stated in numerous Zionist writings that borrowed the accusation of anti-Semites, of Jews as "a 'parasitic' people."[46] "Jews endured anti-Semitism for nearly two millennia before finally succumbing themselves to the opinions of the anti-Semites."[47] Zionism's goal "was to create a new Jewish type who would invalidate the hostility of the anti-Semite for the extremely persuasive reason that the new Jew would be almost identical to the anti-Semite himself and would, to all intents and purposes, have ceased to be a Jew.[48] Selzer argues that the source of the European Israelis' prejudice against the Middle Eastern newcomers after 1948 was the way the latter "raised the fearful specter of Oriental or Asiatic primitivism as a Jewish characteristic and threatened to undo the whole grand psychic achievement of Israel," as "they were a living refutation of…the vitally important Zionist claim that the Jew is *not* Oriental."[49]

Conclusion

Cultural cleansing has served throughout history as a means of domination. Indeed, it is one species of the broader genus of ethnic cleansing. It comes in many varieties, ranging from destruction of monuments to the eradication of mother tongues, but it always aims at destroying a people's memory and identity. Sometimes, as in the cases of Bosnia and Palestine, it comes with other kinds of ethnic cleansing in an attempt to remove evidence, such as place names and even graveyards, of those who were expelled.

The other essays in this volume concentrate specifically on cultural cleansing in Iraq since the invasion at the start of the third millennium CE. Not all of the techniques of conquerors that have been dealt with here necessarily apply in this case. The Arabic language and the religion of Islam in its main sectarian forms are too firmly entrenched for many outsiders to imagine replacing them, although indeed there were some naïve Americans who dreamed at the outset of the occupation that this would bring into being a fertile field for Christian evangelization. The conflict that ensued following the invasion did at least temporarily undermine the Iraqi and pan-Arab identity by stirring up a virulent sectarianism. Inadvertently, the conquerors' initial indifference to protecting the country's ancient heritage – as in not acting to prevent the looting of museums and by using heavy machinery to dig trenches at the site of Babylon – actually contradicted the attempt to undermine the Arab and Islamic identities of Iraqis that pose real threats to imperial objectives. If the invaders were seeking to undermine the country's loyalties to the Arab/Islamic world, destroying the pre-Islamic heritage, which they might have imagined as the basis for some sort of purely Iraqi identity, was counterproductive to such a goal.

Notes

1. Robert Bevan, *The Destruction of Memory: Architecture at War*, London: Reaktion Books, 2006, pp. 8, 210.
2. See Samuel P. Huntington, *The Clash of Civilizations and the Remaking of World Order*, New York: Simon & Schuster, 1996, pp. 139ff and Huntington, "The Change to Change: Modernization, Development, and Politics," *Comparative Politics*, April 1971, pp. 293ff.
3. See John Alden Williams, *Themes of Islamic Civilization*, Berkeley and Los Angeles: University of California Press, 1971, pp. 2–3.

4. Quincy Wright, *A Study of War*, 2nd ed., with a Commentary on War since 1942, Chicago: University of Chicago Press, 1965, p. 111.
5. John Noble Wilford, "Languages Die, but Not Their Last Words," *New York Times*, September 19, 2007.
6. Richard C. Foltz, *Religions of the Silk Road: Overland Trade and Cultural Exchange from Antiquity to the Fifteenth Century*, New York: St. Martin's Griffin, 1999, pp. 96–7.
7. Alistair Horne, *A Savage War of Peace: Algeria 1914–1962*, Harmondsworth, UK and New York: Penguin Books, p. 61.
8. Walker Connor, "Nation-Building or Nation-Destroying," *World Politics*, Spring 1973.
9. Lucian W. Pye, "Chapter 3: Identity and Political Culture," in Leonard Binder et al. (eds.), *Crises and Sequences in Political Development*, Princeton: Princeton University Press, 1971, p. 116.
10. Connor, "Nation-Building or Nation Destroying," pp. 341–2.
11. Raymond Grew, "Italy," in Raymond Grew (ed.), *Crises of Political Development in Europe and the United States*, Studies in Political Development, Princeton: Princeton University Press, 1978, p. 278.
12. Charles W. Anderson, Fred R. von der Mehden, and Crawford Young, *Issues of Political Development*, Englewood Cliffs, NJ: Prentice-Hall, 1967, p. 78.
13. Connor, "Nation Building or Nation-Destroying," pp. 319ff, 328, 322.
14. Ibid., p. 350.
15. Richard W. Cottam, *Nationalism in Iran*, 2nd ed., Pittsburgh: University of Pittsburgh Press, 1979, pp. 118ff.
16. Nader Entessar, "Chapter 16: Ethnicity and Ethnic Challenges in the Middle East," in John Mukum Mbaku et al. (eds.), *Ethnicity and Governance in the Third World*, Aldershot, UK: Ashgate, 2001, p. 156.
17. Bevan, *Destruction of Memory*, pp. 25–6.
18. Ibid., p. 27.
19. Ibid., p. 42.
20. Ibid., p. 47.
21. See Colin Kaiser, "Crimes Against Culture – the Former Yugoslavia," *UNESCO Courier*, September 2000, http://www.unesco.org/courier/2000_09/uk/signe2.htm, accessed November 14, 2008.
22. For one rare comparison of their experiences, see Joseph Schechla, "Bosnia and Palestine: So Close, and Yet So Far," *al-Majdal Quarterly Magazine*, no. 35, Autumn 2007, http://www.badil.org/al-majdal/2007/Autumn/article04.htm, accessed November 19, 2008.

23. Michael Adams, *Signposts to Destruction: Israeli Settlements in Occupied Territories*, London: The Council for the Advancement of Arab–British Understanding, n.d., p. 13.
24. Yoav Stern, "JNF to Erect Signs in Parks, Citing Destroyed Palestinian Villages," *Haaretz*, February 6, 2008, accessed May 16, 2008.
25. Meron Benvenisti, *Sacred Landscape: The Buried History of the Holy Land Since 1948*, Maxine Kaufman-Lacusta (trans.), Berkeley, Los Angeles, and London: University of California Press, 2000, p. 5.
26. Ibid., p. 4.
27. Ibid., p. 8.
28. Esther Zandberg, "The House Remembers," *Haaretz*, November 16, 2003, http://www.haaretz.com/hasen/pages/ShArt.jhtml?item No=361047, accessed March 2, 2008.
29. Benvenisti, *Sacred Landscape*, pp. 17ff.
30. Ibid., p. 47.
31. Ibid., pp. 47, 53.
32. Ibid., pp. 53–4.
33. Meron Benvenisti, *City of Stone: The Hidden History of Jerusalem*, Maxine Kaufman Nunn (trans.), Berkeley, Los Angeles, and London: University of California Press, 1996, p. 240.
34. Benvenisti, *Sacred Landscape*, p. 296.
35. Yigal Hai, "In Jaffa, a War Wages over Graves," *Haaretz*, April 2, 2008, accessed May 16, 2008.
36. Benvenisti, *Sacred Landscape*, pp. 273ff.
37. Yoav Stern, "Arabs Rally Against Construction of Jerusalem Museum on Muslim Cemetery," *Haaretz*, November 6, 2008, http://www.haaretz.com/hasen/spages/1035063.html, accessed November 19, 2008, and Gershon Baskin, "Encountering Peace: A City of Tolerance, Not a Museum of Tolerance," *Jerusalem Post*, Internet Edition, November 4, 2008, http://www.jpost.com/servlet/Satellite?c id=1225910072333&pagename=JPost%2FJPArticle%2FShowFull, accessed November 19, 2008.
38. Nicole Nasser, "Israeli Politics of 'Archeology' in Jerusalem," *Online Journal*, February 14, 2007, accessed May 23, 2008.
39. Meyrav Wurmser, "Post-Zionism and the Sephardi Question," *Middle East Forum*, Spring 2005, accessed May 13, 2008.
40. Bat-Zion Eraqi-Klorman, "The Forced Conversion of Jewish Orphans in Yemen," *International Journal of Middle East Studies*, February 2001, p. 23.
41. Joel Greenberg, "The Babies From Yemen: An Enduring Mystery," *New York Times*, September 2, 1997, http://www.nytimes.com/1997/09/02/world/the-babies-from-yemen-an-enduring-mystery.html, accessed May 9, 2008.

42. William Pfaff, "Eugenics, Anyone?" *New York Review of Books*, Vol. 44, No. 16, October 23, 1997, and Raphael Falk, "Eugenics Denied: Response to William Pfaff," *New York Review of Books*, Vol. 45, No. 1, January 15, 1998.

43. Michael Selzer, *The Aryanization of the Jewish State*, New York: Black Star Publishing Company, 1967, pp. 29, 32; also see Benjamin Beit-Hallahmi, *Original Sins: Reflections on the History of Zionism and Israel*, New York: Olive Branch Press, 1993.

44. Beit-Hallahmi, *Original Sins*, p. 128.

45. Selzer, *Aryanization of the Jewish State*, p. 35.

46. Ibid., pp. 36–7.

47. Ibid., p. 38.

48. Ibid., p. 48.

49. Ibid., p. 50.

PART II

Policy in Motion: The Assault on Iraq's Incomparable History

3

ARCHAEOLOGY AND THE STRATEGIES OF WAR[1]

Zainab Bahrani

The destruction and looting of cultural heritage in the Anglo-American war and occupation of Iraq has been the subject of a great deal of press reports and discussions in academic journals and conferences in the past five years, ever since the initial invasion of 2003 culminated in the widespread plundering of museums and libraries. These discussions, however, have remained at the level of unease over the unfortunate collateral damage of the war and occupation; damage that has included a patrimony, which is seen not as a loss for Iraq as a state or for the people of this land but primarily for what is described as "our global cultural heritage." Since ancient Iraq is the land that archaeologists and ancient historians refer to as Mesopotamia, the cradle of civilization, the place of the rise of urbanism, the invention of writing and complex social structures, Iraq's ancient past is therefore considered to be of great importance to the entire world.[2] However, this international outcry over the destruction and theft of antiquities as a global heritage is a double-edged sword. On the one hand there is no doubt in the importance of raising public awareness on the matter of the particular importance of Iraq's archaeological profile to the world. On the other hand the academic conferences, papers and publications that have emerged from it, as well as general popular press books and the endless news articles on the matter have all circumvented a major point. Cultural destruction in war is not always a result of accidental or "collateral" damage. It is not just a loss of the world's global heritage. It is a destruction of history in a country under occupation.

The Assault on Iraqi History and Collective Memory

Most of the attention that this subject has received has been mainly phrased as a concern for "the cradle of world civilization." However, as in other wars in other times and places, the destruction of monuments and historical archives works to erase the historical landscape and the realms of memory around which people define their collective identities. There has been a remarkable silence on this aspect of the cultural and historical destruction in Iraq. Even though, as an area of research and of scholarly and political public discussions and publications, this type of destruction has been recognized and analyzed when such acts have taken place in other countries, and when they were perpetrated by other peoples. For example, the attacks on monuments and architectural structures that were conceived to be markers of a particular ethnic group's presence in a region – for example, minarets, orthodox churches, and the famous bridge at Mostar – have now become dominant aspects of the historical accounts of the breakup of the former Yugoslavia, perhaps even iconic of that war in some ways.[3] These standing monuments, stone, brick and mortar, came to be equated to linguistic or religious-ethnic groups or nationalities, their presence unwanted and erased from the landscape at the same time that people were either forcefully relocated or killed, each group considering that their ethnic identity and historical relation to place were made tangible or intangible by the presence or absence of monuments.

The earliest course of events in the 2003 war, in terms of the destruction of the ancient Mesopotamian past, is well known. In the first few days following the end of the US "Shock and Awe" campaign on Iraq, when Baghdad was under US military control, Iraq's main museums, libraries and archives were looted and extensively damaged by fire. Most of the damage to museums and libraries occurred between April 10 and 12, 2003.[4] Due to the focus of the international press, it was the Iraq Museum that received the greatest amount of attention. This museum is generally considered to be one of the three or four most important museum collections in the world as it houses a remarkable range of excavated antiquities and Islamic art and manuscripts from Iraq itself rather than being a collection formed by market-bought objects or antiquities acquired through imperial wars and colonization (such as the British Museum in London or the Louvre Museum in Paris, for example).

During the event of the looting of the Iraq Museum in Baghdad, a Bradley tank and a number of US troops were in the area, some meters away from the main entrance. At one point, a curator from the museum staff walked over and asked for assistance but was told by the tank commander (who, to give him credit, actually radioed his superiors to request permission) that no orders had been given to help. At the time, Donald Rumsfeld appeared on our television screens in the US and declared that these events were a positive sign of the liberation of an oppressed people; "stuff happens," he said. In the United States, those of us who opposed the war from the start, and who implied that the US bore some responsibility for its negligence were dismissed as anti-American radicals, even in the mainstream press. But by 2007, Barbara Bodine, the US Ambassador at the time, revealed to Charles Ferguson in his documentary film *No End in Sight* that direct orders had come from Washington stating that no one was to interfere with the looting.

In the press and among most archaeologists, the events of that April are still described as another consequence of the occupation that was not foreseen and was, like so many other aspects of the occupation, due to the lack of foresight of the Bush administration.[5] The looting spree in the museums and libraries was just the tip of the (proverbial) iceberg of a catastrophic scale of historical destruction that was to come in the following five years, and it was not simply the result of poor planning or the inadvertent damage of war. Even if this could not be avoided, or was not foreseen (an excuse that I personally find rather weak given the fact that numerous archaeologists and other scholars had warned both the US and UK governments against exactly such a scenario months before the war), there are areas of cultural destruction that were entirely avoidable and sometimes pre-planned.

First, there is the Pentagon's strategic decision to use the main cultural heritage sites of the country as US and coalition military bases. These sites include (among others) Ur, the legendary birthplace of Abraham; Babylon, the famed capital of Mesopotamian antiquity; and Samarra, the Abbasid Islamic imperial city. The digging, bulldozing, filling of sand bags and blast-barricade containers, the building of barracks and digging of trenches into the ancient sites have destroyed thousands of years of archaeological material, stratigraphy and historical data. Walls and standing structures have collapsed as a result of shootings, bombings and helicopter landings. The idea that there was no pre-planning or high-level military decision making in choosing these ancient sites as major camp installations is difficult to believe.

Despite the commonly held view, these activities are not only ethically questionable because they inadvertently damage cultural heritage sites during an otherwise ethically conducted act of *jus belli*. On the contrary, they are against both the Iraqi Cultural Heritage Law and against International Laws of War and Occupation. In other words, like human rights abuses, the destruction of a people's cultural heritage and history has elsewhere been regarded as a war crime. To be precise, similar to the case of torture, International Law has regarded such activities as war crimes when people or states other than the US have been responsible for them. The war which was presented as a *jus belli* but was launched on the basis of a series of false claims publicized by the G.W. Bush administration, has disregarded international law in several arenas and cultural heritage is another one of them. This kind of abuse of heritage sites is perhaps difficult to understand when the historical sites are unfamiliar. A simple reversal may help illustrate the needless destructive acts of the occupation forces.

Imagine if you will, if, say, Stonehenge were to be taken over as a military barracks that housed thousands of troops and required the digging of the earth in order to provide plumbing and sewerage in the middle of the ancient site itself, while trenches were dug around the megaliths and perhaps some of the smaller monoliths were relocated, and used as blast walls to protect the troops at the checkpoint entries to the base. When leading archaeologists come to point out the damage, they are asked: "Are you suggesting that we risk the lives of our troops?" This is the situation today at some of the most important cultural heritage sites of Iraq.

At other ancient sites, we have a second situation of massive but preventable destruction. This is the looting of countless Mesopotamian archaeological sites. The looting occurred because the State Board of Antiquities and Heritage has a dearth of funding or equipment for site guards like those in other antiquities-rich countries such as Egypt, Italy, Turkey or Greece, and because the US and UK governments have had little interest in including such site protection in the multi-trillion-dollar budget of the occupation. Despite the noble pledges of commitment to the rescue of cultural heritage and rebuilding of the museum and libraries that were made in 2003, the reality is similar to that of the situation with electricity and water. Almost nothing has been done. The Iraqi government is no better. It has shown a remarkable lack of interest in preserving historical sites, whether they are of pre-Islamic or Islamic eras. For example, the ancient area of the ninth century Abbasid royal city of Samarra was chosen as the place for building an Iraqi police barracks. More recently, the Iraqi government has actually cut what little money that had been allocated for these sites. Worse yet, in the summer of 2007 Iraqi troops marched into the National Library and physically assaulted librarians and other staff when they wished to take over the National Library as an observation point.[6]

At the time when the first news of the Iraq Museum looting emerged, there were also allegations made in the Western press and media that the curatorial staff had been responsible. These charges were never substantiated, although people's lives and reputations were seriously damaged as a result. In the de-Ba'athification plan of Paul Bremer, any qualified curators, archaeologists and professors who had remained in Iraq through the terrible years of the embargo, were removed from their positions. In the following five years, many more scholars left the country, forced into exile because of direct threats to their lives; others were not so fortunate and have just become part of the "collateral damage" of war.

Another seriously disturbing development is apparent when it comes to the account of the destruction of Iraq's cultural heritage. A situation has arisen now that the voices of Iraqi archaeologists are mostly dismissed as politically motivated whereas the archaeologists who work with the US or UK government and military are now taken as the unbiased and objective assessors of the situation. In addition to the destruction and erasure of history therefore, we can add the silencing of the voices of Iraqi scholars.

What has happened under the US command of Iraq with regard to cultural heritage, museums and libraries was in opposition to both the 1954 Hague Convention and the principles of the Geneva Conventions. When I first pointed this out, writing on the morning after the looting and destruction of the museums and libraries in 2003,[7] I did not realize that the looting of the museums and libraries would be only the beginning of an immense historical annihilation that was to come, the processes of which I would have the unfortunate privilege of seeing for myself in 2004 while working on the closing of the military camp at Babylon with my colleague Maryam Umran Moussa.[8] Yet given the horrors of that time and in the face of the current death and destruction that have become the day to day existence of the average Iraqi it is difficult for me, as an archaeologist from Iraq, to focus on issues of cultural heritage alone. After all, archaeology and libraries have received some attention by various non-governmental organizations (NGOs) and government ministries, more so than the civilian death count or the contaminated drinking water or the hospitals full of dying children. Yet the destruction of history as an act of war is no small matter.

In academia, the general stance has been that notions of cultural heritage and history, the relation of people to monuments, is not to be universalized like the human subject, whose rights we fight for, because attitudes to history are culturally constructed. Furthermore, the currently favored view in archaeology and anthropology is that this kind of a relation of people to the past is a Western one, and as such it is part of a Western order that we impose on others. My own scholarly view diverges from these current positions and the Iraq war has only made this clearer to me. The appropriation of the notion of historical consciousness for the West is simply a continuation of past colonial attitudes under a new liberal guise. The historical accounts of antiquity make clear that the relationship of people to monuments, to natural and constructed landscapes, and to historical narratives themselves is a very ancient one, certainly as old as the Early Dynastic Mesopotamian cities of the third millennium BC. In my view, having lived in the midst of this war and seen its violence on a daily basis, the horror of war is not the horror of body counts alone. Wars and occupation also cause damage to the living that cannot be quantified. Historical destruction must be seriously assessed as an act of war.

In the United States and Great Britain, the constant debate about the exact amount of looted archaeological sites or stolen antiquities continues in the press and among archaeologists. Since the first days of the war in 2003 there has been a barrage of reports, of sound bites from self-styled experts on Iraq's history or cultural heritage (many having never been in Iraq), reports from journalists who sat in the Rashid or Palestine hotels in Baghdad while their Iraqi employees went out on the streets, reports of coalition government representatives who minimize the effects of the damage or shift all the blame to the previous regime, and reports of representatives from various governments, each claiming to have done the most, or making a pledge to do the most, for the rescue of cultural heritage in Iraq while they remain silent about the civilian deaths. Living in Iraq itself one saw precious few of the projects that have been announced as the valiant rescue of Iraq's heritage. Worse yet, some of the projects and funding agencies appear to be geared more for the benefit of European and North American consumption rather than being of much use to heritage in Iraq itself. In a country taken over by violence, one should expect no more.

After the United Nations (UN) building collapsed in a 2003 bombing, the UN pulled out of Iraq and other NGOs followed suit, stating that it was simply too dangerous for their employees to remain. A number of institutions began working on projects to reconstruct the museums and libraries or to train Iraqi scholars from the safety of distance provided by cites such as Amman, London and New York. In addition, some of the accounts that I have read on cultural heritage issues in Iraq are more in the genre of sensationalizing narratives that set out to heroize the Western protagonist and give either little or no credit to the Iraqi archaeologists and scholars who have been doing all the work inside Iraq itself. As a result of some of these accounts, one might say that the destruction of cultural heritage in Iraq becomes salvaged into a narrative of rescue and reconstruction where in fact there is nothing but catastrophic loss. This appropriation of the very narrative of the events, of the historical account of what has happened to historical sites and cultural institutions and who has been working to rescue and preserve these is a facet that I could not foresee in March and April of 2003. Cultural heritage is a pawn in this game of war in more ways than one.

The people of Iraq continue to endure many forms of violence on a daily basis. Some of these are direct forms of physical violence, while others are psychological forms of violence. The loss or destruction of historical monuments can and does have a devastating effect on people. That is why throughout history such destruction has been calculated into the strategies of war. This is the reason that iconoclasm and destruction or the relocation of monuments have occurred as deliberate acts of war throughout recorded world history, and why ethnic cleansing works through the annihilation of people by means of eradicating any trace of their past. The recognition of cultural destruction as an act of warfare is not new. It was the reason that international legal conventions were written in opposition to such acts, especially after World War II.

Today, as I write this chapter while I sit at my desk in New York City, the death toll for US troops in Iraq stands at 4,183; we see the latest count on the scrolling text at the bottom of our television screens. Conversely, the rising numbers of Iraqi dead never appear in our news reports; the Pentagon does not keep count, and neither does the Iraqi government for that matter.

Meanwhile in Iraq itself, water and electricity infrastructures still have not been repaired after over five years of occupation. Hundreds of thousands of people have been killed, exiled or forcibly displaced, women's rights have been obliterated and the rich cultural heritage and historical archives of the country have been extensively looted and destroyed.

At the same time, a new US government initiative that designates $14 million for the assistance of Iraq's historical patrimony, its museums and libraries, was announced. Speaking in early October 2008 at the Iraqi embassy in Washington DC, then first lady Laura Bush publicized this generous grant made in order to remedy the unfortunate collateral damage done to cultural heritage, and the years of neglect of archaeological sites and cultural institutions under Saddam Hussein's regime.[9] However, a large part of this is money that has already been distributed to American universities in the US, and a great deal of it will actually go to institutions in the US rather than to repairing things that were destroyed under the watch of the occupation or even wrecked directly by the US military in Iraq.

Of course there are good things about this grant and it will certainly be put to positive use in American universities, for example in providing Iraqi scholars with training in the latest technological and scientific methods. The irony here is not to be missed. Part of the money is specifically designated for educating Iraq Museum professionals in curatorial expertise in the US, an offer of lessons in how to be good custodians of your cultural heritage from the country that was responsible for its destruction.

In the US little is heard about the placing of American or Multi-National Force military bases on ancient heritage sites, or about the bulldozing and digging by US forces at legendary historical places like Babylon and Samarra. Satellite images show that one ancient site dating to the early second millennium BC was totally leveled in order to accommodate the expansion of the US base nearby.[10] While different sectarian factions in Iraq bombed each other's mosques and churches because of religious prejudices and intolerance, the occupation's forces participated in the destruction of the historical sites of ancient Mesopotamia in their own way.

The looting of the museums and the torching of the libraries in April of 2003 were famously explained by Rumsfeld as an act of democratic freedom by a previously oppressed population; "freedom is messy," he said. Speaking for the Bush administration in 2003, he also told the American public that the looting could not have been foreseen by anyone. Rumsfeld knew very well when he said this that the looting was indeed foreseen, since dozens of archaeologists, other academics and museum professionals had warned of exactly such a scenario. Some had actually gone to the Pentagon to be assured by US government officials that guards would be placed at museums and libraries as soon as US forces took over the country. Even if we take Rumsfeld at his word and accept that the looting in April 2003 could not have been predicted, he still needs to explain the Pentagon decisions, made under his command, that involved direct US destruction of ancient sites or the removal of national archives, against the wishes of the Iraqi people and government. In addition, the occupation of a number of archaeological and historical sites as US and coalition military bases continues today. These acts are clear violations of the international conventions on the safeguarding of cultural heritage of occupied territories.

In October of 2008 the Pentagon launched another "public relations" initiative that would allocate $US 330 million for pro-American propaganda inside Iraq. This operation would pay for such things as pro-American television and radio programs as well as print news spun from pro-US occupation perspectives. It is clear that this propaganda is aimed at the Iraqi people, but we should realize that some of this spin is also aimed at consumers here in the West, so that we might believe that the humanitarian intervention in Iraq was a success.

Part of the new campaign, seemingly aimed specifically at academics, includes something called the Minerva Research Initiative (MRI) funded by some $US 50–75 million. A website by that name has been set up by the Pentagon, in conjunction with the Social Science Research Council.[11] According to its website, the MRI aims to provide a new military–academic interface, calling on all academics to submit proposals for research and articles to this site. The major lure of the MRI appears to be not only potential financial support for research projects (to be peer reviewed by the Social Science Research Council in conjunction with the Department of Defense) but for the select few, there will be access to the contested Iraqi archive, now housed in the Hoover Institute at Stanford University.

As the destruction of historical sites and occupation of these sites as military bases continues despite the constant requests of the State Board of Antiquities and Heritage of Iraq, the attitude towards the stolen archives demonstrates a general policy of disregard for the people and their history. The US continues to refuse the return of archives that were taken out of Iraq and shipped to the United States. As Saad Eskander the Director of the National Library and State Archives of Iraq put it, rather than improving their stance on the protection of cultural heritage, there has in fact been "an escalation in its [US] violations of international conventions that goes against the principles of the rule of law, self determination and human rights that are supposed to govern the so called free world."[12] The archive at the Hoover Institute is reported to consist of tens of millions of records kept by Saddam Hussein's regime on the Iraqi people: all of the records on private citizens who may have been dissidents, records of those who disappeared, records of human rights abuses, the collective punishments and murdering of the population. Iraqis did not have access to these documents under the violent and repressive regime of Saddam; they are denied access to them now in a so-called free and independent Iraq.

In April 2003, Rumsfeld also described the plundering of the museums and libraries as the "messy birth pangs of democracy." But we now know that at the Iraq Museum that houses one of the world's most important collections of antiquities, no less important historically than any of the major museums in Western capitals, the looting was at least partially inspired by the concept of antiquities as free market goods. These are not the ideals of democracy, but of financial profit. It seems that at least one group of looters that entered the museum were professional art thieves who knew exactly what to take, the difference between a real antiquity and a plaster copy, and what objects would fetch the highest prices in the international illicit art market. The former Director of the Iraq Museum, Donny George Yohanna, has written that months before the war he heard reports from the UK and elsewhere in Europe of people boasting that the war would enable better-qualified Western custodians to take over the antiquities of Iraq, which were, after all, global cultural heritage (he now lives in exile, having been forced to leave when threats were made against his family because they are Christians).[13] Of course there were other looters at the Iraq Museum; many were like the people who went into various government buildings, took furniture and equipment wherever they could find it, and plundered because of their hatred of the regime. However, there is no question that professional art thieves were involved at the museum. A large number of artifacts from the Iraq Museum collections were found later in Western Europe and the United States, as well as several countries in the Middle East, stopped by border control. These objects had obviously been smuggled out of Iraq for sale in the lucrative international market of stolen antiquities.

In the years that followed the museum looting, we also saw an increase in the pillaging of archaeological sites, especially in the south of Iraq, the heartland of ancient Sumer and Babylonia, where there are thousands of ancient sites. Some amount of looting already existed there in Saddam Hussein's era, especially during the days of the embargo, but the rate of the looting increased dramatically after the invasion and occupation of Iraq. Like the major museum thefts, this kind of looting is not for local consumption. It feeds the appetite of the illicit international market in antiquities. The looting has now somewhat subsided, thanks to the appointment of more site guards and the distribution of patrol cars to them, organized and funded in part by the US Department of State as well as by the Italian government. The destruction of the record of the past through the damage done to archaeological sites, whether in the era of Saddam Hussein and the embargo or in the first years of the occupation, can never be repaired.

The Willful Violence of Cultural Destruction

In comparison to the continuing violence in Iraq, the deaths, the forced relocations and exile of the population, the destruction of cultural heritage and the confiscation of archives seem like a minor detail of war, the loss of some bits of paper and old artifacts, but we should not forget that such forms of destruction do great violence to the inhabitants of the land. To Americans, the looting and destruction of museums and libraries that took place soon after the fall of Baghdad is most commonly seen as an example of the phenomenal lack of foresight of the Bush administration. We dismiss much of what happened during the invasion of 2003 and under the continuing occupation as poor planning or, at worst, the stupidity and ineptitude of the early days of the invasion. In fact, however, a large part of the cultural destruction took place not in the first days of the invasion, but during the last five and half years of occupation. Clearly, not all of it was accidental.

The occupation of heritage sites as military bases that I have discussed above is a clear example of a strategic and pre-planned use of historical landmarks and monuments. Besides the legendary city of Babylon, which was turned into the headquarters of South Central Command of the Multi-National Forces, at Samarra, the top of the ninth century minaret was blown off by a rocket-propelled grenade while it was in use as a US sniper post. When such acts occur in other wars and are perpetrated by other people we have no qualms about speaking of them in terms of historical erasure and calling them crimes of war. Why do we not do the same now?

There is also now the potential of historical destruction in the current plans for the demolition of old city centers, for example in the historical heart of Kerbala and Najaf. The planning by the Iraqi government in collaboration with international construction firms is presented in terms of modernization and reconstruction, but these plans will re-shape the medieval city centers, just as the blast walls and checkpoints have reorganized the urban space of Baghdad and facilitated the forced relocation of the population.

The building of "enduring bases" across Iraq and the colossal US embassy in Baghdad should also be taken into account in that they are part of a construction program that contributes to the militarization of urban space, the demolition of historical areas, and the extensive erasure and rewriting of the historical fabric of the land. How can we think of the larger issue of territoriality and control in Iraq without taking into account the continuing obliteration of the past and memory through the removal and suppression of archives, or the erasing and reconfiguration of the historical terrain through the destruction of ancient monuments and historical sites? These things should not be dismissed as accidental collateral damage; they are direct acts of war and it is precisely through such destruction that empires have always re-mapped space.

Notes

1. Parts of this chapter have appeared in Zainab Bahrani, "The Battle for Babylon," in Peter Stone and Joanne Farchakh Bajjaly (eds.), *The Destruction of Cultural Heritage in Iraq*, Melton, UK: Boydell & Brewer Ltd, 2008, and Zainab Bahrani, "Desecrating History," *Guardian*, April 9, 2008.
2. For a history of ancient Mesopotamia, see Marc Van De Mieroop, *A History of the Ancient Near East, ca. 3000–323 B.C.*, Oxford: Blackwell, 2004.
3. See Robert Bevan, *The Destruction of Memory: Architecture at War*, London: Reaktion Books, 2006.
4. See Bahrani, "The Battle for Babylon"; K. Nashef, *The Destruction of Iraqi Cultural Heritage* (in Arabic), Beirut: Dar al Hamra, 2004; and Donny George, "The Looting of the Iraq Museum," in Stone and Bajjaly, *Destruction of Cultural Heritage in Iraq*.
5. For example, see the discussion "Robbing the cradle of civilization: Five years later," *Salon*, http://www.salon.com/news/feature/2008/03/20/iraq_roundtable/print.html, accessed December 2008.
6. Saad Eskander, personal communication with the author in 2007.
7. Zainab Bahrani, "Looting and Conquest," *The Nation*, May 14, 2003.
8. Maryam Umran Moussa, "The Damages Sustained to the Ancient City of Babel as a Consequence of the Military Presence of Coalition Forces," in Stone and Bajjaly, *Destruction of Cultural Heritage in Iraq*.

9. Laura Bush, "Remarks at the Launch of the 'Iraq Cultural Heritage Project'," October 16, 2008, http://www.whitehouse.gov/news/rele ases/2008/10/20081016-1.html, accessed December 2008.

10. See Elizabeth C. Stone, "Patterns of Looting in Southern Iraq," *Antiquity*, No. 82 (2008), pp. 125–38.

11. See Thomas Asher, "Making Sense of the Minerva Controversy and the NSCC," Social Science Research Council, http://www.ssrc.org/ essays/minerva/, accessed December 2008.

12. Saad Eskander, "Minerva Research Initiative: Searching for the Truth or Denying the Iraqis the Rights to Know Truth?" Social Science Research Council, October 29, 2008, http://www.ssrc.org/essays/ minerva/2008/10/29/eskander, accessed December 2008.

13. George, "Looting of the Iraq Museum."

4

THE CURRENT STATUS OF THE ARCHAEOLOGICAL HERITAGE OF IRAQ

Abbas al-Hussainy

The complexity and cultural richness of Iraqi heritage is unquestionable. It is the site of advanced urban settlement dating back to the fourth millennium BC. The ancient sites of Mesopotamia have bequeathed us an impressive array of monuments, texts and artifacts, providing modern archaeologists a remarkable historical record. Iraq's culture heritage, moreover, is marked by an exceptional human and natural variety. In the human dimension, countless peoples and religious communities have contributed to the cultural contours of the Iraqi nation, and in land itself, one finds equal variety: from the Gulf to Shatt al-Arab, to the great Tigris and Euphrates rivers, to the fertile lands in the sediments plains, to the mountain chains. The diversity of Iraq, in terms both human and natural, has greatly enriched the cultural imagination and production of the peoples of Mesopotamia. It is in light of this cultural richness and heritage that the scourging of Iraq in the recent modern era is so particularly troubling.

The Destruction

The extraordinary cultural output of Iraq will be considered in the latter part of this chapter, with a concise survey of the major periods, sites, cities, museums, and libraries. At the outset, it is sufficient to note that more than 12,000 registered archaeological sites constitute the bulk of Iraq's incomparable cultural legacy. Unfortunately, all of those priceless elements have been exposed to a level of destruction that no other country's cultural heritage has ever suffered. An inquiry of this level of cultural destruction should thus be centered on the core questions of an historical account of this devastation and the identification of those responsible for it.

The modern assault on Iraq's cultural legacy began as early as the second half of the nineteenth century. Initially, in the absence of a strong national state, thousands of archaeological objects were illegally exported to Asia, Europe and America. This cultural wasting slowed with the founding of the Iraqi state in the aftermath of World War I and the promulgation of law and regulations to protect antiquities, which banned the trespassing and unauthorized digging of archaeological sites and halted the sale of antiquities abroad. These new legal controls stemmed the flow of Mesopotamian artifacts into the international market for antiquities.

The Iraq–Iran war, however, once again exposed Iraqi heritage to exploitation and destruction. A great many important sites, especially those located close to the borders, suffered war damage. Moreover, Iraqi military activities exposed archaeological sites to further damage. Some sites served as military headquarters and were exposed to wear and damage through regular attendant traffic, such as the site of Der in Badra. Other sites were used as observation points because of their elevation, such as Drehem in Diwaniya and some sites between Ash-Shumali and Numaniyah. Other archaeological sites were damaged by the construction of air bases, such as Tallil, first used as a military base by the British during the Mandate era. The area of ancient Ur is the location of the Tallil air base, also used during the Gulf War. After 1991, as the central government weakened and as a result of the harsh economic embargo, illegal excavations ensued, causing extensive damage to the cities of the south, including Diwaniya, Semawa, Wasit, and Nasiriyah. Accordingly, thousands of cultural objects were looted and numerous sites and museums in those cities suffered damage and neglect. These cultural losses were compounded by environmental wreckage, notably with the Iraqi regime's punitive destruction of the Salt Marshes in the Shi'ite south, following the 1991 uprising/rebellion.

However, these earlier assaults on Iraq's Mesopotamian heritage pale in comparison to the wreckage inflicted by the occupation of Iraq from 2003 onward. Indeed, the scope of the cultural destruction suggests of occupation authorities a profound indifference to Iraq's cultural legacy if not outright complicity in the cultural wasting of the Iraqi nation. All of Iraq's major museums were affected, with damage to the Iraqi National Museum qualifying as catastrophic; thousands of objects were stolen or destroyed. Equal if not greater devastation affected the Sumerian sites, some of which quite simply ceased to exist. Great ancient cities and archaeological sites were thoroughly destroyed including Isin, abu-Hatab, Bezikh, Adab, Larsa, Shmet, Umma, Umm Al-Hafriyat, Tulul al-Dhaher,[1] az-Zebleiat,[2] and Tell al Wilaya.[3] Additional sites were used as military camps for occupying troops, including Babylon, Kish, Ur, and Samarra. In some cases even the offices of the antiquities departments were seized and occupied for military purposes.

Responsibility for the cultural wasting of Iraq is manifold. At the simplest level, unscrupulous antiquities markets in Europe and the United States and elsewhere have driven cultural looting throughout the modern era, up to the present era of occupation. More precisely, blame can be placed on the Iraqi state up to 2003, and to the occupation authorities thereafter.

The modern Iraqi state bears blame on several levels. In addition to launching wars that exposed Iraq's cultural sites to damage, the Hussein regime sponsored restoration projects that served purposes of propaganda rather than genuine historical interest. Most infamously was the "restoration" of Babylon which was rebuilt from inappropriate and anachronistic building materials. The ancient Neo-Babylonian palace was reconstructed with Saddam Hussein's name inscribed on the bricks, in the style of Nebuchadnezzar II. To the discredit of their vocation, some Iraqi archaeologists participated in this farce.

In the aftermath of the 1991 Gulf War, government officials engaged in illegal excavations, using violence against all local opposition in Diwaniya, Semawa, Wasit, and Nasiriyah. They aimed not only at looting but also the deliberate destruction of the historical identity of Southern Iraqis. Some very important sites were affected in this way, including Isin, Adad, Shurrupak, abu-Hatab, Bezikh, Larsa, Shmet, Umma, Tulul al-Dhaher, az-Zebleiat, and Tell al Wilaya.

The damage to these sites, including looting, is sometimes explained as the result of the desperate conditions of the local populace, hence diverting blame from the guilty governmental officials to the local populace. In fact, economic conditions in the affected regions – while difficult – were no worse than the rest of the country. Moreover, the population of the affected areas tended to leave these archaeological sites unmolested, given folk beliefs about evil spirits occupying these sites, while other sites were treated with respect as they served as graveyards.

Much of the cultural destruction of Iraq during this period was concentrated in the south. The Hussein regime, following the 1991 Gulf War and the southern revolts, waged an official campaign of vengeance and terrorism against the south, whose aim was nothing short of its destruction – including the people, their heritage and their environment. Southern Iraqis have the longest history of civil society and heritage and the regime set to extirpate all traces of those cultural markers.

It is estimated that more than 350,000 people were killed and buried in mass graves during the assault. Some 3 million date-palm trees were uprooted and the famed salt marshes deliberately dried up in a wanton act of environmental state terrorism. The regime mounted a propaganda campaign of lies, alleging that the people of the south were not Iraqis but foreigners – i.e. Persians – who moved into the area only recently. These claims are clearly contradicted by the cultural remains of both Sumerians and Akkadians in the region.

Specialists of the southern people report that, despite the recent emergence of Shi'ism, people of the south largely persist in the ancient traditions and use artifacts of their predecessors. There is also linguistic evidence of descent from the ancient Sumerians and Akkadians in the numerous words and place names from both languages that have survived in local dialects.

The Saddam Hussein regime was further involved in the construction of intrusive infrastructure in vulnerable areas including Tell Khaled in Diwaniya. The regime also sponsored agricultural projects, like those of the Greek company Sapanious, which had a deleterious impact on the archaeological heritage.

In this regard, the case of the Third River Project, ostensibly designed to increase agricultural production, deserves special criticism in that it resulted in the destruction of many Sumerian sites in the old dry river bed of the Euphrates. Other sites were damaged as a result of building roads in the vicinity. These neglectful policies extended to so-called rescue operations such as the one at Tell al-Makhada. The site was rescued on paper only, by the staged removal of only the upper surface while deeper layers were left in the hands of the construction company that built over them the road between Diwaniya and Najaf.

Regretfully, the State Board of Antiquities and Heritage bears responsibility for excavations that occurred during the 1990s. The Board adopted a policy of rewarding the discovery of recoverable artifacts while paying no reward or incentive for the discovery or preservation of permanent structures. Resultantly, archaeological structures were left unprotected, and moreover, clumsy excavation became an economic – rather than historical – pursuit for many. Cuneiform tablets, in particular, were copied and sold as original as was the case at the Shmet and Bezikh sites.

Additionally, the training of professional antiquities staff was neglected. The State Board of Antiquities and Heritage did little to raise suitable levels of expertise and care while, at the same time, displaying hostility to PhD holders. Consequently, many such experts chose to teach in the universities instead. At present, the Board retains only six PhDs on its staff, some of whom are on the verge of retirement.

The shortage of trained staff reached such a degree that some critical sites are severely understaffed, such as Semawa, which constitutes more than 600 sites including Uruk. There is only one staff archaeologist on site with a BA degree. Basra is even worse off, with no trained archaeologist in the antiquities office. Contemporary Iraq lacks the necessary staff for major sites, like Mosul and Nasiriyah, where the minimal tasks of protection and documentation cannot be adequately performed.

Though much blame falls on the Iraqi government for its acts of neglect and caprice vis-à-vis Iraqi heritage, the most significant destruction of Iraq's treasures has occurred under the Anglo-American occupation regime since 2003.

Under the eye of occupation forces, significant damage was inflicted to sites converted to military encampments, including Babylon, Kish, Ur and Samarra. The Babylon site was bulldozed to build a helicopter landing base. The soldiers also used the earth to fill sand bags and that "sand" was undoubtedly full of artifacts. In another dramatic case, occupation forces turned the medieval *khan* between Karaba and Najaf, called the Khan of Rubua into a military base. Soldiers collected discarded weapons and explosives, dumped them in a well within the building and detonated the munitions, causing the collapse of the Khan's roof.

The site of Ur was likewise converted for military aims and occupation forces proceeded to expand their military encampment without any permission from the State Board of Antiquities and Heritage or any oversight from archaeologist experts who might have directed American forces away from vulnerable sites. As a result, all of the stairs of the royal cemetery have been severely damaged and some of the large hulls are now cracked. The site is littered with trash. Kish suffered parallel damage when it too was used by the occupation forces as a military camp.

The powerlessness of Iraqis to protect cultural heritage was made personally evident when, on May 24, 2007, I served as chairman of the State Board of Antiquities. An American military convoy arrived at my office at the Iraqi Museum and demanded to enter the compound. When I refused to grant admission, they broke down the gates. I refused again to allow them to enter the museum building itself. They proffered a strange letter in Arabic, addressed to "Dear Colleague" but without a signature, declaring this group to belong to the US Embassy in Baghdad, and that they were authorized to enter the museum. I reiterated that this was insufficient. At this point I threatened to call the United Nations Educational, Scientific and Cultural Organization (UNESCO) and report the incident and potential damage to the Iraqi Museum. Only then did they leave.

It is regrettable that I must also report that there were foreign archaeologists who came to occupied Iraq. They proceeded to conduct highly suspect excavations without the permission of the Iraqi state. Particularly disturbing is the case of the Italian Giovanni Pettinato who announced the discovery of some 500 cuneiform tablets at Eridu. He subsequently claimed a find ten times that number. Then, in a strange twist, he explained that he meant stamps on bitumen and not actual tablets. All of this is highly suspect since it is impossible to believe that a professional archaeologist could mistake stamps for tablets. This bizarre case remains a mystery since until now it is not clear if any tablets were in fact discovered. Nor has there been any satisfactory explanation of how a civilian archaeologist got access to the sites through his country's military presence in occupied Iraq. It should be noted that such activities would seem to be a breach of the Hague Convention of the protection of cultural heritage in war.

As a result of neglect and continual assaults, Iraq's archaeological heritage is severely compromised. There exists extensive damage to all major sites in Iraq, including Ur, Uruk, Nippur, Babylon, all the khans (al-Rubua, al-Utashi, al-Musala,[4] al-Hamad, al-Nus, etc.), al-Kefel, Ctesiphon, Aqerquf,[5] Assur, Nimrud, Nineveh, Hatra, Kirkuk citadel, Arbil citadel, the old town of Basra, the Islamic capital Wasit, the Islamic capitals of Kufa, and Samarra, as well as all the major museums and all of the libraries.

A survey of archaeological damage would be incomplete without mention of relevant acts of terrorism and criminality. Armed elements have attacked unique monuments including al-Khilani and al-Gailani, mosques in Baghdad as well as al-Sarafiya bridge, al-Askari golden dome in Sammara, Anna minaret, al-Khder in Kbesa, Yehya ben al-Qasem, and Aon al-Deen in Mosul, and many shrines across Iraq, though especially in areas controlled by armed factions as in parts of Baghdad, Diyala, Ramadi, and Salahadin.

An Overview of the Iraqi Cultural Heritage

To enable the non-specialized reader to absorb the terrible loss Iraqis and all humanity has suffered, it is essential to provide a historical survey of Iraqi culture. Such a concise survey can be divided into two main historical periods, the ancient and the Islamic. Each of these periods has several important divisions, as summarized below.

The Uruk and Early Dynastic Periods[6]

This "ancient" period in Iraq dates back to the fourth millennium BCE when the inhabitants of ancient Iraq invented the world's first system of writing, using reeds and clay tablets. Among the most significant sites for the fourth and third millennia BCE are: Uruk, Eridu, Shurrupak, Badtebera, Lagash, Umma, Ur, Nippur, Abusalabikh, Kesura, Puzur-Dagan, and Kish.

The Akkadian Empire

This era began when Sargon the Akkadian (2334–2279 BCE) unified the Sumerian city-states, establishing the first empire in the history of the world. This earlier unification of city states in the south had occurred c.2371 BCE under Lugal-Zagesi, but Sargon established a far reaching empire, well beyond the lands of southern Mesopotamia. The city of Akkad served as the seat of an empire that extended from the Gulf to the Mediterranean sea, including Elam and Anatolia. The most prominent sites from this period are: Babylon, Sippar, Marad, Tell Brak (in Syria), Kutha, and Eshnunna.

The Ur III Empire

During the rule of the last Akkadian King, Sharkalisharri, the Gutians conquered Akkad and destroyed it. Utu-hengal, the Sumerian king of Uruk, waged a liberation struggle to drive out the Gutians. In the ashes of the Gutians, Ur-Nammu, one of the

Sumerian leaders, successfully established a new empire that is known as the Ur III Dynasty (2112–2004 BCE). The capital city was Ur itself. The cultural influence of the Sumerians spread out to distant lands as far as Elam, Anatolia, the Indus Valley, Meluhha, Dilmun, and Magan. It can be said that there is an archaeological level dated to the third dynasty of Ur in all the sites in Iraq and some outside as well.

The Old Babylonian Period (Also Known as the Ammorite Period)

This period began at the end of the reign of Ibbi-Sin, the last king of the Ur III dynasty. Naplanum, the king of Larsa, founded the dynasty of Larsa (2025–1763 BCE). Then Ishbi-Erra established an independent dynasty in Isin. It is known as the first dynasty of Isin (2017–1794 BCE). The Elamites subsequently conquered Ur and destroyed it. For this reason part of the old Babylonian period is known as the Isin-Larsa period. Subsequently, the dynasties were established at Babylon I, Der, Eshnunna, Sippar, Mari, Marad, and Assur and Uruk.

The Reign of Hammurabi

The celebrated King Hammurabi unified the competing dynasties to establish the third empire in the ancient history of Iraq. It ended in 1595 BCE when the Hittites conquered the city of Babylon. The empire was left to the Kassites who ruled until c.1160 BCE. The capital city, initially Babylon, was later built anew, in Dur-Kurigalzu, to the west of Baghdad. Subsequently, the Elamites conquered Babylon and plundered the sanctuary and cult statue of the most important Babylonian god, Marduk, as they had done to the sacred precincts when they conquered Ur in 2004 BCE desecrating relics of the Sumerian god Sin.

The Assyrian Empire

Although the Assyrians established their first dynasty of Assyria in the time of Shamshi Adad I in the north of Mesopotamia they were subject to the Babylonian Empire in the time of the king Hammurabi and his successors. In c.911 BCE, the Assyrians established the first Assyrian Empire and the fourth empire in the history of ancient Iraq. They ruled an area from the Gulf in the south to Anatolia in the north and from Elam in the east to Egypt in the west. The Assyrian Empire fell to an alliance between Babylonian King Nabopolassar and the Median King Kashtaritu (Cyaxares) in c.612 BCE. The most important Assyrian capital cities are Assur, Nimrud, and Nineveh.

The Neo-Babylonian Period

This era began when Nabopolassar established the eleventh dynasty of Babylon, making Babylon the capital for his empire, the fifth empire in the ancient history of Iraq. The most famous Neo-Babylonian ruler was Nebuchadnezzar II who ruled the same extensive territory as the preceding Assyrian Empire. There are numerous, dispersed sites of this era remaining, some within Iraq, others outside. These ruins include beautiful monuments such as the gate of Ishtar and the Street of Processions of Babylon, as well as many temples. Babylon was the place of the legendary *hanging gardens* which Herodotus mentions and were considered to be among the wonders of the ancient world. This empire ended when the Achaemenid King Cyrus conquered Babylon in 539 BCE.

The Late Periods

This period began with the fall of Babylon and is divided into the eras of the Achaemenid rule, Alexander the Great, and the Seleucid dynasty followed by the Parthians and the Sasanian. The most important cities are Hatra, Ctesiphon, and Seleucia on the Tigris, Hera, Manathera, and the ruins of some castles.

The Islamic Heritage

The Islamic period was initiated with Islam's expansion following the battle of Qadisiya between the Sassanians and Muslim forces.

The history of the Islamic period is divided into the Caliphate: Omayyad, Abbasid, Ottoman and later periods. There are five Islamic capital cities associated with this period: Basra, Kufa, Wasit, Baghdad, and Samarra. There are also numerous traditional buildings in several cities of Iraq that belong to this period, including mosques, sepulchers, religious schools, khans, baths, forts and castles. In addition, there are also traditional houses of architectural interest in all Iraqi cities, notably in Basra with its ornaments of Shanasheel, as well as in Hilla, Najaf, Kerbala, Baghdad, Kirkuk, Mosul and Erbil.

Iraq has many museums and libraries with holdings from the era of the Caliphates, notably, the Iraqi National Museum, the Military Museum, the Modern Fine Arts Museum, the Natural History Museum, and the Baghdad Museum. In addition, there are private museums as well as provincial museums, including those at Nasiriyah, Mesan, Diwaniya, Najaf, Babylon, Ramadi, Tikrit, Mosul, Erbil, and Sulaymania. There is also the National Library and State Archives in Baghdad as well as public libraries in the provinces.

Notes

1. Or Tullul al-Dhahir.
2. Or Zibliyat.
3. Or Alwelaia.
4. Or Al-Musalla.
5. Also known as Tell abu Shijer.
6. While archaeological sites and settlements in Iraq go back to about 8000 BC, the earliest evidence for complex urban societies, the rise of cities and the invention of writing begins in the fourth millennium BC.

5

NEGLIGENT MNEMOCIDE AND THE SHATTERING OF IRAQI COLLECTIVE MEMORY[1]

Nabil al-Tikriti

Those who control the present, control the past. Those who control the past, control the future.

George Orwell

Where one burns books, one will soon burn people.

Heinrich Heine[2]

Years ago, while roaming the stacks of one of the world's truly great research libraries, an epiphany bubbled to the surface of my substance-enlivened consciousness. Instead of seeing the usual information-packed inanimate objects lying on shelves, I suddenly envisioned a cacophony of passionate debates, insults, romances, genocide defenses, patriarchy justifications, and all the other phenomena one might find in such a vessel filled with millions of texts in hundreds of languages. As they were organized both topically and regionally, that night the books on my floor of specialization harangued me in shelving blocs – fiery Albanian nationalists here, pious Hanafi jurisprudents two rows across, followed by stern Ottoman apologists and whispering Sufi sensualists. I pondered what the complete absence of such books would mean. At least the cacophony would end, I figured – but what then?

While this personal anecdote might resemble a form of insanity meriting a call to burly men in white coats, I introduce it to illustrate the role of written knowledge to humankind. Without such texts, there are no recorded debates. Without such records, one must re-invent every argument – and loud new texts may successfully come to dominate that recently silenced conversation.

This chapter addresses a limited form of such an outcome – the cultural patrimony lost since the 2003 Anglo-American attempt to remake Iraq. One scholar, Keith Watenpaugh, has categorized such losses as "mnemocide," defined as the murder of cultural memory.[3] Nada Shabout and others have spoken about a "systematic campaign to erase Iraq's collective memory."[4] Official pronouncements were opaque in terms of intent regarding the protection of cultural property. However, Bush administration policies have clearly proven mnemocidal in effect – regardless of original intent. If such policies have not constituted active murder of cultural memory, at the very least they must be categorized as passive and negligent mnemocide.

Invasion Policies

When addressing the looting of April 2003, it is widely stated that US military planners either planned poorly for the post-invasion occupation, committed insufficient troops to secure vital facilities, or both. While these points have been effectively confirmed by a series of internal and external reviews,[5] such a limited explanation ignores the knowledge made publicly available prior to the invasion concerning the value of cultural facilities; downplays the selection process for deeming certain strategic and economic sites worthy of protection in spite of limited military resources; fails to mention several active seizures of Iraqi collective assets; largely shifts blame away from Pentagon planners and towards commanders in the field; and shields the Bush administration from all intentionality vis-à-vis the protection of Iraqi cultural facilities. Although many excuses have been provided, the fact remains that throughout several days of widespread looting the US chain of command continued to operate without interruption. Civilian officials based in Washington clearly had charge of operational priorities.

Prior to the invasion, a vibrant and public discussion of the necessity to protect Iraq's rich cultural patrimony culminated in a document submitted to the US Department of State by a number of regional experts, listing and ranking facilities requiring protection in case of invasion.[6] Pentagon officials were briefed by several Iraq experts about the potential for looting of cultural treasures, the location and significance of specific facilities, and the legal imperatives concerning protection of cultural patrimony.[7] Although the experts' list of significant cultural facilities was publicly recognized and discussed – and the facilities in question never targeted by the US military during the invasion – it was completely discounted by Pentagon planners once the looting began. Instead, such planners opted to protect certain Iraqi facilities chosen according to American perceptions of their economic or military value.

Specifically, Iraq experts prioritized protection of the National Museum and several other facilities of cultural, historical, or national value. However, throughout the first week of the occupation in Baghdad, planners instead chose to station troops for protection of sites considered important *for US strategic interests*.[8] Such sites suffered minimal looting damage at most, and in some cases no damage whatsoever. Strikingly, the only one of over twenty ministry headquarters judged worthy of protection was the Ministry of Oil, which held the records most useful for US economic engagement – or exploitation – in Iraq. All other ministries, vital for maintenance of Iraqi state cohesion, bureaucratic management, or the rule of law, were left completely unprotected – as their functions and assets were not considered vital for US interests. The same criterion was applied to all cultural facilities.

Matthew Bogdanos, a colonel in the Marine Corps Reserve who served during the 2003 invasion and led the US military investigation into the Iraqi National Museum looting, provided several military explanations suggesting that in most aspects US actions were correct, legal, and defensible. Since the museum facility had been used as a defensive position during the hostilities and chaos between April 8 and 11, 2003, it forfeited its protected status. If troops had attacked the looters with sufficient firepower to secure the facility, little would have remained of the complex. Sending only a few troops or a single tank to prevent the looting would have risked unacceptable American casualties. Troops were under orders not to fire "warning shots" under any circumstances, apparently in a bid to reduce the possibility of violent escalation and subsequent civilian deaths. While Bogdanos has conceded that the absence of a US troop presence at the museum after the looting had subsided by April 12 was "inexcusable," this should be characterized as a military planning mistake reflecting American lack of urgency, insufficient troop strength, and the dangers of "catastrophic success."[9]

While Bogdanos' explanations are persuasive in isolation, certain points prove problematic if one steps back and examines the hostilities as a whole. The lack of "boots on the ground" obliged military planners considering the "economy of risk" to transfer such risk from US troops to Iraqi civilians while rendering cultural facility protection impossible during the first week of the occupation.[10] While planners were unwilling to risk troop casualties for the protection of the Iraqi National Museum – let alone the less famous cultural facilities discussed further below – no such hesitation was evident for the protection of the facilities deemed of military or economic value. Meanwhile, the orders troops were given not to fire warning shots apparently limited their response options to either lethal fire or non-response. On the one hand, such orders prevented soldiers from firing in the air to restore order during the looting. At the same time, these orders appear to have encouraged other troops in a similar situation later in the same month to open up with lethal fire on a protesting crowd in Fallujah, causing 17 deaths. In yet another case, during the same week that massed crowds were engaging in widespread looting throughout Baghdad, American troops reportedly killed an armed guard at the Qadiriyyah manuscript collection on the assumption that all *armed* Iraqis were hostile. Such calculations intended to externalize casualties in the name of force protection and minimizing military casualties, contributed to the vulnerability of Iraqi cultural facilities in the midst of chaos. They also demonstrated the relative valuation of American military planners.

The occupying powers, primarily the government of the United States, argued that the cultural destruction experienced was not intentional. Yet, it is nevertheless true that it transpired with the direct acquiescence of civilian war planners who had been quick to trumpet their strategic genius and operational efficiency in the days and weeks of "shock and awe" prior to the mass looting of April 2003. For this reason, US government liability for losses sustained by Iraqi cultural facilities in the wake of the 2003 invasion remains an issue open for future pursuit.[11]

Several hours of looting can be considered a failure of policy, but several days of looting can only be seen as a policy of failure. In addition, several facilities continued to suffer damage long after the first week of occupation. All but a handful have received absolutely nothing in the form of American assistance. Most of the initial traumas suffered by these collections began two or more days after the April 8, 2003 entry of US troops into Baghdad and continued for several days – until international media attention appears to have forced a policy change on or around April 14, 2003.[12] Several of the more important facilities were concentrated in two small areas which had a sufficient US troop presence (two or three tank crews) in the area to prevent the events described below. However, when Iraqi staff members asked US soldiers to protect the facilities in question, the invariable response was either that "we are soldiers not policemen," or that "our orders do not extend to protecting this facility."[13] It later emerged that such responses were offered only after checking with superiors up the chain of command.[14]

Why might US officials allow such destruction to visit Iraq's national patrimony? When considered against the extensive background of efforts to protect equivalent facilities of cultural patrimony in Europe during World War II, coupled with the general lack of equivalent efforts in Asian arenas during that same conflict, it seems reasonable to suggest that a lack of common cultural sympathy was at play.[15] American sympathy toward Iraqi cultural losses at times seemed to resemble that of an individual who sympathizes with his neighbors who have lost their photographs and heirlooms in a fire. However, he feels no sense of personal loss at his neighbor's losses and is not averse to retaining his neighbor's property title, seized after the fire.

At the time, political leaders of the invading powers promised to provide a fresh start for Iraqi society. Prior to the Anglo-American invasion of Iraq in March 2003, several Bush administration officials promised a complete remaking of Iraqi society in the interests of spreading democracy, freedoms, liberty, and a "new Middle East." Not surprisingly, the creation of something new necessarily entails the destruction of what preceded it. The more ambitious the creation, the more extreme the destruction. Certain American officials hoped that such looting would clean the slate and smooth the way for their reconstruction of Iraqi society in an image more amenable to their tastes. John Agresto, in charge of the Ministry of Higher Education and Scientific Research in 2003–04, initially believed that the looting of Iraq's universities was a positive act in that it would allow such institutions to begin again with a clean slate, with the newest equipment as well as a brand new curriculum.[16]

In an effort to "blame the victim," apologists for US occupation policy have whenever possible assigned blame for the cultural destruction to Iraqi actors. While most of the looting of government facilities appears to have been carried out by indigent locals, attacks on several cultural sites were carried out by organized provocateurs whose identity remains a mystery years after the event. Some commentators have accused certain Iraqi staff members of being Ba'athist operatives who looted their own facilities.[17] Outside of credible claims concerning such insider vandalism at the National Library and Archives, no collection appears to have been intentionally damaged by staff. Indeed, most staff members continued to work in trying circumstances, initially without pay or assurance of future job security.[18]

Baghdad Archives and Manuscript Collections

While international attention has focused primarily on the immense destruction done to the country's pre-Islamic archaeological assets, domestic Iraqi and regional attention has focused equally on the losses suffered by the country's Islamic and modern cultural patrimony, including certain key manuscript collections, archives, art museums, monuments, and artifact collections.[19] Although several reports have addressed the state of some or all of these collections, much of the information concerning these collections remains inconclusive due to a continuing lack of transparency in the Iraqi domestic sphere. There, reports are therefore open to correction and clarification in the future.[20] To be fully certain of the post-invasion status of these collections, a national survey remains necessary. Until such time, the account that follows provides a summary of what is now known of the current conditions of several key facilities and collections.

The *Iraqi National Library and Archives* (INLA), the country's primary research facility and publication deposit library, featured particularly strong collections of Arabic periodicals, government documents dating back to Ottoman rule, and over a million books. Located directly across from the Ministry of Defense, it was burned and looted on two occasions, April 10 and April 12–13, 2003.[21] The fires at the National Library were set professionally, with accelerants. Although the burn damage seemed complete from outside the building, it later emerged that the main reading room and lobby suffered most of the damage. An iron door leading to the stacks had been sealed.[22] According to Saad Eskander, the INLA Director-General since December 2003, three days prior to the invasion staff members were instructed to destroy all archival material related to Ba'athist rule. In the event, Eskander stated that the burning and looting was carried out by a mix of poor people looking for quick profit and regime loyalists intent on destroying evidence of atrocities. Altogether, an estimated 25 percent of the library's book holdings were destroyed. The newspaper and periodical collection, said to be one of the largest in the Arab world, appears to have emerged largely without damage.[23]

As frustrating as the lack of protection for the INLA in April 2003 has been the overall lack of assistance of the international community to help rebuild and reconstitute the facility. Italian and Czech institutions have been the notable exceptions. Over six years have passed since the initial destruction, and the US government has to date provided a modest set of vacuum cleaners and funded staff training initiatives through the National Endowment for the Humanities (NEH). Harvard University's Committee on Iraqi Libraries found itself unable to provide advanced preservation training to INLA staff in the US when these Iraqi librarians were refused visas. The committee was able, however, to provide preservation workshops to Iraqi staff in Sulaymania and Amman.[24] While such absence of assistance and presence of impediments can be blamed on poor coordination and a lack of domestic attention, from an Iraqi perspective it appears to be at least a case of misplaced priorities and at most an intentional policy of passive neglect.

Perhaps the most valuable collection held by the INLA included the *Ottoman/Hashemite Archives*, which boasted government documents dating from the Hashemite (pre-1958) and Ottoman (pre-1917) eras. Prior to the invasion, this collection was removed from INLA and placed in the basement of the General Board of Tourism. Although this collection escaped the initial round of burning and looting, in August 2003 the basement was flooded in unknown circumstances. In October 2003, the cache was discovered and transferred to the warehouse of an Iraqi businessman associated with the Coalition Provisional Authority (CPA). Following a visit by a US Library of Congress delegation, the documents were transferred in December 2003 to cool storage in the former Iraqi Officers' Club complex. Since these documents were stored for a period in cool rather than frozen storage – with inconsistent electricity at the cooling facility – they continued to deteriorate, albeit at a slower rate than when first discovered in the flooded basement in 2003. Saad Eskander has estimated that 60 percent of these Ottoman and Hashemite documents have been irretrievably lost. This collection, which may represent the highest priority for textual preservation in all of Iraq, has in recent years been undergoing steady preservation efforts by the reconstituted INLA staff.

Established in 1920, the *Ministry of Endowments and Religious Affairs Central Library* (Awqaf Library) is the oldest public manuscript collection in Iraq. A modern two story facility located near the Ministry of Health, the library held *waqfiyya* religious endowment documents and approximately 7,000 manuscripts, mostly concentrated in religious fields. The library also held over 45,000 printed books, including some 6,000 rare Ottoman Turkish published works. The facility was completely destroyed by fire on April 13 or 14, 2003, more than four days after looting had started elsewhere in the city. According to staff members, the library suffered a well-organized and intentional looting and burning by foreign provocateurs.[25] These Arabic-speaking teams carted away some 22 trunks of manuscripts and used accelerants to burn the entire facility within 15 minutes. They filmed their actions the entire time. Ten trunks were burned in the fire, destroying approximately 600–700 manuscripts. Most of the burned and stolen manuscripts came from three prominent family collections temporarily stored at the Awqaf Library for their protection.[26] Since staff members had taken steps to protect the collection, approximately 5,250 out of the facility's total 7,000 manuscripts were moved to an off-site storage space prior to the burning and looting. These manuscripts were then placed under armed protection in what remains an undisclosed location. As this location remains unknown to the general public six years after these events, only time will tell whether these manuscripts will one day be returned to a reconstituted Awqaf Library. There has never been an official investigation of this case of organized destruction. To date, this facility has received no meaningful international assistance.[27] Any future reconstitution of this collection and reconstruction of this facility will inherently be complicated by the post-2003 splitting up of the Ministry of Endowments into three directorates, one each serving Shia Muslims, Sunni Muslims, and all religious minorities including Christians.

The *Iraqi House of Manuscripts* (Dar al-Makhtutat al-'Iraqiyya), with approximately 47,000 manuscripts, was by far the largest such collection in Iraq.[28] Prior to the invasion, all manuscripts were moved to a bomb shelter, while microfilms were moved to two other undisclosed locations. As far as is known, this bomb shelter housed nearly 800 steel trunks, containing nearly 50,000 manuscripts and several thousand rare books.[29] Considering that the bomb shelter where the manuscripts were stored was not included on the US military's "no target" list, it is indeed fortunate that it was never bombed. On three occasions in April 2003 looters tried and failed to force the doors and loot the shelter, but on each occasion locals reportedly chased the looters away and burned their vehicles. In late April 2003 US forces attempted to remove trunks and transport them to the National Museum, which was by then under US protection. Due to growing mistrust of American intentions following the looting earlier that month, neighborhood locals protested and successfully prevented this attempted move.

As the Iraqi House of Manuscripts facility is based in a set of houses appropriated by the state in 1983, it is unclear whether the collection will ultimately be returned to that same location. Since 2003 at least three different directors have been appointed to manage the collection, which remained until recently locked away in the bomb shelter. Although the shelter was said to be climate-controlled, it is unclear whether long-term storage in this location might have damaged the collection. The former director, Osama Naqshbandi, has claimed in recent years that some manuscripts were removed by US forces in 2003. Since this statement somewhat contradicts what he said in May 2003, some observers worry that the collection may have been disturbed over the years. The collection has reportedly been recently moved to another site, and rumors have surfaced that the Kashif al-Ghita Foundation has been exerting pressure to be allowed access to the collection in order to carry out microfilming. There is concern that some of the collection may have been sold off in the past five years, and that Kashif al-Ghita's desire for access may not be entirely innocent.

The *Iraqi Academy of Sciences* is a fully independent research facility dating back to the Hashemite period. Considered an "Iraqi Académie Française," the Academy held collections of manuscripts, periodicals, foreign-language books, and unpublished theses.[30] According to staff members, the pillage started after a US tank crew crashed through the facility's front gate, rolled over and crushed the facility's main sign, removed the Iraqi flag flying at the entrance, and left. Following that cue, neighborhood indigents swarmed over the facility and stripped it of all computers, air conditioners, electrical fixtures, furniture, and vehicles. The fact that the Academy was not burned and that many books were not looted suggests that its looting was not as organized as was the case with some other facilities. Although several hundred manuscripts had been transferred in recent years to the Iraqi House of Manuscripts, the Academy still held over 2,000 manuscripts and 58,000 published works in April 2003.[31] Over half of the Academy's collection of 58,000 published works was looted, and all manuscripts left on site were taken during the looting. Since a published catalogue of the Academy's manuscript collection was incomplete, and all on site catalogues were lost with the manuscripts, it is not entirely known what has been lost.[32] Since 2003 the Academy has returned to operation, but it is still unknown at this time how much of the collection has been reconstituted.

The *House of Wisdom* (Bayt al-Hikma), a semi-private center supporting research in the arts and humanities, was completely burned and looted. Located right next to the Ministry of Defense, on the site of a thirteenth century *madrasa* complex and the first Iraqi parliament, it housed a lecture auditorium, music hall, printing press, computer lab, Western publications library, and a library of Middle Eastern publications. The main building complex was extensively looted on April 11–12, 2003, and partially burned.[33] Staff who witnessed the looting were convinced that the looters were instigated by unknown provocateurs. As the House of Wisdom was not officially authorized to collect manuscripts, its collection only held about 100 manuscripts. Although a small collection, some of these manuscripts were of high value. The entire collection was lost.[34] Outside of limited US funding targeted for repurchasing their own holdings from the local book market in 2003, the House of Wisdom has received no significant international assistance. The current status of certain other collections within Baghdad remains largely unknown.[35]

The *Iraqi Jewish Archives* was found partially flooded in a former intelligence bureau basement in May 2003. Promptly frozen and removed by CPA officials for restoration efforts by the US National Archives and Records Administration (NARA), the cache has remained in the US since its removal. According to a 2003 NARA report, the collection included "16th–20th century Jewish rare books, correspondence and document files, pamphlets, modern books, audio tape and parchment scrolls."[36] The NARA report estimated that $US 1.5–3 million would be required to fully rescue and preserve the collection. However, in May 2005 National Public Radio reported that documentation restoration efforts were stalled due to shortage of funds.[37] Some resentment has been expressed by Iraqi observers about the immense effort undertaken by occupation officials in 2003 to salvage this cache when considered against the relative lack of urgency demonstrated for the Ottoman/Hashemite Archives referred to above. At the same time, palpable tension has arisen concerning the eventual disposition of the collection. The Babylonian Jewry Heritage Center has expressed interest in displaying recovered parts of the collection in its museum outside of Tel Aviv following the completion of NARA preservation efforts.[38] Former Iraqi National Museum Director Donny George has stated that CPA officials had signed a protocol allowing for a two-year loan of the materials to the US for preservation, after which they were meant to be returned to Iraq. NARA officials and the Library of Congress have not yet stated their intentions concerning the return of these materials to Iraq or elsewhere. Although this cache should be considered of Iraqi collective provenance, copies should be made of the entire collection for preservation backup and research retrieval.

In 2007 it emerged that American soldiers in Mosul had taken a roughly 400-year-old *Torah* out of an abandoned building and arranged for the manuscript's smuggling out of the country. A book dealer then took the Torah and sold it to a Reform Jewish congregation in suburban Maryland. Media reports stated that the

Torah was "rescued," even though it had survived for centuries in Mosul only to be whisked from its place of refuge and turned over to an individual who broke the manuscript into 60 pieces in order to complete the act of smuggling.[39]

As with the Mosul Torah, in certain ways US officials participated in the reordering of Iraqi informational assets after the invasion. Contrasting the *laissez-faire* attitude displayed toward the looting of manuscript collections was the active military takeover of certain contemporary Iraqi government document collections, control over which would be highly beneficial for US interests. For example, in the course of the post-invasion search for weapons of mass destruction, Pentagon officials centralized millions of pages of captured *Iraqi government documents* in a single collection currently held in Qatar. This collection has not yet been completely catalogued, although most of it appears to have been digitized, with the digital images held at the National Defense University. Defense Secretary Robert Gates has pledged that the original documents will ultimately be returned to Iraq once conditions allow and that the collection will be open for researchers once correct monitoring and usage systems have been established. There is a great deal of sensitivity over this collection and those like it because individuals named in documents of the former Iraqi government could be blackmailed. As the situation somewhat parallels that of the Stasi Archives of East Germany, similar precautions and protections are likely to be instituted before research access will be allowed.

Kanan Makiya removed the *Ba'ath Party Archives* from the Iraqi Ba'ath Party Headquarters in 2003, stored them at his family home within the Green Zone for some years, and at some point transported the collection to California with US government logistical assistance. Since that time, Makiya's Iraq Memory Foundation (IMF) has claimed stewardship over the cache, and has turned the collection over to Stanford University's Hoover Institute. INLA Director-General Saad Eskander has forcefully contested the IMF's rights to dispose of the cache, and the matter remains under dispute.[40]

Provincial Manuscript Collections

Prior to 2003 there were several provincial collections in Iraq, with most governorate seats boasting at least one modest manuscript library.[41] There were especially notable collections in Basra,[42] Mosul,[43] Najaf,[44] and Kerbala.[45] The post-2003 state of these collections remains almost completely unknown in the public realm. This lack of public information encourages opaqueness in the management of such collections and the potential sale of manuscripts. It is therefore imperative that a national survey of these collections be made as soon as security conditions allow.

One of the more tragic, if somewhat tragi-comic, stories of the damages sustained in the course of the 2003 invasion concerns the events which affected the *Mosul Center for Turkish Studies* and the *Basra Center for Gulf Studies*.[46] Prior to the invasion, Mosul's collection of Ottoman documents and manuscripts was reportedly sent to Basra's Center for Gulf Studies and Basra's collection of "Iranian documents" was sent to Mosul. Apparently the Iraqi government had decided on a provincial preservation strategy whereby if Turkish forces should enter from the north, they would only find Persian documents, and if Iranian forces should enter Basra, they would only find Ottoman documents. Unfortunately, the Center for Gulf Studies was completely burned in the war, and Mosul's entire collection of Ottoman documents was lost. The "Iranian documents" held in Mosul are said to be fine. An Iraqi academic, although not in a position to know all the collection's details, reported that to the best of his knowledge the Ottoman collection held somewhere between 10,000 and 15,000 items, a mixture of manuscripts and documents. Mosul's former Center for Turkish Studies was renamed the *Center for Regional Studies* in 2004.

Relative Human Valuation and the Collapse of Collective Memory

Why is it that those who lose everything in a fire, flood, or some other natural disaster lament the loss of their family photographs and heirlooms more than their car, stereo, or appliances? Even though such elements of transportation, entertainment, and consumerist ease of living ensure the minimum requirements necessary for a "bourgeois" lifestyle, they do so devoid of any material individuality. What sets us apart from others are antiques, photographs, records, heirlooms, and other artifacts, especially those that document our familial or individual pasts. By connecting us to our past, the existence of such items also promises to preserve the connection into a remembered future. Without such artifacts, there is no memory.

Are mass societies so different from the abstracted individuals and families presented here? Considering the 2003 destruction of several prominent cultural treasures of the Iraqi national patrimony, it would seem not. In Iraq's case, during a period of great chaotic flux, one country under occupation lost a great deal of its connection to its past while certain occupying powers profited from that loss in a variety of ways.

While all humans are created equal, certain types of individuals are treated more equally than others. Some 5.4 million individuals have died from war-related causes in Congo in the past ten years,[47] yet have attracted far less attention worldwide than the several hundred thousand who have died from conflict in Iraq since 2003, the 1,191 Lebanese who died from violence in the summer of 2006,[48] or the hundreds of Palestinians and dozens of Israelis who have died from domestic attacks since sectarian conflict broke out in 2001. How does one account for this hierarchy of human valuation, whereby certain lives and deaths are valued by the international community far more than others? One can attribute such valuation to corporate pressures on media presentation (whereby human valuation follows their relevance as sources of advertising revenue), tribal and/or national solidarity (whereby all groups only value members of their own group), financial holdings (whereby only the wealthy are valued), racism, relative economic or political power, and many other factors. In addition to each of these factors, one might add relative cultural valuation, measured by the amount of material records of the past held by a society.

None of these factors are constant, with all of them capable of adjusting quite quickly in times of conflict.

Why is it that societies boasting few material records of the past tend to be valued less than those in possession of them, and why is there such a desire for individuals and societies to collect artifacts demonstrating past value? The absence of such artifacts signifies a lack of connection to the past, which in turn signifies cultural poverty to those with strong roots somewhere, local or otherwise. In times of peace, families anchor their social value in such artifacts. Very little can be done to change quickly what is normally a slowly evolving collection of such connections to the past. In times of war, however, individuals and societies can quickly gain or lose such stature in a situation of great flux.

One of the major effects of the "mnemocide" suffered in Iraq is to reduce the relative human valuation of the individuals who are the bearers of that cultural memory. One example of this phenomenon is the lack of respect shown by US soldiers at Iraq's Unknown Soldier Monument in Baghdad. While quartered in the Iraqi equivalent to Washington's Vietnam Memorial in the summer of 2003, soldiers closed the facility to the general public, parked armored personnel carriers in the marble courtyard, laid cots throughout the hall of martyrs, and posted exercise notices over the names of deceased Iraqi soldiers who fell fighting in the 1980–88 Iran–Iraq war.[49] Soldiers normally tend not to wish the degradation of other soldiers' memories. However, in this case the general cultural alienation and lack of relative human valuation was sufficient to trump such norms of respect.

Certain neo-conservative ideologues in 2003 hoped that new texts, debates, and ideas would come to dominate Iraq's collective memory once the past had been silenced like the hypothetically silenced library that introduces this chapter. Nada Shabout has suggested that CPA Head Paul Bremer and others engaged in a "systematic campaign to erase Iraq's collective memory," by facilitating the destruction of Iraq's modern art museum, political monuments, and other artifacts of recent Iraqi creativity.[50] Unfortunately, the push to remake Iraq has proven quite destructive of Iraq's collective memory, and by extension, its "social capital," defined as "a measure of how closely people in the community are interconnected." Although the process of social capital destruction in Iraq had arguably been building for several decades, the looting of April 2003 pushed Iraqi society over a psychological precipice evidenced by the complete breakdown of collective memory.[51] This social capital, once shattered, has proven exceedingly difficult to reconstruct.[52]

Notes

1. I would like to thank the US Institute of Peace for the support necessary to continue this research. I would also like to thank Jean-Marie Arnoult, Mary-Jane Deeb, Hala Fattah, Donny George, McGuire Gibson, Amanda Johnson, Charles Jones, Hakim Khaldi, Lital Levy, Ibrahim al-Marashi, Edouard Méténier, Osama Naqshbandi, Jeffrey Spurr, and Zayn al-Naqshbandi for various instances of informational and logistical assistance that went into the carrying out of this research. Further information concerning contacts and sources can be obtained either through my 2003 site report (cited below), or through contacting me at: naltikriti@yahoo.com.
2. Heinrich Heine, nineteenth century German poet, in his 1821 play *Almansor*, cited in Nikola von Merveldt, "Books Cannot Be Killed by Fire: The German Freedom Library and the American Library of Nazi-Banned Books as Agents of Cultural Memory," *Library Trends*, 55:3 (2007), pp. 524, 532.
3. Eliza Woodford, "Symposium: The Destruction of Civilization and the Obligations of War," *University Record Online*, The University of Michigan, September 29, 2003, http://www.ur.umich.edu/0304/Sept29_03/10.shtml, accessed December 2008.
4. Laura Wilkinson, "There is more to be mourned than Iraq's ancient treasures," *Daily Star*, April 18, 2008, http://www.dailystar.com.lb/article.asp?edition_id=10&categ_id=4&article_id=91145#, accessed December 2008.
5. For an example, see Nora Bensahel et al., *After Saddam: Prewar Planning and the Occupation of Iraq*, Santa Monica: RAND, 2008, http://www.rand.org/pubs/monographs/2008/RAND_MG642.pdf, accessed December 2008.
6. Prof. McGuire Gibson of the University of Chicago made several appeals to US officials for Iraqi cultural protection in the weeks prior to the invasion. Bill Glauber, "Casualty Count Could Include Iraq Antiquities," *Chicago Tribune*, March 10, 2003, http://www.museum-security.org/03/032.html, accessed December 2008. For a

general discussion of US military policy concerning Iraqi cultural assets during the 2003 invasion, see Chalmers Johnson, "The Smash of Civilizations," 2005, http://www.tomdispatch.com/index. mhtml?pid=4710 and Zainab Bahrani, "Looting and Conquest," *The Nation*, May 14, 2003, http://www.thenation.com/doc/20030526/ bahrani; websites accessed in December 2008.

7. Such briefings included a January 2003 meeting held at the Pentagon, attended by high ranking representatives from the Departments of Defense and State, the American Council for Cultural Policy (ACCP), the Association of Art Museum Directors, and the American Association for Research in Baghdad. In 2005, allegations – since denied – arose that representatives of the ACCP had not acted in good faith at such meetings, using them to gain knowledge useful for illicit trade in cultural property, https://listhost.uchicago. edu/pipermail/iraqcrisis/2005-November/001396.html, accessed December 2008.

8. These sites included the Ministry of Oil, the Saddam (Baghdad) International Airport, the Palestine Meridian and Ishtar Sheraton hotels, the Republican Palace, and several other locations that were later included in the "Green Zone" of international governance.

9. Matthew Bogdanos, "Thieves of Baghdad," in Peter G. Stone and Joanne Farchakh Bajjaly (eds.), *The Destruction of Cultural Heritage in Iraq*, Woodbridge: The Boydell Press, 2008, pp. 109–17.

10. For a discussion of the "economy of risk" during these hostilities, see Thomas W. Smith, "Protecting Civilians...or Soldiers? Humanitarian Law and the Economy of Risk in Iraq," *International Studies Perspectives*, 9 (2008), pp. 144–64.

11. For an excellent reference work and orientation to the relevant legal issues, see Patty Gerstenblith, "From Bamyan to Baghdad: Warfare and the Preservation of Cultural Heritage at the Beginning of the 21st Century," *Georgetown Journal of International Law*, 37:2 (2006), pp. 245–351. Prof. Gerstenblith argues that international law concerning cultural patrimony was not broken in the course of the 2003 invasion, and that international law should be revised in order to reflect a series of developments first witnessed in conflicts which occurred after the 1954 Hague convention.

12. From May 25 to 31, 2003, I visited Baghdad and interviewed a number of officials responsible for various manuscript collections, libraries, and academic research facilities. For the original situation report based on that visit, posted on the Iraq Crisis list on June 8, 2003, see Nabil al-Tikriti, "Iraq Manuscript Collections, Archives, and Libraries Situation Report," (hereafter: al-Tikriti,

2003), http://oi.uchicago.edu/OI/IRAQ/docs/nat.html, accessed December 2008.

13. Iraqi directors first approached US field commanders when looting broke out on April 10. Despite reassurances to the contrary, no protection was extended until April 14, after the looting had become an international scandal. Al-Tikriti, 2003. For an eyewitness account of the Iraqi National Museum looting, see Donny George, "The Looting of the Iraq National Museum," in Stone and Bajjaly, *Destruction of Cultural Heritage in Iraq*, pp. 97–107.

14. According to Zainab Bahrani, "by 2007, Barbara Bodine, the U.S. ambassador at the time, revealed to Charles Ferguson in his documentary film *No End in Sight* that direct orders had come from Washington stating no one was to interfere with the looting," *Guardian*, April 9, 2008, http://commentisfree.guardian.co.uk/zainab_bahrani/2008/04/plundering_iraq.html, accessed December 2008.

15. For a discussion of US cultural protection policy during World War II, see Kathy Peiss, "Cultural Policy in a Time of War: The American Response to Endangered Books in World War II," *Library Trends*, 55:3 (2007), pp. 370–86.

16. Rajiv Chandrasekharan, *Imperial Life in the Emerald City: Inside Iraq's Green Zone*, New York: Vintage Books, 2006, p. 187. John Agresto later revised his judgment of the looting's legacy on Iraqi higher education.

17. On June 8, 2003, British architectural historian and television presenter Dan Cruickshank – who had visited Iraq in late April 2003 – first reported this claim vis-à-vis Iraqi National Museum staff on an ITV documentary entitled *Raiders of the Lost Art*. The allegation has since been repeated in some form or another by several subsequent commentators.

18. In my own interviews and site visits, I encountered nothing to suggest that archival staff acted improperly vis-à-vis their respective collections. It seems self-evident that efforts of Iraqi staff to preserve their cultural heritage in the midst of invasion, social chaos, and occupation should be recognized and rewarded by the international community – not attacked by interested external parties.

19. The focus here is on collections with unique holdings. Academically-affiliated research collections, which also suffered a great deal of loss, should in time and with sufficient support be able to duplicate and expand their pre-invasion holdings.

20. The most significant reports to date concerning the post-invasion state of Iraq's manuscript collections, archives, and libraries include those by the following: Nabil al-Tikriti (2003), Jean-Marie Arnoult

(2003), Ian Johnson (2005), Edouard Méténier (2003), Zayn al-Naqshbandi (2004), Jeff Spurr (2005), Keith Watenpaugh et al. (2003), and Library of Congress (2003). For links to each of these reports, see the Middle East Librarians Association Committee on Iraqi Libraries (MELA) website: http://oi.uchicago.edu/OI/IRAQ/mela/melairaq.html, accessed December 2008.

21. For further detail, see Ian M. Johnson, "The Impact on Libraries and Archives in Iraq of War and Looting in 2003 – a Preliminary Assessment of the Damage and Subsequent Reconstruction Efforts," *International Information and Library Review*, November 2005; Jeff Spurr, "Indispensable yet Vulnerable: The Library in Dangerous Times. A Report on the Status of Iraqi Academic Libraries and a Survey of Efforts to Assist Them, with Historical Introduction," Middle East Librarians Association Committee on Iraqi Libraries, August 2005.

22. Immediately following the initial round of destruction, staff and volunteers associated with a cleric named 'Abd al-Mun'im welded the door shut and began to remove as many books as they could transport to the cleric's al-Haqq Mosque in Sadr (formerly Saddam) City. The percentage of books removed was initially said to number roughly 40 percent of total holdings, but Saad Eskander later stated that the amount was closer to 5 percent of the total, and that many of the books suffered in the move and the storage conditions at the mosque. For more details, see Keith Watenpaugh, Edouard Méténier, Jens Hanssen, and Hala Fattah, "Opening the Doors: Intellectual Life and Academic Conditions in Post-War Baghdad, a Report of the Iraq Observatory," July 2003; and Saad Eskander conference presentation, posted by Ian Stringer, *Iraq Crisis List*, November 9, 2004.

23. Saad Eskander conference presentation, 2004.

24. For further details concerning international assistance to INLA since 2003, see Jeff Spurr, "Iraqi Libraries and Archives in Peril: Survival in a Time of Invasion, Chaos, and Civil Conflict, a Report 2007," http://oi.uchicago.edu/OI/IRAQ/mela/update_2007.htm, accessed December 2008.

25. Although the staff was convinced – as were most Iraqis – that Kuwaitis were behind this looting and burning, they admitted that they had no evidence to prove the assertion. Al-Tikriti, 2003.

26. The three family collections included the Kamal al-Din al-Ta'i collection (250 manuscripts), Salih Salim Suhrawardi collection (350 mss), and the Hasan al-Sadr collection (589 mss). Al-Tikriti, 2003.

27. The library's collection of published books appears to have been a total loss. In addition to the 6,000 Ottoman Turkish books, the flames also consumed three large collections of medical books boasting close to 4,000 volumes and 5,300 books concerning Ja'fari (Shi'i) jurisprudence. For more details concerning the Awqaf Library, see al-Tikriti, 2003; Zayn al-Naqshbandi, "Report on the Central Awqaf Library," *Iraq Crisis List*, June 28, 2004, http://oi.chicago. edu/OI/IRAQ/zan.html, accessed December 2008.

28. This facility was formerly known as the "Saddam House of Manuscripts" (Dar Saddam lil-Makhtutat). As a result of damages sustained in provincial collections during the 1991 uprising, and in accordance with longstanding Ministry of Culture efforts to centralize all holdings, several manuscript collections were absorbed into this main collection in the 1990s. Al-Tikriti, 2003.

29. These trunks reportedly included around 500 trunks of Iraqi House of Manuscripts manuscripts, some 200 trunks from other collections, and 83 trunks of rare published books. Some 3,000 manuscripts (mss) from the following collections were housed in the shelter along with the main collection: Iraqi Academy of Sciences (667 mss), Mosul Central Library (301 mss), University of Mosul Library (122 mss), University of Tikrit Library (40 mss), Kirkuk Central Library (40 mss), University of Mustansiriyya Library, and the University of Basra Library. Al-Tikriti, 2003.

30. It also boasted an internet computer lab, printing press, lecture rooms, and offices for affiliated researchers. For more information, see al-Tikriti, 2003; Watenpaugh et al., "Opening the Doors."

31. These manuscripts included 93 unpublished works by the Iraqi historian 'Abbas al-'Azawi and a Selçuk-era work by the medieval Sufi figure, "Umar al-Suhrawardi. Roughly half of the al-'Azawi collection had been returned by May 2003.

32. A handwritten catalogue of Academy manuscript holdings disappeared along with all of the manuscripts. In addition, although the entire collection had been copied, the copies were looted along with the originals.

33. For further information, see al-Tikriti, 2003; Watenpaugh et al., "Opening the Doors."

34. The manuscripts included a ninth century Qur'an, a twelfth century copy of *Maqamat al-Hariri*, an Ibn Sina philosophy text, and a nineteenth century al-'Alusi manuscript concerning Baghdad. There were no microfilms or microfiche taken of this collection. The facility also held several research collections relevant to Iraqi history, including several thousand copies of Ottoman, British, French, and

US documents. As many of the Ottoman originals were held by INLA, it is possible that their information is now lost.

35. Such collections include the Qadiriyya Mosque (1,833 mss), the Deir al-Aba al-Krimliyin collection (120 mss), and the al-Hidaya Library (500 mss).

36. "The Iraqi Jewish Archive Preservation Report," October 2, 2003, posted in January 2004, http://oi.uchicago.edu/OI/IRAQ/mela/Iraqi-JewishArchiveReport.htm, accessed December 2008.

37. http://www.npr.org/templates/story/story.phpstoryId=4645146.

38. Judy Lash Balint, "Back to Babylon," *Jerusalem Post*, August 12, 2005, http://pqasb.pqarchiver.com/jpost/index.html?ts=1137441164, accessed December 2008.

39. The Mosul Torah set off a heated discussion on the Iraq Crisis List in June 2008. One example includes the following posting: https://listhost.uchicago.edu/pipermail/iraqcrisis/2008-June/002037.html.

40. The saga of this archive has also attracted a great deal of attention: http://chronicle.com/free/2008/01/1335n.htm, http://www.nytimes.com/2008/07/01/books/01hoov.html, accessed December 2008.

41. Such collections included the al-Mufti (120 mss) and Salah al-Din University (402 mss) libraries in Arbil, the al-Awqaf (6,000 mss) and al-Shaykh Muhammad al-Khal (350 mss) libraries in Sulaymania, the Al-Jamal al-Din library (180 mss) in Suq al-Shuyukh, and an unknown cleric's private collection (300 mss) in Diwaniyya. Al-Tikriti, 2003.

42. Such collections included the Basra Center for Gulf Studies and the Bash A'yan al-'Abbasiyya Collection (1,200 mss).

43. Such collections included the Mosul Center for Turkish Studies, the Ninewa Governorate Artifacts Inspectorate Library (Maktabat Mufatashiyya Athar Ninawah), the Ninawah Governorate Awqaf Library, Deir Mar Behnam Collection, Deir Mar Matti Collection, Karakosh Library Collection, al-Jalili Madrasa Collection (400 mss), and the Dr. Mahmud al-Jalili Collection (60 mss). The two Christian collections were moved to Baghdad prior to the invasion, and their status is unknown, as with most of the other collections.

44. Such collections included the Amir al-Mu'minin (3,000 mss), al-Hakim (1,600 mss), and Kashif al-Ghita libraries (3,000 mss).

45. The most prominent collection is the Hussein Mosque's Dar al-Makhtutat (1,200 mss).

46. The information for these two facilities was reported to me in a 2004 conference by an Iraqi academic who may not wish to be named publicly. This same informant reported that all Dohuk, Erbil, and Sulaymania collections were in fine condition as of June 2004.

47. http://www.theirc.org/news/irc-study-shows-congos0122.html, accessed December 2008.
48. Report of the Commission of Inquiry on Lebanon Pursuant to Human Rights Council Resolution, S-2/1, p. 26: http://www2.ohchr.org/english/bodies/hrcouncil/docs/specialsession/A.HRC.3.2.pdf, accessed December 2008.
49. For photographs, see Sinan Antoon, "Monumental Disrespect," *Middle East Report*, 228 (2003).
50. Nada Shabout, "There is more to be mourned than Iraq's ancient treasures," *Daily Star*, April 18, 2008, http://www.dailystar.com.lb/article.asp?edition_id=10&categ_id=4&article_id=91145#, accessed December 2008.
51. For a textured discussion of this phenomenon in Iraq, see Bernadette Buckley, "Mohamed is Absent. I am Performing: Contemporary Iraqi Art and the Destruction of Heritage," in Stone and Bajjaly, *Destruction of Cultural Heritage in Iraq*, pp. 283–306.
52. Shankar Vedantam, "One Thing We Can't Build Alone in Iraq," *Washington Post*, October 29, 2007, p. A03, http://www.washingtonpost.com/wp-dyn/content/article/2007/10/28/AR2007102801477.html, accessed December 2008. Vedantam applied the work of sociologist Peter Bearman and political scientist Anirudh Krishna to the case of Iraq, arguing that social capital cannot be inculcated by externally driven reconstruction efforts alone.

PART III

Policy in Motion:
The Present and the Future

6

KILLING THE INTELLECTUAL CLASS: ACADEMICS AS TARGETS[1]

Dirk Adriaensens

Looting, Arrests and Murder: The Occupation of Iraq Begins

When considering the widespread campaign of assassination that has targeted so many of Iraq's professional middle class, it is essential to recognize that the killing spree of Iraqi academics began in April 2003, with the first wave of assassinations coinciding with the invasion of the country.

Despite the chaos that followed the illegal US-led invasion of Iraq, the attitude of the invaders towards Iraq's education system and its academic community rapidly became clear.

On April 11, 2003, a number of Iraqi scientists and university professors sent an SOS e-mail complaining that American occupation forces were threatening their lives.[2] The appeal stated that looting and robberies were taking place under the watchful eye of occupation soldiers.

These soldiers, the e-mail added, were transporting mobs to the scientific institutions, such as Mosul University and different educational institutions, to destroy scientific research centers and confiscate all papers and documents to stop any Iraqi scientific renaissance before it had a chance to begin.

The e-mail also noted that occupation forces had drawn up lists of the names, addresses and research areas of the Iraqi scientists to assist them in their harassment tasks in light of the chaos and anarchy that existed after the toppling of the Iraqi regime on April 9.[3]

One early target of such harassment was Dr. Huda Salih Mahdi Ammash, dubbed "Mrs. Anthrax," who was taken into custody by coalition forces on May 4, 2003. A US Central Command news release issued after her capture described Ammash as: "a Ba'ath Party Regional Command member and weapons of mass destruction scientist. She was No. 53 on the U.S. Central Command 'Iraqi Top 55' list." But Andrew Dwinell, the co-publisher of South End Press, says United Nations weapons inspectors did not believe Ammash aided in the production of biological weapons or other weapons of mass destruction and that Ammash's detainment was politically motivated.[4]

Dr. Ammash, an environmental biologist, professor and dean at Baghdad University, received her PhD from the University of Missouri. She has earned international respect for her publications, particularly her documentation of the rise in cancers among Iraqi children and war veterans since the Gulf War. In *Iraq Under Siege* she writes: "Iraqi death rates have increased significantly, with cancer representing a significant cause of mortality, especially in the south and among children."[5] Dr. Ammash's other publications include: "Impact of Gulf War Pollution in the Spread of Infectious Diseases in Iraq" (Soli Al-Mondo, Rome, 1999), and "Electromagnetic, Chemical, and Microbiological Pollution Resulting from War and Embargo, and Its Impact on the Environment and Health" (*Journal of the [Iraqi] Academy of Science*, 1997).

Dr. Ammash was never charged with any crime and US authorities refused her legal access. Eventually they had to release her. A close Iraqi friend comments:

> She is without a job or any financial support. The occupation won't allow her to get any money from her accounts. She was very sick for a while because of the cruelty of the interrogations. The American troops during raiding Dr Ammash house took every single paper in her house. Even the computer and the trash and the bathroom tissue in the house, the CD's and all her books and journals. They are all in Democratic Washington DC. When they released her they never gave her back the things they took from her house. At that time, I visited her family next to her door. It was a

disaster, and believe me, it was all about the DU [depleted uranium] issue. Dr Ammash had her own Pathogenic and hematological lab. This is one reason she could conduct her advanced researches.

Others were not so lucky. Dr. Mohammed Munim al-Izmerly was tortured to death after his arrest in April 2003; he died in American custody from a sudden blow to the back of his head caused by blunt trauma, possibly from a bar or a pistol.[6] His battered corpse turned up at Baghdad's morgue and the cause of death was initially recorded as "brainstem compression." It was discovered that US doctors had made a 20cm incision in his skull. According to another Iraqi professor who knew Dr. Izmerly, "The occupation was desperate for one confession that Iraq's program of WMD was still active, but with all the torture they couldn't get that out of him. His family in London accused the Pentagon officially of killing him during interrogation based on false allegations."[7]

The Campaign of Assassination

According to US officials, on February 26, 2004 it was reported that a senior Iraqi scientist who had been involved in Iraq's nuclear program was found murdered in Baghdad. It was the ninth assassination of Iraqi scientists in the previous four months, reported Geostrategy-Direct, the global intelligence news service.[8] The article notes that the latest killing was that of Iraqi aeronautical scientist Muhyi Hussein. The official comment of the US afterwards was a typical example of disinformation, given the fact that the Iraqi academics had already highlighted that their lives were threatened by the US invaders: "Although the reason for the assassination campaign is unclear, U.S. officials believe the killings represent an effort to conceal the scope of Iraq's nuclear program."

Whilst almost any academic in any scientific field could be accused of involvement in some sort of weapons program, it quickly became clear that "scientists" were not the only targets.

On January 21, 2004, the *LA Times* reported on the killing of politics professor Abdul Latif al Mayah:

> Gunned down only 12 hours after advocating direct elections on an Arab television talk show, Abdul Latif Mayah was the fourth professor from Baghdad's Mustansiriya University to be killed in the last eight months, his death the latest in a series of academic slayings in post-Hussein Iraq. Salam Rais, one of Mayah's students, claimed, "His assassination is part of a plan in this country, targeting any intellectual in this country, any free voice. He is the martyr of the free world."[9]

Jeffrey Gettleman reported that hundreds of intellectuals and mid-level administrators had been assassinated since May 2003 in a widening campaign against Iraq's professional class, according to Iraqi officials. "They are going after our brains," said Lt. Col. Jabbar Abu Natiha, head of the organized crime unit of the Baghdad police. "It is a big operation. Maybe even a movement."[10]

American and Iraqi officials say there is no tally of all the professionals assassinated. However, Lt. Akmad Mahmoud, of the Baghdad police, has claimed that there had been "hundreds" of professionals killed in Baghdad. Mr. Saadi, a Baghdad city council member who works closely with the police, estimated the number to be between 500 and 1,000.[11] The *Independent* stated on December 7, 2006 that "more than 470 academics have been killed. Buildings have been burnt and looted in what appears to be a random spree of violence aimed at Iraqi academia."[12] As of January 15, 2009, the B*Russell*s Tribunal's list of murdered Iraqi academics contained 413 names.[13] The Iraqi minister of education announced that 296 members of education staff were killed in 2005 alone.[14] On March 15, 2007, Minister of Higher Education Abduldhiyab al-Aujaili declared that since the 2003 US invasion more than 100 university professors have been abducted. He said the ministry has almost lost hope for the return of those who had been abducted and the violence targeting Iraqi universities has terrorized faculty members. "Houses of hundreds of professors have been stormed and hundreds of them have been arrested though later most of them were released," he observed. According to al-Aujaili, the rising violence has forced "thousands" of Iraqi professors to flee the country.[15] Human Rights Watch estimates that 331 school teachers were slain in the first four months of 2006 and at least 2,000 Iraqi doctors have been killed and 250 kidnapped since the 2003 US invasion.[16] The International Medical Corps reports that populations of teachers in Baghdad have fallen by 80 percent and medical personnel seem to have left in disproportionate numbers.[17] "Up to 75 percent of Iraq's doctors, pharmacists and nurses have left their jobs since the U.S.-led invasion in 2003. More than half of those have emigrated," according to a Medact report of January 16, 2008.[18] Roughly 40 percent of Iraq's middle class is believed to have fled the country by the end of 2006; most are fleeing systematic persecution and have no desire to return.[19] At least 303 Iraqi and 30 non-Iraqi media professionals have died under US occupation.[20]

Hana Al Bayaty, coordinator of the Iraqi International Initiative on Refugees,[21] concludes that

> The modern Iraqi educated middle class, vital now and in the future to run the state, the economy, and build Iraqi culture, has been decimated. Following systematic assassinations, imprisonment, military raids and sieges, threats and discrimination, most of what remained of that class left the country. The absence of this middle class has resulted in the breakdown of all public services for the entirety of Iraqi society.

Even beyond the loss of life and accumulated human knowledge that such loss represents, the effect of these killings on Iraq's academic community has been catastrophic, with thousands fleeing the country and those who remain frightened into silence. On April 30, 2004, the *Christian Science Monitor* noted that Dr. Saad Jawad still speaks out. However, like other university professors across Iraq, he is increasingly afraid that saying what he thinks – or saying anything political at all – could get him killed. "To tell the truth, at the time of Saddam Hussein, we used to speak to our students freely... Ministers, for example, were criticized all the time. But now, a lot of people are not willing to say these kinds of things because of fear."[22] Another academic, Sadoun Dulame, described this process of intimidation: ripping open an envelope containing a small, hard object, Dulame discovered the unwanted gift Iraq's academics have learned to dread. "They sent me a bullet," he said, describing the letter he received in March 2004. "They said in Arabic: 'You cost us just one bullet, no more, so shut your mouth'."

On October 30, 2006, the following message arrived:

> I am sure you have heard about the assassination of Dr. Issam Al-Rawi. Dr. Al-Rawi was the head of the Iraqi University Professors Union. He helped unveiling all the crimes committed against his colleagues by pro-government militias including Badr and Jaish Al-Mahdi and other security gangs. His death is a great loss. He refused to leave, even though like the others he was threatened many times to leave Iraq. He felt that he was mostly needed to protect his colleagues to keep the Iraqi universities going on in this critical time of his beloved country. Dr. Al-Rawi got killed because he believed that one day things would get better in Iraq and he has worked hard to see that day coming. I guess his assassination concludes how far that day is!!

Dr. Issam al-Rawi was a major source for the B*Russell*s Tribunal and the Spanish Campaign Against the Occupation and for the Sovereignty of Iraq (CEOSI) list of murdered Iraqi academics, and he was one of the first to bring notice to the dreadful situation of the Iraqi academics. His list was initially translated and handed over to the B*Russell*s Tribunal by Dr. Souad Naji Al-Azzawi, a former Vice President of Mamoun University of Scientific Affairs; she testified in the culminating session of the World Tribunal on Iraq in Istanbul June 2005.[23] Shortly before being attacked, al-Rawi was interviewed on TV, urging Iraqis to leave aside the sectarian violence. He was attacked in Al-Dawoodi neighborhood, West Baghdad, where he lived, shortly after leaving his home for Baghdad University. Two other professors were with him; they were both wounded.

In January 2005, Charles Crain remarked in *USA Today* that in a country with distinct political, ethnic and religious fault lines, the university killings seem to follow no pattern. The dead have been Shi'ites and Sunnis, Kurds and Arabs, and supporters of various political parties. "They have a common thing: they are Iraqis," al-Rawi said.[24] While leaving his house on October 30, a white four wheel drive vehicle blocked al-Rawi's car, then shots were fired at him. The vehicle, a 2004 Land Cruiser, is almost always used by the high-ranking officials of the Ministry of Interior and this vehicle is the "trade mark" of the death squads backed by some high-ranking officers and officials inside the ministry. There were four people in the vehicle: the driver, two shooters and one passenger who provided protection to the shooters. The car escaped in front of a National Guards checkpoint near the Al-Mansour area. On October 19, the occupation forces and the "Iraqi" Special Police Forces had raided al-Rawi's office (the League of the Iraqi University Professors, which he founded).[25] Al-Rawi had issued a communiqué on October 28 condemning the raid and the damage to the offices: the doors were broken, the library was a mess; his office and that of his deputy were searched.[26]

Omar Al Hajj, a professor at the University of Technology in Baghdad has pointed out that "Death squads accused of killing Iraqi professionals and scientists are the same forces that invaded Iraq, looted its museums and stole its banks... They are also the same parties, which abduct businessmen and foreigners for high ransoms."[27]

On December 2, 2007, hundreds of university students and professors took to the streets in Amara protesting the abduction of a technical institute dean and urging the government to put an end to mounting attacks against Iraqi intellectuals. "Today's demonstration denounces attacks against the Iraqi intelligentsia, which security forces remain unable to halt...," a professor from Missan University, Dr. Bassim al-Rubaie, told the independent news agency Voices of Iraq (VOI). He continued, "supported by foreign bodies, organized gangs from all over Iraq are seeking to empty Iraqi universities and institutes of professors. Other gangs aim at financial gains from the release of hostages."[28]

A Case Study: Baghdad's College of Dentistry

The college of Dentistry at the University of Baghdad was established in 1953 as a department of the Medical College. In

1958 it became a separate College belonging to the University; it was in this year that the first group of new dentists was graduated. The Teaching Hospital of the College was founded in 1991, and the hospital possesses many laboratories, clinics and new centers. In all, today the college is composed of two buildings and contains roughly 400 dental units. The College also runs continuing education courses in all the fields of dentistry.[29] Throughout the occupation, Baghdad University's College of Dentistry has continued to educate students, with more than 50 currently pursuing their degree.[30]

The College started with four dental chairs and it slowly grew into a major college at the University by relying on new Iraqi teaching staff. The college's staff includes 305 teaching staff (30 professors, 51 assistant professors, 71 lecturers and 153 assistant lecturers), 106 technicians and dental assistants, and 190 employees.

Iraq's healthcare system was once a showcase for the rest of the Middle East. Its dentists often studied in Britain or the US, and the country's dental schools boasted high standards. More than a decade of international sanctions, followed by years of occupation, have left healthcare in Iraq little better than that seen in developing countries.

On December 20, 2004, Hassan Abd-Ali Dawood Al-Rubai, Dean of the College of Dentistry at Baghdad University, was assassinated while he was leaving the college with his wife. Under a year later, on November 15, 2005, Fakhri Al-Qaysi, a faculty member of the Dentistry College, was critically injured in an assassination attempt; he subsequently fled the country.

Others followed. On April 24, 2007, a bomb hidden in a student's locker exploded at the Dentistry College as students were preparing to attend classes, killing at least one student and wounding several others.[31] Munther Murhej Radhi, Dean of Baghdad University's Dental College, was murdered in his home on January 23, 2008.[32] Ten days later on February 2, 2008, gunmen attacked a convoy of Abdul-Kareem al-Mohammedawi, Deputy Dean of the College, killing two guards and wounding two others in the Zayouna district of eastern Baghdad.[33]

Days later a spokesman for the Iraqi Ministry of Higher Education said US forces raided the Faculty of Dentistry at al-Mustansiriya University in central Baghdad. Taqi al-Musawi, the President of al-Mustansiriya University, confirmed the incident. "The forces broke the faculty gates and destroyed its laboratories… They did not arrest the guards but seized their weapons." He strongly denounced the incident, pointing out it was the second of its kind at his university in less than ten days.[34]

On February 17, 2008, Iraqi "security" forces broke into the College of Dentistry at Baghdad University. They arrested the former dean of the college Dr. Osama Al Mulla, Dr. Riyadh Uttman, and three college employees, taking them all to an unknown location. They also beat up one student.[35] Iraqi blogger Lubna commented on this incident:

There's a systematic plan to empty Iraq silently from its brains. The game goes like this: THEY threaten the BRAIN. The BRAIN leaves Iraq. If the BRAIN refuses to leave, then THEY kill the BRAIN! And so many BRAINS had to leave Iraq because of the threats they've received. So they had to choose between their lives and staying in their country. The cultural structure of our society is beings slowly disrupted day by day, and that – in my opinion – is the greatest loss of my Iraq.[36]

An eye-witness of the raid recalls further:

The army took 2 doctors and 3 guards, they placed them in the Humvees and no one knows where they are now… I reached the college immediately after they took the doctors… I asked around and reached the true (or what people believe is the true) story. Sunday morning between 10 and 11am a patrol of Humvees for the Iraqi Army or the national guards parked at the gate of the dentistry college and soldiers wearing uniforms entered the college and arrested (or I'd better say Kidnapped) 2 doctors…Dr. Osama Al-Mola (orthodontist, the chief of orthodontic department and former temporary dean) and Dr. Ryiadh Al-Kaisy (a pathologist and the chief of the pathology department) with three other post graduate students (some say 3 of the college guards) and no one knows where did they take them, at the afternoon they headed to Dr. Fakhri Alfatlaoy's clinic (orthodontist and former dean's assistant for the students affairs) and kidnapped him from his clinic because he wasn't in the college at the time they raided the college.[37]

An Iraqi citizen wrote to President Bush:

Dear President Bush,

The war on Iraq and the Iraqi people has caused untold misery to millions of Iraqis, worse than Hitler inflicted on Europe and the Jews. All of this planned holocaust will paint your administration and other nations that supposed to be free and democratic and being much worst than any Nazi.

This morning, 2-17-2008, College of Dentistry, Baghdad University was raided by Military type persons in 8 Hummers and kidnapped 7 professors to destinations unknown, similarly as it was done about a year ago at the Ministry of Higher Education.

Your war and your Surge have failed and is failing if such atrocities are allowed to take place. YOU opened a Pandora Box and unleashed the worst nightmarish terror of death and destruction on a nation and its people, your name will be linked forever with this modern day Holocaust.

This to inform you and hope that you still have time to save your name and your country's regard in the whole world.

Emad.[38]

On March 3, 2008, Amnesty International released the following statement:[39]

Ryadh al-Qaysi and Fakhri 'Abd Fatlawi, professors at Baghdad University's Faculty of Dentistry, and four other Baghdad University staff members who were arrested on 17 February, have been released. However, one professor, Ussama al-Mulla, remains in the custody of the Iraqi security forces and is at risk of torture and ill-treatment.

On 17 February, armed men wearing Iraqi security uniforms entered the Faculty of Dentistry. They went to the office of the Dean of the Faculty and threatened him at gunpoint, telling him they had arrest warrants for 10 university staff. The three professors were arrested, along with four other staff members. The staff members were originally taken to al-Salihiya police station in Baghdad. The whereabouts of Ussama al-Mulla are currently unconfirmed.

The arrest warrants were apparently issued by an official body, and related to the investigation into the murder of the previous Dean of the Dentistry Faculty.

At the time of the arrests, a number of students who protested against the arrests were detained in a room within the faculty and beaten by the same security forces before being released.

Such are the living conditions in Iraq.

More than 80 faculty members from the University of Baghdad have been killed since the beginning of the invasion in 2003.[40]

Violence on Campus

The exodus of academics has dramatically lowered educational standards.[41] However, the brain drain and assassination of academics are not the only reasons for the collapse of the educational system; educational institutions and students are themselves targeted.

On December 11, 2006, a car bomb exploded in a parking lot of Al-Ma'amoon College in the Al-Iskan district of Baghdad, killing one person and injuring four. One student was killed and another six injured in a roadside bomb that exploded on the same morning in front of al-Mustansiriya University.[42] A little over a month later, on January 16, 2007, at least 65 students were killed and another 110 injured in a double attack at the university.[43] Then, on January 29, 2007, an attack against a girls' school in Baghdad left five students dead and another 20 injured.[44]

Mohammed Abdul-Aziz, a statistician with Iraq's Ministry of Education, told Integrated Regional Information Networks (IRIN, the UN Office for the Coordination of Humanitarian Affairs' news and analysis source) that at least 110 children had been killed and 95 injured at schools since 2005;[45] these numbers do not include children killed or injured in transit to and from school.[46]

On December 3, 2007, unknown gunmen opened fire on a mathematics teacher at the Ali al-Hadi preparatory school in al-Qebla district in western Basra, killing him in front of his students.[47] A month later in Mosul, on January 31, 2008, unknown gunmen kidnapped five university students. A Ninewa police source relayed "Unknown gunmen abducted five of Mosul University students in Ein al-Beidha district, south of Mosul... the students were getting back to their homes in al-Sharqat district, 80 km south of Mosul."[48] Then, on April 6, 2008, gunmen kidnapped 42 university students near Mosul; they were freed later that day.[49]

The intimidation campaign against the institute of education persists.

An Educational System on the Verge of Collapse

A former teacher from a high school in Amariya commented in October of 2006:

> Education in my area is collapsing... Children can't get to school because of road blocks. The parents of others have simply withdrawn them from the school because of the fear of kidnapping... If children have to travel by car, we are much less likely to see them. When I left, we had 50% attendance. We see parents when they come in to ask for the children to have a "vacation," and they admit they are too scared to let them come. Between September 8 and 28 two members of the staff were murdered. The staff was supposed to be 42. Now there are only 20.[50]

The violence unleashed since the start of the invasion has driven thousands of students away, with enrolment off by more than half at some universities in the 2007–08 academic year alone.[51] Universities in other parts of the country are open, but have become deserted.[52] According to statistics from the Ministry of Education, only about 30 percent of Iraq's 3.5 million school-aged children were attending classes in early 2007, compared to 75 percent in the previous school year.[53] The NGO Save the Children reported similar statistics in the spring of 2007: 818,000 primary school-aged children, representing 22 percent of Iraq's student population, were not attending school.[54]

A joint study by Iraq's Ministry of Education and the United Nations Children's Fund (UNICEF) found that of those who do not attend school, 74 percent are female. Aid agencies estimate that thousands of Iraqi parents do not send their daughters to school for security and economic reasons and because of the general insecurity in the country itself.[55] Agencies add that schools and universities are likely to continue emptying for years to come if there is no let-up in current levels of violence and the displacement it causes.

A UNICEF report on the state of education for Iraqi children concluded that:[56]

- Many of the 220,000 displaced children of primary school age had their education interrupted.
- An estimated 760,000 children (17 percent) did not go to primary schools in 2006.
- Only 28 percent of Iraq's 17-year-olds sat their final exams in summer, and only 40 percent of those sitting exams achieved a passing grade (in south and central Iraq).

In 1982, UNESCO awarded Iraq a prize for eradicating illiteracy.[57] At the time, Iraq had one of highest rates of literacy for women – by 1987 approximately 75 percent of Iraqi women were literate.[58] In 2004, UNESCO estimated that the literacy rates for adults – after a year of Anglo-American occupation and twelve years of UN-sponsored sanctions – stood at 74 percent. Three years later, in June of 2007, Education International estimated that only 65 percent of adults were literate (54 percent of women and 74 percent of men).[59]

Actions to Protect Iraqi Intellectuals

The first organized attempt to create awareness about these murders, was made by the International Coalition of Academics Against Occupation, which published the following appeal on July 25, 2004:[60]

Even after the "transfer of authority" the U.S. Government remains in de facto military occupation of Iraq. The idea that the escalation of violence can be put to an end by the "interim" government, while 140,000 U.S.

> troops remain in control of major Iraqi cities like Mosul and Baghdad, is far from the reality on the ground.
>
> Overlooked by the U.S. Press is the escalating assassination of Iraqi academics, intellectuals, and lecturers. More than 250 college professors since April 30, 2003, according to the Iraqi Union of University Lecturers, have been the targets of assassination.

From September 2004 onwards, press reports about these assassinations appeared on a regular basis. Many of these can be read at the BRussells Tribunal website.[61]

The second attempt to bring focus to the destruction of Iraqi higher education came from the BRussells Tribunal, which began its campaign in December 2005, in cooperation with CEOSI.[62]

The campaign aimed to break the silence, appealing to organizations which work to enforce or defend international humanitarian law and to put these crimes into the public domain. It also appealed to the special rapporteur on summary executions at the United Nations Office of the High Commissioner on Human Rights (UNHCHR) in Geneva that an independent international investigation be launched immediately to probe these extrajudicial killings.[63] The response was overwhelming. To date, the petition has been signed by some 11,000 academics and intellectuals worldwide, among them four Nobel Laureates, who vowed to help create awareness and make a concerted effort to stop this extermination.[64]

The BRussells Tribunal established a list of the assassinated academics in order for mandated human rights authorities to investigate the killings and find a way to protect Iraq's academic and cultural wealth.[65] Despite these attempts, to date nothing has been done and no case has been seriously investigated inside Iraq.

Since the campaign started, the BRussells Tribunal has received many letters of support as well as comments and useful information from inside Iraq. Hundreds of Iraqi academics from inside the country and/or recently exiled have signed the petition, despite the danger this could bring to them.

One professor wrote:[66]

In Iraq, everybody knows that the Badr Brigade, the armed militias of Islamic Revolution in Iraq are among the assassins of the academics in Iraq. Those armed forces turned into national guards of the Interior Ministry, so they have a license to kill now!! The petition idea is very good, but the response from the Iraqi academics will not be so great since the real criminals are still free to kill any of us under the blessing of occupation. Killing the educators and the academics would make it easier for the illiterate religious fanatics to govern uneducated people, terrified for their lives.

Another professor wrote:

We, as University lecturers, are going through exceptional conditions in which any one of us may get killed intentionally or otherwise. It became normal that we greet one another when we meet, we wish each other safety and thank God to be still alive. Messages of threats to kill became something very usual. I myself got threatened after being elected Head of the Department of (omitted for safety reasons) at the college and was consequently obliged to move to another college.

Below are some facts concerning Iraqi academics:

1. Murdering involves University and other academic institutes as well, teachers of different ages, specializations, and political and religious beliefs.
2. Assassins are professional people, and we never heard till now that one murderer got arrested.
3. Murdering takes place everywhere: on the road, at work, and home as well.
4. Nobody has taken responsibility, and reasons have not been clarified.
5. Murdering is carried out by fire-shooting, some got killed with 3 and others 30 bullets.
6. The number of those killed in the University of Baghdad alone has exceeded 80 according to formal reports.
7. People are afraid to ask for details about those crimes.
8. Many of the killed are friends, one is Prof. Sabri Al-Bayati, a Prof. on Arts was killed on 13/6/2003 near the college. Another is Prof. Dr. Sabaah Mahmood Dean of the college Al-Mustansiriya University who was killed near the college 2003. Prof. Dr. Abdullateef al Mayaahi was killed with more than 30 bullets. He occupied the post of Director of

the centre of Arab studies in the Mustansiriya University. I suggest that you correspond with the presidents of Universities to get data and details of these killings from the presidents of the universities of Baghdad, Mustansiriya, Basrah, Kufa, Mosul....

9. Many famous professors, doctors have left Iraq to save their lives.

Here's a message from an Iraqi professor, who has been able to escape the Iraqi Armageddon:

I am a female Iraqi academic forced to leave Iraq on 2 August 2006. On 17 July 2006 I was kidnapped, tortured and threatened to be killed with my daughter if didn't leave Iraq within a few days. I have a PhD in [omitted] and was a member of staff at [omitted], University of Technology in Baghdad, Iraq.

I had no time to contact the Iraqi Academic Association to report the incident because I hid when I received the threat until I fled Iraq.

Thank you for your effort to document the assassinations and threats to Iraqi academics. The real situation in Iraq is much worse than anything mentioned in the news or any report. Not all the incidents were documented in your website. Personally, I knew many academics at University of Technology were threatened and forced to flee Iraq after the occupation and for one reason or another they might not have the time to report the threats to the Iraqi Academic Association. Among them Head of Control and Systems Eng. Dept., Prof Dr Ali Althamir, Spectrum specialist at Applied Sciences Dept., Dr Mohammad Radhi, a member of staff at Building and Construction Dept., Dr Ghanim Abdul Rahman and many others.

One particular reaction was especially important. It shows that Iraqi academics indeed want to oppose this situation, but are obstructed by the Quisling-government from doing so.

OK I will give you some names. In fact the list is so big I will do a scan and send it to you as I wish we can do something about that, and I am ready to work with you on that, but please keep my name secret for security reasons.

Give me a couple of days. Then you'll receive a list of more than 100 Iraqi professors who were murdered. As well as I have my own stories about that.

The head of our dept. was killed a month ago. I arranged for a rally in the university and I invited all the media. I wrote a press release, I tried to make it official, I mean not only among the students. And you know what? Many important people in the university and the government told me we should not show the weakness of our government. I became very disappointed. I didn't know how to work on that and if no one helps you it will be useless.

I hope we can raise our voice this time.

In these circumstances, solidarity campaigns are essential to create awareness about the atrocities that are taking place and support the academic community in Iraq in their efforts to raise their voice against the killings of their educators, and safeguard them from further decimation.

The number of assassinations has not decreased since the B*Russell*s Tribunal started its campaign. According to its sources, the contrary is true. Since the end of 2005 hundreds of academics have been assassinated and an end to the killings is not on the horizon. The B*Russell*s Tribunal continues receiving e-mails on extrajudicial killings. Before this book went to press, the latest was from Dr. Saad Jawad on January 15, 2009:

My name is Prof. Saad N. Jawad, a political scientist from Baghdad University. I am now a fellow at LSE [London School of Economics], [in] London. While going through the updated list of the killed Iraqi academics published by your esteemed organisation, I found that the names of the following colleagues, god rest their souls in peace, are missing from it. May I ask you to kindly include them in the coming updated list? Thank you very much.

1. Prof. Khalil Ismail al-Hadithi, Prof. of Political Science, College of Political Science, University of Baghdad, killed in Amman, Jordan, 23 April 2006.
2. Prof. Husain Ali al-Jumaily, Prof. of Political Science, College of Political Science, University of Baghdad, killed in Baghdad 16 July 2006.
3. Mr. Khalid Hassan Mahdi Nasrullah, administrative Secretary of the College of Political Science, University of Baghdad, kidnapped and killed after four days of kidnapping and torture, 27 March 2007.

The Occupation is Responsible

Iraqi professors direct most of their ire towards the failed Anglo-American occupation. Dr. Bakaa, former president of al-Mustansiriya University (2003–04), commented that he had received almost no funding for research since the occupation. Buildings destroyed during the First Gulf War were rebuilt in two months' time under the Hussein regime, yet the Americans have repaired nothing. When professors are threatened or killed, there is never any investigation.[67]

Dr. Saad Jawad adds that "Iraqi professors are being killed by everyone, and nobody has told us if any killers have been caught. Nothing has been done. One U.S. soldier was kidnapped and Baghdad is on full alert, but the killing of an Iraqi professor? Nothing happens."[68]

In fact, neither the Iraqi "government," nor the occupation forces can guarantee security, education, healthcare, electricity or any other basic need. To the contrary: there are clear indications that the US and UK can be held responsible for many of the "terrorist" and death-squad activities (this is further explored later in this chapter).

Were the assassinated academics Ba'athists? The answer is that they were educators. The term "de-Ba'athification" was a war slogan used by the US and its allies in a bid to destroy the Iraqi national state[69] – its administrative apparatus,[70] public services,[71] properties,[72] archives,[73] registries of public and private ownership,[74] natural resources,[75] revenues[76] and reserves[77] (leading Iraq to the brink of economic collapse[78] and abject poverty[79]) as well as its economic foundations,[80] laws[81] and the judicial system,[82] museums,[83] libraries,[84] army and police,[85] health[86] and education[87] systems, art,[88] print media,[89] radio[90] and television.[91]

This destruction is not a consequence of war but rather a studied plan prepared before the invasion.[92] Strictly speaking, and according to definitions under international law, this destruction is genocidal in nature.[93]

The systemic liquidation of Iraqi academics has nothing to do with them being Ba'athist or not. It follows from the imperialist character of the invasion of Iraq, and the attempt to render null and void Iraqi sovereignty.[94] The US imperial project, based on privatization[95] and ruin,[96] indeed outright looting,[97] plunder[98] and confiscation,[99] and in direct violation[100] of international law, has created the objective and political conditions for the rise of puppet-government-controlled death squads[101] and US-drafted mercenary security contractors[102] that kill and terrorize Iraqi academics and others with impunity.[103] The various actors that make up these death squads help to destroy the Republic of Iraq, kill and expel its people, annihilate its middle class, all this with the active (or tacit) support of the occupation authorities, in a campaign of counterinsurgency that resembles the many "dirty wars" of the US during the past 50 years. It is the largest heist in history, and it is backed with murderous force.[104]

Instead of bringing stability to Iraq, the Anglo-American occupation is bringing chaos and terror, inciting civil war and sectarian strife, in order to defeat the National Popular Resistance and to break the aspirations of the Iraqi people to live in a sovereign state and decide their own future. The real division in Iraq[105] is between those who go along with the US project and those who oppose it.[106]

Urgent Actions are Needed to Save Iraq's Academics

Organizations that work to enforce or defend international humanitarian law should put these crimes high on their agendas. In concrete terms, the UN human rights system, including the recently streamlined Human Rights Council, the International Committee of the Red Cross, responsible for ensuring general respect for the laws of war, and the conference of the High Contracting Parties to the Geneva Conventions, should ensure that their mandates are fulfilled, lest these mandates be deemed worthless by the international public. International human rights organizations can play a role in bringing pressure to bear on inter-governmental organs to act. Whereas violators regard international humanitarian and human rights law as a luxury easily dispensed with, in reality, for the sake of humanity, it must be asserted as the bare minimum upon which we can claim civilization.

An independent international investigation should be launched immediately to probe these extrajudicial killings. This investigation should be carried out by the UN Special Rapporteur on extrajudicial, summary or arbitrary executions under the auspices of the UN Human Rights Council, establishing not only the facts and circumstances of those killed but also the responsibility of perpetrators, and others accountable. The fact that the number of assassinated academics in Iraq is so high should not be taken as an excuse for inaction, nor the budgetary restrictions of the UN human rights system. It is not for the international public to suggest to the UN human rights system how to best fulfill its mandate. We should demand, however, that it fulfills it.[107]

Suggested further possible actions for the academic community include:

- Helping end the silence that surrounds the ongoing crime of the assassination of Iraqi academics and the destruction of Iraq's educational infrastructure, and support Iraqi academics' right and hope to live in an independent, democratic Iraq, free of foreign occupation and hegemony. Academic institutions and organizations can declare solidarity with their Iraqi colleagues. An example of such an action is the *Declaration of the General Assembly of the Conference of Spanish University Rectors* (CRUE) of November 14, 2006.[108]
- Academics worldwide can forge links between their universities and Iraqi educators, both in exile and in Iraq. This can take the form of internet exchanges, direct faculty and student exchanges, joint research projects, and general support, direct (research grants, material assistance) and indirect (public campaigns to highlight the plight of Iraqi academics and students). Student organizations can link with Iraqi student organizations in much the same way.
- Universities can set up and grant scholarships to Iraqi exiled lecturers. Organizations that are active in facilitating

scholarships for Iraqi academics include the Council for Assisting Refugee Academics (CARA)[109] and the Iraq Scholar Rescue Project.[110]

- Educators can mobilize colleagues and concerned citizens to take up the cause of the salvation of Iraq's intellectual wealth, by organizing seminars, teach-ins and forums on the plight of Iraq's academics, like the Madrid International Seminar on the Assassination of Iraqi Academics and Health Professionals that was held between April 22 and 23, 2006.[111]

Notes

1. Thanks to the B*Russell*s Tribunal members Dr. Ian Douglas, Abdul Ilah and Hana Al Bayaty, for their valuable contribution to the information in this chapter and their relentless efforts to start and guide our campaign on the assassinations of Iraqi academics.
2. "US Threatens Iraqi Scientists," *Islam Online*, April 12, 2003, http://www.islamonline.net/english/news/2003-04/12/article02. shtml, accessed December 2008.
3. See "Sensing Foul Play, Iraqis Take Arms to Stop Looting," *Islam Online*, April 11, 2003, http://www.islamonline.net/english/ news/2003-04/11/article13.shtml, accessed December 2008, and "Iraqi Regime Collapses, Baghdad Under U.S. Control," *Islam Online*, April 9, 2003, http://www.islamonline.net/English/ News/2003-04/09/article09.shtml, accessed December 2008.
4. Nate Carlisle, "Amash Should be Freed, publisher says," *Columbia Daily Tribune*, May 15, 2003, http://www.freerepublic.com/focus/ f-news/912256/posts, accessed December 2008.
5. Dirk Adriaensens, "The Real Story Behind the Arrest of Dr. Huda Saleh Mehdi Amash," http://www.casi.org.uk/discuss/2003/ msg02406.html, accessed December 2008.
6. Alissa J. Rubin, "Suspicion Surrounds Death of Iraqi Scientist in US Custody," *Los Angeles Times*, May 28, 2004, http://www. commondreams.org/headlines04/0528-07.htm, accessed December 2008.
7. An e-mail sent to the B*Russell*s Tribunal.
8. "9 Iraqi Scientists Murdered in Last 4 Months: US Believes Killings Effort to Conceal Scope of Iraq's Nukes Program," *WorldNetDaily*, February 26, 2004, http://www.worldnetdaily.com/news/article. asp?ARTICLE_ID=37299, accessed December 2008.

9. Nicolas Riccardi, "Another Voice of Academia is Silenced in Iraq," *Los Angeles Times*, January 21, 2004, http://www.brusselstribunal. org/academicsArticles.htm#another, accessed December 2008.

10. Jeffrey Gettleman, "Assassinations Tear into Iraq's Educated Class," *New York Times*, February 7, 2004, http://www.nytimes. com/2004/02/07/international/middleeast/07ASSA.html?ex=13914 90000&en=1d4f662cec46b775&ei=5007&partner=USERLAND, accessed December 2008.

11. Ibid.

12. Lucy Hodges, "Iraq's Universities are in Meltdown," *Independent*, December 7, 2006, http://www.independent.co.uk/news/education/ higher/iraqs-universities-are-in-meltdown-427316.html, accessed December 2008.

13. "List of Killed, Threatened or Kidnapped Iraqi Academics," B*Russell*s Tribunal, continuously updated, http://www.brussels-tribunal.org/academicsList.htm, accessed December 2008.

14. Katherine Zoepf, "Iraqi Academics are Marked for Death, Human-Rights Groups Say," *Chronicle of Higher Education*, July 7, 2006 (Vol. 52, No. 44), http://www.topsy.org/IraqiAcademics.doc, accessed December 2008.

15. Saad Albazzaz, "196 Professors Killed, More Than 100 Kidnapped Since US Invasion," *Azzaman*, Editorial, March 15, 2007, http:// www.azzaman.com/english/index.asp?fname=news\2007-03-15\ kurd1.htm, accessed December 2008.

16. See Michael E. O'Hanlon and Jason H. Campbell, "Iraq Index: Tracking Variables of Reconstruction and Security in Post-Saddam Iraq," Brookings Institution, October 1, 2007, http://www3. brookings.edu/fp/saban/iraq/index.pdf, accessed December 2008, and Jeremy Laurance, "Medics Beg for Help as Iraqis Die Needlessly," *Independent*, October 20, 2006, http://www. independent.co.uk/news/world/middle-east/medics-beg-for-help-as-iraqis-die-needlessly-420850.html, accessed December 2008.

17. Elizabeth Ferris, "Statement," Brookings-Bern Project on Internal Displacement, February 14, 2007, http://www.reliefweb.int/rw/ rwb.nsf/db900SID/AMMF-727BUF, accessed December 2008.

18. Luke Baker, "Iraq Healthcare in Disarray, report says," Reuters, January 16, 2008, http://www.reuters.com/article/latestCrisis/ idUSL16828588, accessed December 2008.

19. Carolyn Lochhead, "Iraq Refugee Crisis Exploding: 40% of Middle Class Believed to Have Fled Crumbling Nation," *San Francisco Chronicle*, January 16, 2008, http://www.sfgate.com/cgi-bin/ article.cgi?file=/c/a/2007/01/16/MNG2MNJBIS1.DTL, accessed December 2008.

20. "Assassinated Media Professionals," B*Russell*s Tribunal, continuously updated, http://www.brusselstribunal.org/JournalistKilled.htm, accessed December 2008.

21. See "Iraqi Oil Revenues for Iraqi Refugees," http://www.3iii.org and Hana Al-Bayaty, "Oil for Iraqi Citizens," *Al-Ahram Weekly*, No. 879, http://weekly.ahram.org.eg/2008/879/focus.htm, accessed December 2008.

22. Annia Ciezadlo, "Death to Those Who Dare to Speak Out," *Christian Science Monitor*, April 30, 2004, http://www.csmonitor.com/2004/0430/p11s01-woiq.html, accessed December 2008.

23. Former professor of environmental engineering at Baghdad University, recipient of the 2003 Nuclear-Free Future Award for her work on environmental contamination after the Gulf War in Iraq and a member of the B*Russell*s Tribunal Committee. Read her testimony in: *World Tribunal on Iraq: Making the Case Against War*. See http://www.nuclear-free.com/english/souad.htm and Dr. Souad N. Al-Azzawi, "Deterioration of Iraqi Women's Rights and Living Conditions under Occupation," B*Russell*s Tribunal, December 19, 2007, http://www.brusselstribunal.org/pdf/WomenUnderOccupation.pdf, accessed December 2008.

24. Charles Crain, "Approximately 300 Academics Have Been Killed," *USA Today*, January 17, 2005, http://www.usatoday.com/news/world/iraq/2005-01-16-academics-assassinations_x.htm, accessed December 2008.

25. Dr. Issam K. Arrawi, "Breaking into AUL Headquarters," October 28, 2006, http://www.brusselstribunal.org/AlRawi.htm#AUL, accessed December 2008.

26. "Note on the Assassination of Dr. Issam Al-Rawi," B*Russell*s Tribunal, October 30, 2006, http://www.brusselstribunal.org/AlRawi.htm, accessed December 2008.

27. Basil Adas, "Dentist Claims Mossad Is Behind Scientist Killings," *Gulf News*, July 29, 2006, http://archive.gulfnews.com/articles/06/07/29/10055723.html, accessed December 2008.

28. "Hundreds Protest Attacks on Intellectuals in Missan," http://en.aswataliraq.info/?p=61871, accessed December 2008.

29. This information was accessed at http://www.baghdentistry.com/work/about.html, this site is no longer active.

30. Joanne Bladd, "Business as Usual," *Arabian Business*, April 2, 2008, http://www.arabianbusiness.com/515183-business-as-usual, accessed December 2008.

31. "Security Developments in Iraq," *Iraq Updates*, April 24, 2007, http://www.iraqupdates.com/p_articles.php/article/16778, accessed December 2008.

32. "Dental College Dean Killed in Baghdad," January 25, 2008, http://www.iraqupdates.com/p_articles.php/article/26584, accessed December 2008.

33. "Factbox: Security developments in Iraq," Reuters, February 2, 2008, http://uk.reuters.com/article/gc05/idUKL3055213520080202, accessed December 2008.

34. "US Forces Deny Raiding Dentistry College," *Iraq Updates*, February 10, 2008, http://www.iraqupdates.com/p_articles.php/article/27146, accessed December 2008.

35. Lubna, "Brains as Targets," *The Untold Story: Blog*, February 24, 2008, http://dijlarq.blogspot.com/2008/02/brains-as-targets.html, accessed December 2008.

36. "Iraq: The Exodus of Academics has Lowered Educational Standards," IRIN, January 7, 2007, http://www.irinnews.org/Report.aspx?ReportId=62983, accessed December 2008.

37. Dr. Mohammed, "Dentistry College Ordeal," *Last of Iraqis: A Stranger in His Own Country: Blog*, February 18, 2008, http://last-of-iraqis.blogspot.com/2008/02/dentistry-college-ordeal.html, accessed December 2008.

38. E-mail correspondence to author.

39. "Iraq: Further Information on Fear of Torture or Ill-Treatment," Amnesty International, March 3, 2008, http://www.amnesty.org/en/library/asset/MDE14/007/2008/en/MDE140072008en.html, accessed December 2008.

40. Joshua Partlow, "At Least 15 Iraqis Die as Building Explodes: Attack Highlights Problems in North," *Washington Post*, January 24, 2008, http://www.washingtonpost.com/wp-dyn/content/article/2008/01/23/AR2008012303402.html, accessed December 2008. The author of the preceding commented: "Iraqi government and police as well as U.S. troops have practically been doing nothing to stop the murderous campaign against these intellectuals. Most of the killings are not investigated and university officials, refusing to be named, say they are not aware of any of the alleged killers being brought to justice."

41. "Iraq: The Exodus of Academics Has Lowered Educational Standards," IRIN, January 7, 2007, http://www.irinnews.org/Report.aspx?ReportId=62983, accessed December 2008.

42. "Human Rights Report: 1 November – 31 December 2006," United Nations Assistance Mission for Iraq, http://www.uniraq.org/FileLib/misc/HR%20Report%20Nov%20Dec%202006%20EN.pdf, accessed December 2008.

43. Kim Sengupta, "Double Bombing Kills 65 Students at Iraqi University," *Independent*, January 17, 2007, http://www.

independent.co.uk/news/world/middle-east/double-bombing-kills-65-students-at-iraqi-university-432440.html, accessed December 2008.

44. "Iraq: Widespread Condemnation of Fatal Attack on Girls' School," IRIN, January 29, 2007, http://www.irinnews.org/Report.aspx?ReportId=66296, accessed December 2008.

45. Ibid.

46. "Iraq: Children's Education Gravely Affected by Conflict," IRIN, March 14, 2007, http://www.irinnews.org/Report.aspx?ReportId=70697, accessed December 2008.

47. "Teacher Killed in Front of his Students in Basra," *Iraq Updates*, December 4, 2007, http://www.iraqupdates.com/p_articles.php/article/24667, accessed December 2008.

48. "Gunmen Abducts Five University Students in Mosul," *Iraq Updates*, February 1, 2008, http://www.iraqupdates.com/p_articles.php/article/26818, accessed December 2008.

49. Maquiladora, "Gunmen Kidnap 42 Iraqi Students," *Free Republic*, April 6, 2008, http://www.freerepublic.com/focus/f-news/1997505/posts, accessed December 2008.

50. Peter Beaumont, "Iraq's Universities and Schools Near Collapse as Teachers and Pupils Flee," *Guardian*, October 5, 2006, http://www.guardian.co.uk/world/2006/oct/05/highereducation.internationaleducationnews, accessed December 2008.

51. "Bombing Latest Blow to Colleges," *Washington Times*, January 18, 2007, http://www.washingtontimes.com/news/2007/jan/18/20070118-101338-1968r/, accessed December 2008.

52. Sandy English, "Violence Escalates Against Students and Teachers in Iraq," World Socialist Website, January 31, 2007, http://www.wsws.org/articles/2007/jan2007/stud-j31.shtml, accessed December 2008.

53. "Iraqi Academics at Grave Risk," *Education International*, January 1, 2007, http://www.ei-ie.org/en/article/show.php?id=56&theme=statusofteachers, accessed December 2008.

54. "Iraq: Children's Education Gravely Affected by Conflict," IRIN.

55. Ibid.

56. "Little Respite for Iraq's Children in 2007," UNICEF, December 21, 2007, http://www.unicef.org/media/media_42256.html, accessed December 2008.

57. English, "Violence Escalates Against Students and Teachers in Iraq."

58. Weam Namou, "Operation Iraqi Freedom Enslaved Iraqi Women," *Global Politician*, April 2, 2008, http://www.globalpolitician. com/24070-iraq, accessed December 2008.

59. The current percentage of literate women has risen from the UNESCO estimate of 2000 (25 percent), http://www.globalpolitician.com/24070-iraq. See "Barometer of Human & Trade Union Rights in Education: Iraq," Education International, June 19, 2007, http://www.ei-ie.org/barometer/en/profiles_detail. php?country=iraq, accessed December 2008.

60. International Coalition of Academics Against Occupation, *The Assassination of Iraqi Intellectuals*, https://listhost.uchicago.edu/ pipermail/iraqcrisis/2004-July/000783.html, this site is no longer active.

61. "List of Articles," B*Russell*s Tribunal, continuously updated, http:// www.brusselstribunal.org/AcademicsResources.htm, accessed December 2008.

62. See the collection at http://www.brusselstribunal.org/Academics. htm and CEOSI's website http://nodo50.org/iraq/2004-2005/docs/ represion_3-01-06.html, both accessed December 2008.

63. "Urgent Appeal to Save Iraq's Academics," B*Russell*s Tribunal, http://www.brusselstribunal.org/Academicspetition.htm, accessed December 2008.

64. "Principal Endorsers of the Campaign," B*Russell*s Tribunal, http:// www.brusselstribunal.org/AcademicsPetitionList.htm, accessed December 2008.

65. "List of Killed, Threatened or Kidnapped Iraqi Academics," B*Russell*s Tribunal.

66. These were e-mails sent to the B*Russell*s Tribunal.

67. Christina Asquith, "Murder, Fear Follow Iraqi Professors On Campus," *Diverse: Issues in Higher Education*, November 21, 2006, http://www.diverseeducation.com/artman/publish/article_ 6690.shtml, accessed December 2008.

68. Ibid.

69. Abdul-Ilah Al-Bayaty, "Why the US Will Lose," *Al Ahram Weekly*, 2–November 9, 2005, http://weekly.ahram.org.eg/2005/767/op8. htm, accessed December 2008.

70. "Testimony of Mohamed Al Rahoo," *World Tribunal on Iraq*, June 25, 2005, transcript on B*Russell*s Tribunal website, http://www. brusselstribunal.org/AlRahoo.htm, accessed December 2008.

71. Dan Murphy, "Iraqis Thirst for Water and Power," *Christian Science Monitor*, August 11, 2005, http://www.csmonitor. com/2005/0811/p01s03-woiq.html, accessed December 2008.

72. "Halliburton Loses $18.6 Million Worth of Government Property in Iraq," Halliburton Watch, July 27, 2004, http://www.halliburtonwatch.org/news/property_missing.html, accessed December 2008.

73. "The Destruction of Iraq's National Library and Archives," The Memory Hole, April 2003, http://www.thememoryhole.org/history/iraq-natl-library.htm, accessed December 2008.

74. Saad Kiryakos, "Destroying Iraq's Public Records," *Global Outlook*, No. 5, Summer–Fall 2003, http://www.globalresearch.ca/articles/KIR307A.html, accessed December 2008.

75. "New UN Resolution Must Turn Over US Control of Iraq's Oil Revenues to Iraqis," Iraq Revenue Watch, May 10, 2004, http://www.globalpolicy.org/security/issues/iraq/dfi/2004/0510resolution.htm, accessed December 2008.

76. Emad Mekay, "Is Iraq Becoming the World's Biggest Cash Cow?" Inter Press Service, March 18, 2005, http://www.globalpolicy.org/security/issues/iraq/contract/2005/0318cow.htm, accessed December 2008.

77. "Bush Administration Not Recovering Stolen Money in Iraq," Halliburton Watch, January 17, 2006, http://www.halliburtonwatch.org/news/wsj011706.html, accessed December 2008.

78. Eric Le Boucher, "The Other Failure in Iraq: the Economy," *Le Monde*, February 18, 2006, http://www.truthout.org/docs_2006/022006H.shtml, accessed December 2008.

79. James Cogan, "IMF Measures Wreak Havoc on Iraqi People," World Socialist Web Site, February 21, 2006, http://www.wsws.org/articles/2006/feb2006/iraq-f21.shtml, accessed December 2008.

80. Daphne Eviatar, "Free Market Iraq? Not So Fast," *New York Times*, January 10, 2004, http://www.globalpolicy.org/security/issues/iraq/attack/law/2004/0112freemarket.htm, accessed December 2008.

81. "Iraqis Angered as Bremer Says He Has Final Say on Iraq's Basic Law," Agence France Presse, February 17, 2004, http://www.commondreams.org/headlines04/0217-06.htm, accessed December 2008.

82. "The New Iraq," *NewsHour with Jim Lehrer*, May 13, 2003, http://www.pbs.org/newshour/bb/middle_east/jan-june03/iraq_05-13.html, accessed December 2008.

83. Patrick Martin, "The Sacking of Iraq's Museums: US Wages War Against Culture and History," World Socialist Web Site, April 16, 2003, http://www.wsws.org/articles/2003/apr2003/muse-a16.shtml, accessed December 2008.

84. "Middle East Librarians Association Committee on Iraqi Libraries," http://oi.uchicago.edu/OI/IRAQ/mela/melairaq.html, accessed December 2008.

85. "Iraqi Security Bodies, Army Dissolved: US Move to Consolidate Control," *Dawn*, May 23, 2003, http://www.dawn.com/2003/05/24/top1.htm, accessed December 2008.

86. Dahr Jamail, "Iraqi Hospitals Ailing Under Occupation," World Tribunal on Iraq, June 21, 2005, http://www.brusselstribunal.org/DahrReport.htm, accessed December 2008.

87. Ahmed Mukhtar, "Where Is This Going?" *Al Ahram Weekly*, June 10–16, 2004, http://weekly.ahram.org.eg/2004/694/re7.htm, accessed December 2008.

88. "Iraqi Art Destroyed in Post-War Looting," Non-Profit News and Information Service, http://www.pnnonline.org/article.php?sid=4525, accessed December 2008.

89. Josh White and Bradley Graham, "Military Says it Paid Iraq Papers for News," *Washington Post*, December 3, 2005, http://www.washingtonpost.com/wp-dyn/content/article/2005/12/02/AR2005120201454.html, accessed December 2008.

90. Mika Mäkeläinen, "Shock and Awe on the Air: US Steps Up Propaganda War," April 5, 2003, http://www.dxing.info/profiles/clandestine_information_iraq.dx, accessed December 2008.

91. "CPJ Sends Letter to Rumsfeld About US Bombing of Iraqi TV: Group continues to monitor reports of missing and detained journalists," International Freedom of Expression eXchange, March 28, 2003, http://www.ifex.org/20fr/layout/set/print/content/view/full/33956?PHPSESSID=caf28d2a1819f3bbeea55d3bfeb31f38, accessed December 2008.

92. Greg Muttitt, "Crude Designs: The Rip Off of Iraq's Oil Wealth," Global Policy Forum, November 2005, http://www.globalpolicy.org/security/oil/2005/crudedesigns.htm, accessed December 2008.

93. "We're Committing Genocide in Iraq," Al Jazeera, http://www.aljazeera.com/cgi-bin/review/article_full_story.asp?service_ID=6634, link no longer valid, and Dr. Ian Douglas, "US Genocide in Iraq," Power Foundation, April–June 2007, http://www.brusselstribunal.org/pdf/NotesOnGenocideInIraq.pdf, accessed December 2008.

94. See "Declaration of the Jury of Conscience," World Tribunal on Iraq, June 27, 2005, http://www.brusselstribunal.org/pdf/WTI-JuryFinalJuly26.pdf, accessed December 2008, and Joe Hendren, "The Hijacking of a Nation," Foreign Control Watchdog, August

2003, http://www.converge.org.nz/watchdog/05/05.htm, accessed December 2008.

95. Antonia Juhasz, "Bush's Other Iraq Invasion," *AlterNet*, August 22, 2005, http://www.alternet.org/waroniraq/24307/, accessed December 2008.

96. "In Less Than Three Years," Assyrian International News Agency, April 2, 2006, http://www.aina.org/news/20060204121313.htm, accessed December 2008.

97. Ghali Hassan, "The Endless Looting of Iraq," *Online Journal*, December 14, 2005, http://www.onlinejournal.com/artman/publish/article_332.shtml, accessed December 2008.

98. Mohsen Khalil, "Bush and Blair Violations to the International Law in the Economic Field," February 4, 2006, http://www.brusselstribunal.org/Moshen.htm, accessed December 2008.

99. "Confiscating and Vesting Certain Iraqi Property," Office of Policy Coordination and International Relations, Executive Order 13290, March 20, 2003, http://nodis3.gsfc.nasa.gov/displayEO.cfm?id=EO_13290_, accessed December 2008.

100. Naomi Klein, "Bring Halliburton Home," *The Nation*, November 6, 2003, http://www.thenation.com/doc/20031124/klein, accessed December 2008.

101. Max Fuller, "Crying Wolf: Media Disinformation and Death Squads in Occupied Iraq," *Global Research*, November 10, 2005, http://www.globalresearch.ca/index.php?context=viewArticle&code=FUL20051110&articleId=1230, accessed December 2008.

102. Louis Nevaer, "Here Comes the Death Squad Veterans," *AlterNet*, June 16, 2004, http://www.alternet.org/waroniraq/18967/, accessed December 2008.

103. Dahr Jamail, "US Coalition Forces Above the Law, According to the CPA," Information Clearing House, May 1, 2004, http://www.informationclearinghouse.info/article5475.htm, accessed December 2008.

104. A.K. Gupta, "The Great Iraq Heist," *ZMagazine*, January 2004, http://www.zmag.org/zmag/viewArticle/13790, accessed December 2008.

105. Hana Al-Bayaty, "The Primary Divide," *Al Ahram Weekly*, August 18–24, 2005, http://weekly.ahram.org.eg/2005/756/re11.htm, accessed December 2008.

106. Abdul Illah and Hana Al Bayaty, "The Politics of Sovereignty," *Al Ahram Weekly*, June 2–8, 2005, http://weekly.ahram.org.eg/2005/745/re2.htm, accessed December 2008.

107. It is interesting to note that since 2004 there is no longer a Special Rapporteur on the situation of human rights in Iraq. http://www. unhchr.ch/html/menu2/7/b/execut/exe_mand.htm.

108. "Declaration Regarding the Widespread Violence in Iraq and the Killing of University Professors," http://www.brusselstribunal. org/pdf/CRUE.pdf, accessed December 2008.

109. Council for Assisting Refugee Academics website, http://www. academic-refugees.org/, accessed December 2008.

110. Scholar Rescue Fund: Iraq Scholar Rescue Project website, http://www.scholarrescuefund.org/iraq/pages/intro.php, accessed December 2008.

111. "US Policy in Iraq: A War Launched to Erase both the Culture and Future of the Iraqi People," http://www.brusselstribunal.org/ SeminarMadrid.htm.

7

WIPING THE SLATE CLEAN

Max Fuller and Dirk Adriaensens

The Purge of Iraqi Academics

Emergence of the Purge

Among the many tragedies that have befallen Iraqi society as a consequence of the Anglo-American led invasion of April 2003, the physical elimination of hundreds or thousands of Iraqi academics has been one of the most heinous and most frequently overlooked. This outcome has every appearance of being a systematic and ruthless campaign of targeted assassination. It has drawn frequent and wide-ranging speculation within mainstream discourse. However, it has also been subjected to far less critical analysis than it has needed. Nor have any of the concrete steps that are urgently needed to protect Iraqi intellectuals been taken. At the same time, the edges of the phenomenon have remained substantially blurred, with no categorical definitions of exactly who has been killed, how or even when. To date, the B*Russell*s Tribunal has campaigned most actively to raise these killings as an issue. The Tribunal has also kept one of the most comprehensive databases recording the killings of Iraqi university teachers and administrators.[1] The earliest recorded instance of targeted assassination in that database is of Falah Hussein, Assistant Dean at Mustansariya University, in May 2003, but the names of two others precede his chronologically without attributing a cause of death. Dozens more killings are listed without confirmed dates.

Although some initial speculation suggested that the killings targeted scientists who had been involved in illicit weapons programs, it quickly became clear that the victims included many who could not have been.[2] By May 2004 the Iraqi academic community had come to recognize itself as a targeted group,[3] and by September, the Association of University Teachers (AUT), established by Issam al-Rawi in June 2003, had recorded the deaths of some 250 academics that had been killed since the occupation began.[4]

In fact, such deaths were part of a wave of killings of leading professionals that the news channel Al Jazeera claimed had taken more than 1,000 lives by April 2004.[5] Undoubtedly, the killings of academics take place within a broader scope of attacks against Iraq's professional middle class that includes medical professionals, journalists, judges and lawyers, as well as religious and political leaders.[6] Within this context it is hard to say whether academics have been specifically singled out as academics or whether the institutionalized academic community has been more effective at documenting its own plight than other sections of the middle class. Regardless of this question, this chapter focuses on the decimation of the academic community, whose plight is not to be understood in isolation, but as a window into the wider horror afflicting occupied Iraq.

Many of the first assassinated academics fell among the waves of targeted killings of members of the Ba'ath Party that became obvious towards the end of 2003.[7] According to the reporting of the Institute of War and Peace, of the party members who lost their jobs in the L. Paul Bremer initiated de-Ba'athification process, approximately 1,000 were lecturers and professors.[8] Andrew Rubin wrote that of the Ba'athists that had been sacked, "a surprisingly large number fell victim to assassination."[9] One of the earliest victims was Dr. Muhammad al-Rawi, the president of Baghdad University and a senior member of the Ba'ath Party, who was assassinated in his clinic in July 2003.[10]

The number of killings has continued to rise. By the end of 2006 the UK's *Independent* reported that over 470 academics had been killed,[11] while the *Guardian* stated that the figure stood at around 500 from Baghdad and Basra Universities alone.[12] There are now around 400 cases recorded on the B*Russell*s Tribunal database. The list is undoubtedly incomplete, as much of the data must be derived from media sources, which make no claim to assemble complete records. Since the murder of Dr. Issam al-Rawi on October 30, 2006, there is no indication that anyone is currently attempting to systematically compile this information on the ground.[13]

Even amid the horrifying levels of violence in Iraq following the occupation, the killings of academics, alongside those of Ba'athists and others, have stood out for their highly selective character. In fact, although the list of killed academics includes a handful of seemingly random deaths, in the vast majority of cases it appears that the victims have been specifically singled out, either as the immediate target of professional assassins or as the object of so-called kidnappings, which resulted in their deaths.

In his assessment of the killings of academics delivered to a UK Cross-Party Commission on Iraq in June 2007,[14] Dr. Ismail Jalili demonstrated that the killings of academics have been widely dispersed by academic discipline, and that their rate appears to have increased over time (Figure 7.1). He has also demonstrated the very high proportion of senior academics that have been killed, with the majority of victims having attained PhDs and over two thirds holding the positions of rector/chancellor, dean or vice dean,

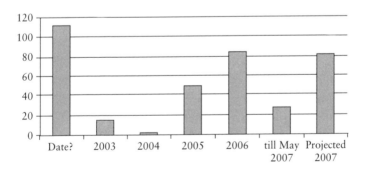

Figure 7.1   Killings of academics and some medical professionals up to May 2007

Note that the vast majority of undated cases fell in the period up to June 2006.

Source: *Iraq's Lost Generation: Impact and Implications*, June 15, 2007, http://www.naba.org.uk/content/articles/HR/IraqHRM/Jalili_Report2007_Iraq_LostGeneration.pdf

department head or professor (Figure 7.2). Since the murder of Dr. al-Rawi, this kind of detailed information has been much harder to obtain and is largely dependent on monitoring of the media.

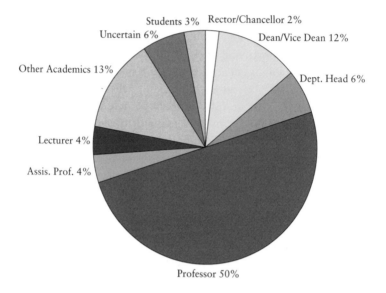

Figure 7.2   Proportions of murdered academics by university post up to April 2006

Source: As Figure 7.1

The majority of killings have taken place within the various universities and higher education colleges in Baghdad, especially Baghdad University itself (Figure 7.3). Basra and Mosul Universities have also seen a substantial number of killings of academic staff. The high levels of murder amongst academics at the universities of these three cities does not appear to correspond with the overall levels of violence in their respective provinces as depicted in various surveys.[15] It is likely that these higher levels reflect the leading position of these universities as well as the potential role of the cities where they are located as capitals in an Iraq divided along the major ethno-sectarian lines.

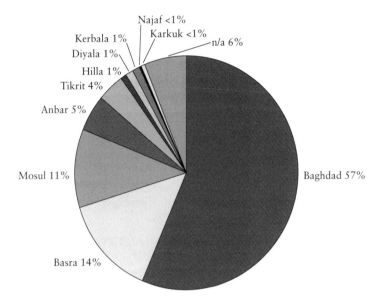

Figure 7.3   Distribution of murdered academics by city of work up to April 2006

Source: As Figure 7.1

Dr. Jalili found no indication that violence against academics has followed a sectarian agenda, with victims belonging to both Sunni and Shi'ite sects, where it was possible to establish such an identity. However, the majority of those killed appear to have been ethnic Arabs, as opposed to Kurds.

Targeted Assassinations

From almost the outset of the occupation Iraqi academics began to fall victim to well-organized teams of assassins who ambushed them as they went about their daily lives, typically killing them instantly. Such killings account for the substantial majority of recorded deaths (Figure 7.4), especially from 2003 to 2005.

Where data exist, most of the victims were killed by small groups of armed men at close range. Sometimes they are executed

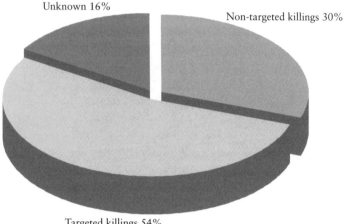

Figure 7.4   The proportion of Iraqi academics that have fallen victim to targeted assassination in relation to the total number of academics killed (includes all cases where there is sufficient data to make a reasonable assessment), March 2003 to December 2007

Source: BRussells Tribunal

at point blank range with handguns; at other times they are subjected to a barrage of automatic fire.

Typical descriptions of such killings take the following form:[16]

- Dr. Sabri Mustapha al-Bayati, Prof. of Geography; faculty member at the College of Art, University of Baghdad. Shot dead just outside arts dept in front of students, June 13, 2004.
- Dr. Mahfoudh al-Qazzaz, Prof. in Islamic History; faculty member at the College of Art, Mosul University. He was killed by a death squad in front of his family at his home, December 20, 2004.
- Gunmen riding in a civilian car targeted Dr. Qais Sabah al-Jabouri, Prof. at the Islamic University in al-Adhamiya, after leaving a university building and showered him with bullets which led to his immediate death, June 6, 2007.

- Unknown men rained down a hail of gunfire on Dr. Zaki Bakir Sajr al-Anji, lecturer in the College of Education, Al Mustansiriya University, and Dr. Husham Abd al-Amire, lecturer in College of Literature, at the same university, killing them as they were leaving the university, August 28, 2005.
- In a drive-by, gunmen killed Dr. Ali Ahmed Husseinin, a professor at the Baghdad Engineering College, in northeastern Baghdad, with a machine gun fired from an Opel Vectra. May 22, 2006.

Such methods, while in many ways typical of contemporary violence in Iraq, are marked by an unusual level of professionalism. Very few of the intended targets survive and the killers, who frequently make use of one or more vehicles to stage their attacks and make their escape, display an intimate familiarity with their victims' lifestyle and movements. Academics have typically been ambushed in their places of work, especially at entrances to compounds, while travelling between home and the workplace, and at or outside their homes. A former general of the Iraqi Army described the pattern in the following terms: "Many of them get killed near their houses or on the way to their work, and others get kidnapped, and we find their dead bodies in the street. When you follow these crimes you will be sure that the criminals have special training and their purpose is to make Iraq empty of any professionals."[17] Killings have often taken place in public spaces and in front of witnesses. Sometimes small groups, including families, have been killed at once; sometimes the victim has been deliberately separated from friends and colleagues.

To date, no one had taken responsibility for the killings and there is no indication that any of the killers have been apprehended or brought to justice. In addition, there is almost no direct evidence of which party or parties are responsible, with two noteworthy exceptions relating to the killings of academics from the University of Mosul. In the first instance, in December 2005, the car of the Kurdish historian Dr. Omar Miran was driven off the road into a gorge by two four-wheel-drives "typically used by the Kurdish security forces" with sirens blazing. Dr. Miran was known as an opponent of Kurdish separatism and his son, Dr. Abdul Qadir Miran, publicly accused the security forces in the region of responsibility for his father's death.[18] Just weeks later, in February 2006, Dr. Abdul Qadir Miran was himself assassinated in his home, together with his wife and children. A mysterious seventh body was also discovered at the scene wearing "full Kurdish uniform," which it is assumed belonged to one of the attackers, whom Dr. Miran slew in self-defense.[19] Beyond these isolated and linked cases, it is unfortunate that very few details of the crimes have been recorded in most instances, making it impossible to know whether, for instance, the same cars are commonly employed.

Death Threats and Intimidation

Alongside the targeted assassinations of academics and other professionals have come explicit and implicit threats of assassination. Such threats have taken a variety of forms. Although no statistics are available, it appears that the threats are most commonly issued in the form of letters. The letters are typically pushed under doors or even delivered though the internal mail within academic institutions.[20] Explicit threats of death carried in the messages, which may be handwritten in childish scrawl,[21] are sometimes reinforced by the inclusion of a single bullet, with a message that might say: "You cost us just one bullet, no more, so shut your mouth"[22] or "Its better to leave your job or you will face what you don't want."[23] The bullet itself has become an effective shorthand, so that often victims of intimidation receive only a bullet. For instance, one lecturer found a bullet on her desk with her name written on it,[24] while it has been reported that many academics have found bullets in their mail boxes.[25] Such intimate yet anonymous forms of delivery serve to heighten the impact with their overtones of proximity, familiarity and impunity.

Threats have also been scrawled on office walls,[26] delivered by phone[27] or, to universities, via the internet.[28] Other forms of explicit intimidation have included visitations in person, such as when a man came to the office of Dr. Abdul al-Latif al-Mayah at

Mustansiriya University and told him to close the Human Rights Center[29] or when a group of armed men "hysterically raided" the campus of Bab Al-Moadham University, roaming corridors and rooms, calling the names of professors from a list and threatening them with death if they show up in the college,[30] and lists of names of people scheduled for death posted on public walls.[31] In this vein, we can perhaps add the leaking of certain death lists, which, to the extent that those on the list are aware of their inclusion, becomes a cost-effective form of mass intimidation.[32] Implicit intimidation has also been reported. For instance, Dr. Harb Zakko, a resident of Baghdad's central Karrada district, was approached through his mother, who had received calls from someone asking her to open the door, saying that they had something for Dr. Zakko. These calls were followed by a call to Dr. Zakko himself at his clinic, asking personal questions. That was enough to convince Dr. Zakko to flee Baghdad.[33] Another doctor who wished to remain anonymous first heard that his name was on a list, then found that a strange car with heavily armed young men had been parked outside his home while he was away at a conference.[34]

As with targeted assassinations, there is very little evidence of who is directly responsible for issuing the various forms of intimidation, but, like the killings themselves, threats and intimidation appear to have become a widespread phenomenon across Iraq. The exact extent of such intimidation is difficult to specify, although one Iraqi academic writing in 2005 described such threats as "very usual,"[35] while a spokesman for the Association of University Lecturers stated in November 2004 that over 400 members had received threats of physical harm.[36] Within the College of Dentistry, the Assistant Dean, Fakhri Al-Qaisi, noted in January 2006 "that most dentistry section professors have received letters of threat."[37] There is no indication that the situation has subsequently changed, with the *Chronicle of Higher Education* reporting in May 2007 that scores of professors throughout Iraq had received bullets sent through internal mail, death threats tacked to their doors or anonymous telephone calls during the months recently preceding its report.[38] According to an article in the *Christian Science Monitor*, academics were claiming that some 2,500 university professors had been killed, kidnapped, or told to leave the country by June 2006.[39]

Explicit messages and demands contained within the threats vary, although by far the most common demand is for the victim to leave the country, hence such threats have become known as "leave or die" messages.[40] Other explicit demands have included leaving a workplace,[41] not taking up a specific post,[42] or just for the recipient to shut their mouth.[43] Only in one case from Basra do we hear that a "leave or die" message was couched in specifically sectarian terms ("get out you dirty sunny, or you will be slaughtered like the camel"[44]), although it has also been reported that some messages claim that a professor favors a particular ethno-sectarian group.[45]

Another category of intimidation that has been reported are messages purportedly from students demanding higher grades. There is little evidence to substantiate that this is a widespread phenomenon or that students are actually the authors of the threats. In one case, a professor at Baghdad University, Ali al Kafif, was said to have been murdered for failing three students after receiving a number of threatening letters. The killer(s) apparently left a note near to his body, which read "Death for those who are responsible for oppression in the classrooms."[46] However, the content of the threatening letters has not been recorded and the message on the note is extremely ambiguous; it might equally imply that Dr. Al Kafif was murdered for his perceived political sentiments.

However, such semantic variations in the language of intimidation belie the unity in the underlying grammar of fear, which essentially serves two functions, both of which are firmly underlined by the actual violence directed against academics and other professionals and extends far beyond even the hundreds or thousands that have actively been subject to intimidation. The first function is to hound them out of their social roles, their homes and, frequently, their homeland. As Dahr Jamail shows (in Chapter 8), the impact on Iraq's academic, medical and professional community in general has been devastating. By April 2007 the International Committee of Solidarity with Iraqi Professors stated that more than 3,000 university professors had fled the country since the invasion.[47]

The second function of such widespread intimidation is to ensure that all those academics who remain in Iraq, whether or not they are the immediate object of death threats, exist within a massively pervasive culture of fear. Dr. Faris Nadhmi, a founding member of the Iraqi Psychological Society and a former lecturer at Baghdad University, describes the climate of fear in Appendix 1 of this book.

Whilst the personal impact of such terror tactics is enormous (analagous to a state of post-traumatic stress), in political terms, its effect is to make academics and others increasingly afraid to speak out. According to Ahmed Mukhtar, the climate of fear had become so pervasive by June 2004 that many professors flatly refused to speak about the killings of their colleagues, or even to admit that they were happening.[48] Talking about the occupation is perceived as particularly dangerous and has become a reason for dismissal,[49] while others live in fear of offending any number of groups suspected of murder and mayhem.[50] The climate of fear even extends to the security guards, who are widely perceived as potential persecutors rather than as protectors.[51] To shield themselves, professors at Baghdad's universities have begun dressing down, putting on Arab headscarves and driving to work in old, scruffy cars.[52]

The climate of fear within universities is also exacerbated by the incursion of religious fundamentalism, which can take a variety of forms. One form is for demands to be issued by anonymous or unknown groups for students to be segregated by gender and for the institution to stop teaching "Western ideals."[53] Students are reported to have felt such pressures to the extent that thousands have requested transfers to campuses where their sect is in the majority.[54] Such incursions also contribute to undermining the non-sectarian and essentially secular character of the Iraqi system of higher education.

Kidnapping and Detention

Whilst kidnapping is generally included in the list of crimes faced by Iraqi academics, it is typically seen as an outlying phenomenon in relation to targeted assassinations, characterized as a symptom of general lawlessness, rather than as part of the specific persecution of the academic community. Hence IRIN commented in October 2004 that "as professionals with stable jobs they [academics] present easy targets for gangs who simply want to get money."[55] A similar point was made by Sabrina Tavernise in May 2005: "The simple quest for money, which fuels the country's widespread kidnapping industry, appears to be the biggest motivation for making targets of doctors."[56]

Although several commentators, including Issam al-Rawi, former head of the AUT, have highlighted the fact that payment of ransom does not guarantee the safe return of the victim,[57] the assumption that a ransom is necessarily involved has tended to prejudice perceptions of authorship, so that it is "gangs" and "local mafias"[58] that conduct kidnappings. One effect of this discourse has been to distance the killings of academics and other professionals from the more endemic "sectarian violence," the victims of which have tended to have been tortured and summarily executed under conditions of detention.[59]

In fact, a significant proportion of the recorded cases of deaths of academics (some 35 percent where sufficient information is available; see Figure 7.5) appear to have occurred under conditions of some form of detention, following the forceful seizure of the victims from their homes, workplaces or in the course of their normal routines. For instance, Dr. Samir Yalda, Assistant Director of the Faculty of Business Administration and Economics at Mustansiriya University, was seized in front of the university gate and his body was found in the street three days later on August 3.[60] In fact, the proportion of killings following forced abduction in relation to overall deaths rose rapidly between 2004 and 2007, to the extent that in 2007 nearly 50 percent of all killings of academics took place in detention and must therefore be seen as a second and potentially distinct phenomenon (Figure 7.6).

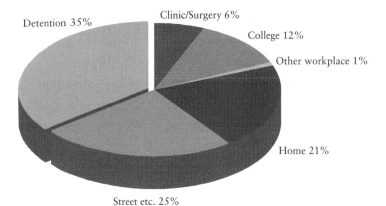

Figure 7.5   Killings of Iraqi academics by place of death, 2003–07

Includes all cases where there is sufficient data to make an assessment

Source: BRussells Tribunal

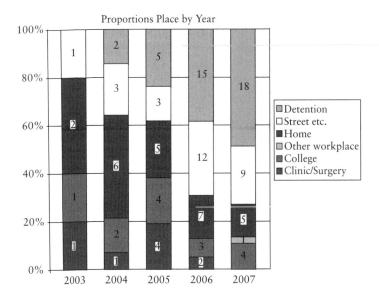

Figure 7.6   Killings of Iraqi academics by place of death over time, 2003–07

Includes all cases where there is sufficient data to make an assessment

Source: BRussells Tribunal

As Issam al-Rawi noted, such killings do not preclude the possibility that a ransom will be asked and paid, although there are only two recorded instances in the B*Russell*s Tribunal database (Wissam al Hashimi, chairman of the Arab Geologists Union, and Uday al Beiruti, an ENT specialist at Al Nahrain University). One thing that is striking is that in all the cases where sufficient data exist, killings within conditions of detention rapidly followed abduction (typically within two days and often after a matter of hours), which suggests that in such cases obtaining a ransom was not the primary motivation. In fact, there is no indication that ransoms are typically demanded at all in such cases.

As with cases of targeted assassinations and threats, very few positive identifications of those responsible for killings within detention have been made. However, in at least six cases, direct accusations or sufficient eye-witness observations have been recorded to offer some evidence of culpability. In the four cases where direct accusations have been recorded, the culprits seem to enjoy an ambiguous identity as both representatives of the new security forces and simultaneously Shi'ite militiamen. In the earliest of the four, Dr. Kadhum Mashhut Awad, Dean of the Faculty of Agriculture at Basra University, is described as having been found cut into pieces after being taken from his home by police. The account goes on to state that he was "assassinated by a death squad of Failaq Badir [Badr Brigade] – Iranian militia working under the American Authority." The next three cases all focus on the supposed Mahdi Army militia associated with the Shi'ite cleric Muqtada al Sadr. In one, Uday al Beiruti, head of the Faculty of Medicine at Nahrain University, is described as being kidnapped from Kadimia hospital by the Mahdi Army after being circled by four new BMWs, but alternative sources claim his abductors were gunmen in Interior Ministry uniforms.[61] In the second, Khalid al Naid, Assistant Dean of the Medical College at Nahrain University, is said to have been taken by "the militia which controls the area of the Medical School." The *Sunday Times* identifies this militia as the Mahdi Army, but it is extremely likely that over and above any informal identity that such "militiamen" might have, the "militia which controls the area of the Medical School" would more formally belong to either the Facilities Protection Service or a National Police Brigade. In the final case, the body of Mahdi Saleh al Any, a "sunni professor," is described as being found two weeks after being "abducted by police" and that he was a victim of al-Mahdi militias. His body was found with drill holes and bullet wounds in the head and chest, entirely consistent with having been killed within a para-legal detention facility.[62]

In the two cases where incriminating eye-witness observations have been recorded, these also suggest the involvement of the security forces. On September 10, 2007, Muayad Ahmad Khalaf was abducted by men in three cars, one of which was described as bearing a government license plate, and in late 2006 the neurologist Dr. Lu'ay Mas'ud was taken away by men in uniform, before his body was found in a waste ground close to the Sadr City (formerly Al Thawa) area of Baghdad. These anecdotal examples convey a significant impression that at least some members of the security forces are involved in the detention/abduction/arrest and murder of academics and that there is a considerable degree of confusion over the identity of the "official" security forces vis-à-vis illegal or para-legal armed actors.[63]

One final case that may shed some light on the authorship of these crimes is that of Dr. Ali Faraj, one of Iraq's top cardiologists. He narrowly escaped being abducted when armed men in ski-masks broke into his Baghdad clinic. The gunmen indicated that they wanted to take him to the Interior Ministry, but prevented Dr. Faraj from making a telephone call to confirm that their orders came from the Interior Minister. Dr. Faraj escaped after a neighbor's guards intervened when they saw him being dragged out to a car.[64]

Even where academics have been abducted and released, there are indications that the motives of their abductors are frequently the same as those that drive the persecution of academics more generally. Most importantly, according to Dr. Muthana al Dhari, a spokesman for the Association of Muslim Scholars, many of those detained "are receiving threats of future abuse if they do not take the necessary steps, which is to leave Iraq."[65] The same point was made in relation to a wave of abductions of top medical specialists, many of whom were ordered by their abductors to leave the country, sometimes with a deadline.[66] According to the author, some of these were beaten and tortured; others were released after a ransom was paid. Thus, as with those academics who receive written or verbal warnings to leave the country, an important objective of those carrying out abductions is to rid the country of certain undesirables and more broadly to create a climate of fear in which a large part of Iraq's former professional class are encouraged to seek refuge abroad or to relocate within the country, effectively becoming internally displaced. Again, this can overlap with demands for payment, as well as with the abduction of family members, as with the abduction of the son of Saadoon Isa, Vice President of Nahrain University, who was released following the payment of a ransom with an explicit message for his father: "Tell him to leave the country because Iraq is not his, it is ours."[67] Thus, within the pattern of abuse directed at academics, it seems appropriate to see many of the cases of kidnapping/detention as part of a more general process of murder and intimidation. By June 2004, according to Zuheir al Maliki, a judge at the Central Criminal Court, only three of many kidnappings had been investigated.[68]

The Authorship of Killings of Iraqi Academics

Motive and Opportunity

The assassinations of academics, doctors and other professionals in Iraq has attracted considerable media attention, with wide speculation about both the authorship of these crimes and the motives behind them. The list of suspected assassins that have been suggested is long, extending from the Ba'athists, Islamists and "insurgents," the Badr Brigade, Mahdi Army and other groups linked to political parties, through the Mossad, CIA and the intelligence apparatuses of every surrounding state, as well as private security companies, all the way to gangs and disgruntled students. Of the various allegations that have been made, a handful stand out for their strength and specificity, their repetition or for the perceived insight of their authors.

The first serious allegation to emerge was that Israel, through its intelligence service Mossad, was responsible for the killings of Iraqi scientists and academics. No hard evidence was produced, but the accusation gained currency through a series of influential statements. The first of these statements was made on French television in April 2003 by an anonymous retired French general, who claimed that 150 Israeli commandos had been sent into Iraq to assassinate 500 Iraqi scientists linked with weapons programs.[69] At the end of 2004 an anti-war conference in Cairo concluded that Israeli secret agents had been responsible for the killing of more than 300 Iraqi scientists since the invasion,[70] although it is unclear on what basis this conclusion was reached.

The charge of Israeli orchestration of the killings was subsequently reinforced by references to information published by the Palestine Information Centre in June 2005, which purported to cite a US State Department document intended for the president, demonstrating Mossad involvement.[71] In fact, the references are not directly to the original publication, but to an anonymous article published on the website aljazeera.com (a news and discussion forum quite distinct from the better-known satellite channel Al Jazeera). There is no trace of the original article to be found online and therefore it is impossible to know to what State Department report any such article referred. Given that the report is also reputed to have incriminated the US Defense Department, it seems extremely unlikely that any genuine such report ever existed.

A further, though slightly less direct, element in the case against Israel was a report by Julian Borger published in the *Guardian* in late 2003.[72] Quoting anonymous former senior intelligence officials and "well-informed intelligence sources," Borger claimed that Israeli advisors operating at Fort Bragg were training US forces in aggressive counterinsurgency techniques that amounted to "basically an assassination programme."

It seemed obvious to many that Israel has a vested interest in preventing the reemergence of Iraq as a competing regional power and specifically that they might want to forestall any possibility of Iraq becoming a nuclear-armed state in the future. It should be noted that while Israel was implicated directly, to many Iraqis such an implication went hand in hand with a belief that Israel and the US were working together, or at least that the US was tolerating such a policy.

The second major allegation to emerge was that pro-Iranian forces were responsible for the killings. This charge began to take hold towards the end of 2005 when the American Association for the Advancement of Science reported that some Iraqi academics claimed the Badr Brigade, the supposedly disarmed military wing of the Supreme Council for Islamic Revolution in Iraq previously based in Iran, was responsible for some of the assassinations.[73] At the same time, the satellite channel Al Jazeera quoted an Iraqi political analyst as stating that Iranian-backed militias were holding teachers of Arabic and history as allies of the Ba'ath Party, on whom they were exacting revenge.[74] The charge came against a rising tide of extrajudicial killings that left scores of bodies on Baghdad's streets each day and in which the Badr Brigade was frequently singled out as a major participant, despite the persistent evidence of involvement by elements of the security forces.[75] It is argued that Iran favors the dismantling of Iraq's secular institutions in order to advance its own hegemony in the region.

The charge of Iranian or pro-Iranian involvement was almost the mirror image of the position held by the occupying forces and new Iraqi authorities, which principally claimed that Ba'athist "insurgents" and foreign fighters were responsible for the killings as part of their efforts to halt progress.[76] Nevertheless, both positions gradually fed into what now appears to have become a more or less established mainstream solution: that extremists on both sides of an internal sectarian conflict have targeted academics in what has even been described as "an orgy of mindless terrorism."[77] This new synthesis found favor with the likes of John Agresto, senior advisor to the higher education ministry in Iraq from 2003 to 2004, who in 2007 insisted that "Their secular nature is what is getting them targeted."[78]

What has been strikingly and shockingly absent from mainstream discourse is even the merest hint that the Anglo-American occupation might be actively responsible for the purge of Iraqi academics. In this failure to grapple with what is clearly the most obvious solution, this mainstream discourse has blindly accepted the contention put forward by representatives of the occupation, such as Brigadier General Mark Kimmitt who is known to have said, "This works against everything we're trying to do here." In fact it is possible to take a far more empirical attitude.

If, as representatives of the British and American states publicly insist, it is their intention to build a functional democratic state that respects human rights, it is clearly in their interests to protect and preserve Iraq's "human capital." Such a strategy would implicitly involve opposing the murder and terrorization of Iraqi academics. If, on the other hand, it is their intention to dominate the country's natural resources, impose a proxy government and possibly even to break the country into smaller, more manageable pieces (divide and conquer), it might very well be in the interests of those powers to destroy the backbone of Iraq as an integrated secular nation with an ideogolical commitment to a centralized economy and a welfare state. Eliminating Iraqi academics might very well constitute one strand of such a strategy.

To determine which of those two mutually independent strategies the occupying powers are pursuing at the level of competing discourses would mean attempting to set public proclamations of "freedom and democracy" against the less well-publicized, but nevertheless high-powered, statements and theories about "natural states"[79] and the necessary federalization of Iraq,[80] notions of "creative chaos"[81] and the strategic imperatives of US global hegemony[82] to determine which of them was setting policy. But in fact we do not have to leave this debate in the realm of conflicting discourses. Despite the fact that there is very little in the way of direct evidence of culpability, we can nevertheless look at what evidence there is in an attempt to determine whether the occupation has done its best to protect and nurture Iraq's "intelligentsia" or whether it has facilitated their murder and removal. Two important case studies will provide a useful foundation for understanding what must be termed a culture of impunity, while an assessment of the creation of the new intelligence apparatus and the forces of the Interior Ministry will lay the basis for recognizing the most likely apparatus of violence.

Case Study 1: Professor Tareq Samarree

The case of Dr. Tareq Samarree is thus far unique[83] in offering a potential window into the "kidnapping" of Iraqi academics.[84] Tareq Samarree held the post of Professor of Pedagogy at Baghdad University prior to the invasion and was a long-standing member of the Ba'ath Party. Professor Samarree was forced from his job shortly after the invasion under the prevailing climate of de-Ba'athification. For the next year and a half he lived an almost clandestine existence at a family farmhouse outside Samarra. On March 3, 2005, Dr. Samarree was forcibly detained at his home by armed men claiming to be from the government. He was taken away and held at the Jadriya detention facility in Baghdad with many other detainees. Dr. Samarree was never formally charged and had no access to the outside world, nor any form of formal judicial process. During his detention he was repeatedly tortured physically and subjected to continual abuse and terror. He was specifically questioned about his role in the Ba'ath Party and the whereabouts of other party members. The detention facility held not only academics but a range of Iraqis including an artist and a Sunni Imam.

Dr. Samarree's ordeal at Jadriya came to an end in November 2005 when US soldiers entered the detention facility and the story of Iraqi prisoner abuse hit the world headlines.[85] Dr. Samarree was among a group taken to a hospital due to the severity of his injuries, but when it became clear that the group was to be returned to Iraqi custody, he and a number of his companions escaped with the assistance of a sympathetic US soldier. Professor Samarree subsequently fled Iraq and has been granted asylum in Europe.

Soon after the discovery of the Jadriya detention facility it was widely reported that the Interior Ministry facility had been run by pro-Iranian militia elements within the Interior Ministry without US knowledge and that an investigation into the facility would be launched by the Iraqi government with US assistance and that efforts to prevent similar abuse at other facilities would receive high priority.[86]

First of all it must be stated that, more than two years later, the promised Iraqi government report into the Jadriya facility has still not been made public and there is no indication that any individuals were held accountable for abuse.[87] It is simply not credible that the US government would have been unable to exert sufficient pressure to make such a report public or to conduct its own investigations if the protection of Iraq's "human capital" was a genuine concern. Nor was any effort made to involve the appropriate international bodies, such as the UN rapporteurs for torture and extrajudicial killings.

Secondly, several sources have alleged that US personnel were well aware of the existence of the detention facility long before its official discovery. Those sources include Hadi al Amiri, the head of the Badr Organization, whose own forces were widely accused of running the facility,[88] and the United Nations Assistance Mission in Iraq.[89]

Thirdly, no attempt was made to protect Professor Samarree, offer him judicial assistance or even to question him regarding his experiences by US authorities. His testimony has now been joined by that of another former detainee at Jadriya, Abbas Abid. Unlike Professor Samarree, Mr. Abid remained in Iraqi government detention following the US intervention, where he continued to be repeatedly tortured.[90]

Whist Dr. Samarree's case may not be typical of the persecution of academics, it provides an insightful test case into the attitude of US authorities towards prisoner abuse in general and specifically the persecution of at least one academic. In the very few cases in which academics have been killed within conditions of detention and any positive identification of the perpetrators has been recorded, it has been strongly indicative of involvement by elements of the security forces. In view of such evidence, the case of Dr. Samarree and the existence of the Jadriya detention facility must be viewed as relevant to the issue of the killing of academics. That so little has been done is instructive of the attitude of the occupying powers.

Case Study 2: The Raid on the Ministry of Higher Education

On November 14, 2006, paramilitary gunmen in the uniforms of Iraqi National Police commandos raided a building belonging to the Ministry of Higher Education in Baghdad's Karrada district and forcibly detained around 100 members of staff from two departments and around 50 visitors, according to the Minister of Higher Education.[91] The raid took place in broad daylight, 1 kilometer from the Green Zone, in an area that contained several high-security compounds, including the department where passports are issued. According to a BBC correspondent the Karrada area is "well protected with a heavy presence of Iraqi troops and several checkpoints."[92] The paramilitary force estimated at between at least 50 and 100 arrived in a fleet of some 20–30 camouflage pickup trucks of the kind employed by the Interior Ministry and established a cordon of the area. They stated that they were from an anti-corruption unit and were carrying out arrests ahead of a visit by the US ambassador.[93] The paramilitaries made their arrests according to lists, confirming the identities of those present by their ID cards. The paramilitaries then made their exit through heavy traffic without opposition.

Within days Prime Minister Maliki declared that this was not a case of terrorism, but a dispute between "militias" and that all of the detainees had been released in a series of police raids.[94] A number of senior policemen, including the district police chief and the commander of a National Police paramilitary commando brigade and three other officers were reportedly detained for questioning over possible complicity.

However, the Education Ministry insisted that only around 70 of 150 detainees (both Sunnis and Shi'ites) had been released.[95] In addition, it reported that some of those released had been tortured (some legs and hands had been broken) and that there were allegations that others had been killed. One released detainee, whose own arm had been broken in detention, described seeing three security guards suffocated to death and hearing a number of senior academics that had been put in a separate room screaming in agony; according to the witness their cries were cut off abruptly.[96] The witness also said that he had not been released as the result of a police raid but that his captors had simply dumped him and others at various locations around Baghdad. His account is partially confirmed by earlier reports, which stated that those released had been blindfolded and deposited in various parts of Baghdad.

Since Maliki's statement that all of the detainees had been released (later reinforced by the National Security Advisor Mowaffak Rubaie), several more detainees were released after undergoing torture.[97] Little more than two weeks after the raid, the bodies of two ministry officials, Dr. Abdil Salam Al Suwaydan, head of the Scholarship department, and Abdil Hameed Hamadani, were found bearing signs of torture and mutilation.[98] No further word has been heard about the remaining dozens of people that the Education Ministry insisted were still missing.

In view of the circumstances surrounding this case, it is very difficult to believe that any forces but officially sanctioned ones could have made such a daring daylight assault in one of the most secure areas of Baghdad. It is equally impossible to believe that any forces but Interior Ministry ones could have assembled a fleet of Interior Ministry camouflage pickup trucks. The designation of the paramilitaries responsible for this abduction as Interior Ministry commandos is fully confirmed by eyewitness testimony, who specified that at least some of the raiders were wearing blue camouflage uniforms of a digitally designed type very recently introduced to National Police commandos by the US, specifically intended to prevent other parties from masquerading as National Police commandos.[99] That the raid was conducted by Interior Ministry forces in fact seems to have been confirmed from the outset by Iraqi government spokesman Ali al-Dabbagh, who claimed the mass detention was the work of militiamen who had infiltrated the Interior Ministry.

Just as in the case of Jadriya, we once again find that officially sanctioned elements of the security forces have been involved with the persecution of academics and that the response of both the Iraqi government and the coalition has consisted of nothing but empty promises of investigation and redress, as well as, in this case, outright lies. Again it must be assumed that the coalition does not have a vested interest in preventing the destruction of Iraqi "human capital."

These two cases underline the most important single piece of evidence in the elimination of Iraqi academics: that to date none of the killers have been caught and we are no closer to a detailed understanding of this horrific phenomenon. Whilst this situation has frequently been characterized as one of lawlessness in mainstream reporting, it is important to recognize that what we actually appear to be witnessing is an institutionalized culture of impunity[100] that is a common aspect of state-sanctioned terror and is endemic in the violence of counterinsurgency conflicts.[101] If there were no alternative paradigm through which to view this killing spree, it would strain credulity to its limits to believe that the agents of foreign governments without military presences in Iraq, rogue agents operating within the security institutions established under US military occupation, armed rebels, foreign jihadis and criminal gangs could have continued to murder so many of Iraq's intelligentsia so brazenly and enjoyed such complete immunity from prosecution. However, an alternative paradigm does exist and one that has the distinction of being at once far more plausible theoretically and infinitely better rooted empirically. That paradigm begins to surface under the policy of de-Ba'athification instituted by Iraq's Coalition Provisional Authority.

De-Ba'athification and the Origin of the Purge of Academics

Within days of the beginning of the occupation it started to become clear that US administrators intended to fundamentally reshape not just Iraq's government, but also the public institutions that made up a major part of the country's social fabric, including those in the field of higher education.[102]

Under the guiding hand of Andrew Erdmann, the US senior advisor to the ministry of higher education, the policy was to wipe the slate clean on the pretext that the new Iraqi state required a symbolic cutting of ties with the old "regime" and that it was necessary to develop a "real education system" despite Iraq's formerly high academic standing.[103] In practice this meant that the upper echelons of the Ba'ath Party were to be excluded and the past was to be, literally, rewritten from a pro-American perspective.[104] An initial step was to hold elections within universities to appoint new presidents, vice presidents and deans, the vast majority of whom were seen as too closely linked to the pre-invasion government. Dr. Tareq Samarree has described the way in which this process worked at Baghdad University.

The day after the fall of Baghdad Dr. Samarree and other senior members of staff returned to the university, where they found US soldiers, anti-Ba'athist slogans and un-uniformed gunmen. A plethora of mass-produced posters spread around the campus carried images of Shi'ite clerics linked with the Daawa Party and the Supreme Council for Islamic Revolution in Iraq. A week later, when payday arrived, Dr. Samarree was warned not to come into the university to collect his salary, as his name had appeared fourth on a list of Ba'athists on public display within the university. On April 22 a meeting was held at the university to discuss a new curriculum and a new academic structure. The atmosphere at the meeting was extremely intimidating despite the presence of US soldiers, with the names of Ba'athists publicly displayed on a screen. Eventually, Dr. Samarree and a colleague decided it would be prudent to leave the meeting, only to find that their cars had been set alight in the car park.[105]

These initial indications of the direction of US policy were crystallized on May 16 with the Coalition Provisional Authority's "Order No 1: De-Ba'athification of Iraqi Society."[106] According to this order the top four rungs of the Ba'ath Party organizational structure (estimated at about 120,000 people) were to be dismissed from their posts and barred from taking up employment in the public sector in the future. A de-Ba'athification Committee was established in November under Ahmed Chalabi,[107] leader of the Iraqi National Congress party, a group which had for many years received funding from the CIA.[108] Thousands of workers within the field of education were subsequently dismissed, including hundreds of senior academics across various scientific disciplines, including some 283 from Baghdad University alone.[109] The purge was very unpopular and some of those dismissed actively campaigned for their reemployment, while thousands of their former colleagues signed petitions appealing against the decisions.[110]

Many of those who were dismissed retreated to their homes or sought refuge abroad against a backdrop of rising intimidation.[111] For the new rulers of Iraq and the opposition parties that they had brought with them, it was very much the Ba'ath Party with whom they were, at least publicly, at war.[112] Party members were accused of organizing opposition to the occupation,[113] filtering down to unsubstantiated allegations that individual academics, such as Sa'ad al Zuhairi, had led groups of irregular Fedayeen forces and committed acts of sabotage against their own institutions.[114] Any line that existed between de-Ba'athification and counterinsurgency was always perilously thin.

In this environment graffiti appeared bearing such slogans as "The blood of Saddam's unbelievers will pay for the lives of all our Islamic martyrs"[115] and many former members of the Ba'ath Party were illegally detained or assassinated. Those murdered included teachers, lawyers, doctors, former members of the armed forces and academics. The pattern was recognized by the end of 2003, when the *Washington Post* reported that over the previous few months of that year, around 50 former senior security officials had been gunned down, while the death toll among neighborhood officials across Baghdad was even higher.[116] In the Sadr City district of Baghdad the death rate in December was as much as one or two per day. According to both the Post and Knight Ridder,[117] local police officers described some of these killings as "absolutely organized" and "meticulously planned," with one stating that the killers had "specific knowledge of the targets' homes and usual driving routes."

In Basra killings of former Ba'athists and government officials, including several teachers, began at the end of 2003. On November 1, 2003, the *New York Times* reported that "over the past month, more than a dozen former senior members of Saddam Hussein's government have been shot dead in the streets of this normally peaceful city – two of them this week alone, both shot in the head at close range."[118] Amnesty International highlighted that in at least seven instances that it was aware of in Basra, former educators who had lost their jobs as a result of the de-Ba'athification Order were invited to reapply for their positions or a pension. Immediately after leaving the Directorate of Education, where they had registered their personal details, including their party rank, the seven men were all gunned down at close range. According to Amnesty many of the killings in Basra were of middle-ranking Ba'athists.[119]

It is impossible to consider the killing of Iraqi academics without taking into account these early killings of Ba'ath Party members for several reasons. Firstly, some of the murdered academics, such as Muhammad al-Rawi, president of Baghdad University, were undoubtedly party members and it is impossible to know at this point in time what proportion of these academics belonged to the Ba'ath.[120] Secondly, in their modus operandi, many of the killings of Ba'athists and academics are essentially identical: brazen, professional-style hits employing detailed knowledge of the victims' routines, making use of cars and carried out under a blanket of impunity despite massive force presence in the areas of attack. It is therefore highly likely that the same or related parties are responsible for both sets of extrajudicial killings. Finally, it must be borne in mind that the de-Ba'athification Committee remains active into 2008,[121] demonstrating that there was no speedy finish to the process of de-Ba'athification.

The Intelligence Apparatus

The advantage of this digression into killings of Ba'athists is that we are able to build up a partial picture of the apparatus that was designed to combat the party and which may well be responsible for at least a proportion of both sets of killings.

One of the earliest reports relating to the battle against the Ba'ath Party was a December 15, 2003 article in the *New Yorker* by Seymour Hersh.[122] In it, Hersh, citing anonymous officials, claimed the Bush administration was planning to stand up a special forces group (Task Force 121), whose highest priority would be the "neutralization" of Ba'athist "insurgents" by capture or assassination, specifically targeting what was referred to as the "broad middle" of the Ba'athist underground.

Shortly before this stark warning the *Washington Post* had announced that US proconsul Paul Bremmer had agreed with the Iraqi Governing Council to the establishment of an 800-strong Iraqi paramilitary unit, whose operatives were to be drawn from former security forces personnel and members of the armed wings of the five main opposition (exile) parties[123] and whose targets would include "supporters of former president Saddam Hussein."[124] The force was to include a domestic intelligence-gathering arm. The unit, which at the time would have been the most powerful force under Interior Ministry command, was to work side by side with US special forces and be overseen by US military commanders, presumably under the umbrella of Task Force 121.

It seems very likely that this paramilitary unit must have overlapped with the teams of CIA-sponsored militia (paramilitaries) knows as Scorpions, that had been operating since the invasion.[125] These teams were recruited from Iraqi exiles and were employed to infiltrate resistance groups, to interrogate suspects and, from time to time, to do "the dirty work," according to an anonymous intelligence official.

Further detail about the new paramilitary intelligence structure was supplied later by the Knight Ridder news agency.[126] Knight Ridder reported that immediately after the invasion the CIA took operatives from the militias of the six largest opposition (exile) parties, which they welded into an organization known as the Collection Management and Analysis Directorate (CMAD), whose task was to "turn raw data into targets." In other words, the same militiamen now widely held responsible for Iraq's internal violence were given responsibility for selecting the opponents in a counterinsurgency conflict. This organization was subsequently to form the nucleus for Iraq's new state intelligence apparatus, with branches in the interior and defense ministries and a special core of operatives picked out to form a national intelligence agency. According to Knight Ridder, the CIA retained control of the intelligence apparatus after the transfer of sovereignty.[127]

Whilst these various units and agencies were ostensibly aimed at combating an armed opposition,[128] at the same time that they were growing and developing, the process of de-Ba'athification was continuing apace. A series of windows relating to the activities of two shadowy groups sheds more light on the process of de-Ba'athification and reveals that de-Ba'athification itself overlapped with the world of paramilitary intelligence operations.

The first window relates to the de-Ba'athification Committee which was established in 2003 under the chairmanship of Ahmed Chalabi, leader of the Iraqi National Congress (INC). A communiqué released by the INC in May 2003, before the official inauguration of the Committee, reveals the existence of armed paramilitary teams.

> Yesterday, on the outskirts of Baghdad in the area of Wahash, one of the debaathification teams of the INC was attacked by two vehicles carrying armed men. A fire fight broke out and two of the INC members were lightly wounded. The INC debaathifaction team was pursued back to the Hunting Club (the INC's Baghdad headquarters), where another fire fight broke out. In the gun battle, 2 of the attackers were seriously wounded.
>
> Two hours later, the American military arrived at the Hunting Club after hearing reports of the fire fight. They subsequently moved to arrest some 35 members of the INC and confiscate their weapons. The American military liaison to the INC intervened with the U.S. forces and explained that they had just arrested U.S. allies. All INC members were subsequently released.[129]

Thus the same political party that the CIA was using to build an intelligence-gathering arm and Bremmer was calling on for paramilitaries was already sending out paramilitary teams to conduct intelligence-based operations in collaboration with an

American military liaison. It is extremely likely that such de-Ba'athification teams fell under the mantle of Task Force 121, whose mission was to kill or capture the broad middle of the Ba'athist underground.

A further window into the activities of the de-Ba'athification Committee occurred in mid-2004, when a doctor who had been abducted accused three members of involvement.[130] The accused included Aras Habid, the head of the INC's intelligence wing, who would almost certainly have been a key figure in the implementation of de-Ba'athification.[131] It was at this point that the US officially severed relations with the INC, and warrants were issued for the arrest of 15 of its members including Habid. But, in fact, the US liaison to the INC, Francis Brooke, claimed that the INC had received prior warning of the US raid and had removed their computers and that nothing of any "intelligence value" was recovered. There is no evidence that Habid was ever apprehended and the INC continued to hold the chair of the de-Ba'athification Committee.[132]

The second group that appears to have a bearing on the process of de-Ba'athification, and that has been particularly prominent in Basra, is a party/militia known as Tha'r Allah (God's Revenge). This group was first mentioned in the western media by Radio Free Europe/Radio Liberty (RFERL) in late 2003, which reported that a group by that name had been operating in Baghdad, and had issued a statement on November 1 in which it claimed that it was "hunting down and killing supporters of the Saddam Hussein regime," specifically those who worked in security and intelligence.[133] The group claimed its membership came from "all the factions" of Iraqi people. Agence French-Presse (AFP) reported that a group by the same name appeared in Basra later that month, where it was under the leadership of Yusuf al-Musawi, who, in a similar vein, claimed that al-Qaeda was working with Hussein loyalists.[134]

Despite its avowed murderous intentions, Tha'r Allah appears to have enjoyed a similar degree of nurturing by the British to that afforded to the INC by the Americans. In one early encounter between the British and Tha'r Allah in March 2004, British soldiers are reported to have apologized to the paramilitary Islamist organization and returned its weapons, stating that, "We are not in the business of charging around arresting people."[135] More significantly, the head of Tha'r Allah, Yusuf al-Musawi, had a place on the Provincial Council and held some sort of intelligence/security portfolio.[136] According to the *Telegraph*, the Deputy Governor had discussed the appointment of a new police chief with a representative of Tha'r Allah in February 2005,[137] while a January 2005 article in the Iraqi *Al-Sabah* newspaper records that al-Musawi, who is the head of the higher supervisory commission of the Basra Council, was appointed as a supervisor for Basra's night time checkpoints, "subordinating for Basra Police leadership."[138] In August 2005, evidence of Tha'r Allah's involvement with political assassinations was given to *The Times*, which interviewed an eye-witness who claimed that Tha'r Allah had tried to assassinate his father, a former naval officer. When the family had fought Tha'r Allah off, they were arrested by the police and tortured for over a week.[139]

Such bizarre fragments were crystallized in a report submitted to the United Nations following a raid on Tha'r Allah conducted by the Basra Governor in October 2005. The raid took place after relations with the British had broken down following their assault on the Jamiyat police station to rescue two undercover British operatives arrested by the Iraqi police in late 2005. The report claimed that Yusuf al-Musawi was an officer in police intelligence and that the raid had resulted in the arrest of dozens of death-squad members and the seizure of their vehicles.[140] The response to the raid from central government was fury and a team with US advisors was quickly sent in to shake up the police force.[141] Al-Musawi himself was never sucessfully prosecuted and he and Tha'r Allah continued to impose their "vigilante justice" on Basra for at least the next two years.

The relationship between Tha'r Allah and police intelligence might have seemed all the more remarkable if it were not for a much earlier exposé of the intelligence apparatus in Basra by British journalist Stephen Grey.[142] Grey reported that the killings of Ba'athists in Basra emanated from the Special Operations

Department set up by the British and based at the Jamiyat police station. Although British sources claimed that the undercover operatives arrested by Iraqi police had been targeting corruption within the Jamiyat, it was later revealed by the *New York Times* that US intelligence officers had been working at the Jamiyat, supplying the names of suspects, despite the fact that they were aware that the names were being "leaked" to death squads.[143] The British cover story, which began with countering Iranian weapons smuggling, appeared to be nothing but. No investigation was forthcoming and the rate of death-squad killings in Basra if anything rose following the British intervention.[144] The firm promise that a British Army officer had made in 2003 that those responsible for the killings of Ba'athists would be caught was nothing but hollow rhetoric.[145]

So in the case of the killings of Ba'athists it appears that immediately after the invasion small paramilitary teams were organized by US and UK intelligence officers drawn from the personnel of the six major opposition parties in exile and tasked with pursuing a counterinsurgency program directed against opponents that included members of the Ba'ath Party. At the same time a vigorous policy of de-Ba'athification was pursued at a social/political level, presided over by one of the same parties involved in the counterinsurgency effort and involving armed de-Ba'athification teams. By the end of 2003 it was clear that dozens if not hundreds of Ba'ath Party members were being assassinated under an umbrella of total impunity. While we cannot conclusively prove that any of the agencies set up under British and American auspices are responsible for the killings or that the occupation authorities had approved of or directed such killings at any level, it seems nonetheless highly likely that both contentions hold true and this inference is strongly supported by the apparent total absence of investigation or preventative action. It is therefore worth remembering that a significant proportion of the murdered academics were members of the Ba'ath Party and that the infrastructure of clandestine violence created under the auspices of US intelligence is by far the most plausible candidate that we know of for their murder and would satisfy the record of impunity that we encounter.

The End of History?

Since the US-led invasion of 2003, two distinct patterns of killings of Iraqi academics have emerged: targeted assassinations and killings within detention. Nevertheless, it seems unlikely that we are looking for more than a single agency at the level of intellectual authorship, as the two sets of crimes have more in common than not. Firstly, if we can assume that death threats are delivered by the same hand that guides the assassin's bullet, there is a demonstrable overlap between the motivation of the gunmen and at least some of those with the power to forcibly detain their victims:[146] both parties seem to wish to rid Iraq of groups or individuals that they have labeled as undesirables. Secondly, and even more importantly, both parties have been able to operate without restraint under the noses of those foreign forces that have assumed the responsibility (both moral and legal) for the safety and security of the civilian population. If we were to speculate about the reason for these differing methods, over and above the fact that several different groups might be carrying out the "dirty work," we could suggest that the apparent shift over time from targeted assassinations to killings within detention might imply: firstly, that the physical infrastructure, i.e. the necessary secret detention facilities such as Jadriya, has gradually expanded,[147] making this second form of killing easier to achieve; secondly, that the list of targets was initially incomplete and that part of the process of continuing such intelligence-based purges is acquiring further data through capture and interrogation;[148] thirdly, that the immediate culprits may have shifted from teams of professional assassins to more formal security agents of the new state operating under an imposed counterinsurgency doctrine;[149] and, finally, that the message of terror and impunity spelled out by killings that take place out of sight may be deemed as more effective than that contained in the threat of instantaneous death. While such implications are indeed speculative, what is clear is that far from finding their operations more difficult to carry out, the killers have become more deeply physically entrenched within a flourishing culture of impunity.

One further dimension to this second phenomenon of killings within detention is that it draws the purge of academics into the mainstream of Iraq's so-called "sectarian violence." Victims abducted by paramilitary units from the Ministry of Interior whose tortured bodies reappear days or weeks later are the hallmarks of the killings of the "Shia militias."[150] Yet there is very little in the way of indication that the killings of academics have followed a sectarian agenda, with victims belonging to both Sunni and Shia sects. If an ethno-sectarian dimension were to exist, it would almost certainly have to relate to the fact that a disproportionate number of the victims have been Iraqi Arabs, but it is inconceivable that Kurdish death squads could be conducting such a campaign across Iraq and the coincidence that various ethno-sectarian interest groups might be pursuing an essentially identical campaign strongly argues that a higher level of orchestration exists.

Recently the legal group Public Interest Lawyers has been making a case for holding an independent inquiry into the deaths of a number of Iraqis purportedly within British custody. To establish the need for such an inquiry, Public Interest Lawyers does not need to prove beyond reasonable doubt the guilt of the British Army, merely to convincingly argue that the deaths were most likely to have taken place under British custody.

If we were to apply a similar criteria to the killings of Iraqi academics we might start from two great axioms of deductive and inductive reasoning: firstly, that when we have ruled out the impossible, whatever remains, no matter how unlikely, must be the truth, and secondly, that, all other things being equal, the simplest solution is the best. It is the first of these axioms that must sway us from hasty or generalized prognoses, but it is the second that should guide the order of any investigation. In mainstream Western narrative these fundamental axioms have been utterly disregarded. In the almost random allegations that have been cited or suggested, the authors have dispensed with the most basic, obvious and simplest of all solutions, not because it is impossible, but because it appears to be impossible to mention.

The starting point for any investigation into the killings of Iraqi academics, which began with the illegal invasion and occupation of a sovereign nation by British and American forces, is with those forces and their political leaders themselves. If we began our investigation from this starting point, we would find that our very own representatives had systematically set about the creation of paramilitary outfits designed to fight a war in the shadows against opponents designated as belonging to a specific political background that overlaps with the identity of at least a proportion of the murdered academics. We would find that certain shadowy paramilitary or militia organizations with links to the de-Ba'athification process, as well as an array of political murders in the case of Tha'r Allah, appear to have been groomed or nurtured by the hidden hand of our occupation. We would find that not only had our representatives systematically failed to prevent these killings or apprehend the assassins, but that in several important cases where thorough and proper investigation might have revealed a great deal about the authors and mechanisms of these crimes, our representatives have shown no interest in establishing even rudimentary and transparent inquiries.

These key facts demonstrate that the US and UK established the forces that offer by far the most likely means for the killings.[151] They are also the only actors realistically capable of creating the culture of impunity that has shielded these killings and that, along with the intelligence-gathering apparatus that they have maintained control of,[152] provides the most likely opportunity for the killings. These two factors alone are more than sufficient to satisfy the criterion that Public Interest Lawyers is attempting to reach in the killings mentioned above. However, as we must also conclude, it is the US and the UK that have the most likely motive. The fact that they have taken no effective action to stem the killings of Iraqi academics or to apprehend their killers is compelling evidence that establishing a free and democratic society in Iraq was never their aim. Whilst we may speculate about any wider geopolitical objectives, we can be concrete about at least one of their chief aims.

Quite outside the bounds of international law, the Coalition Provisional Authority imposed a new series of laws for Iraq, subsequently enshrined in a constitution presented under conditions of war and foreign military occupation, that set out the transformation of Iraqi society into a model of neo-liberal economic design.[153] Within this paradigm it must be suspected that Iraqi academics, immersed in the experience of decades of a centralized welfare state, are likely to constitute one among many poles of opposition. That this is the case is spelt out no better than in the creation of an American University on Iraqi soil, whose object is to train a future generation of administrators; the existing generation is quite simply redundant.[154] For the immediate future, decimating Iraq's professional middle class ensures that the country remains dependent on US and other foreign expertise, providing a powerful means of political leverage.

Beyond this, Iraq's secular academic institutions represent a backbone of the nation in the face of federalism and potential partition along ethno-sectarian lines that were entrenched within the opposition parties in exile prior to the invasion.[155] That a proportion of the violence directed against academics is veiled in the trappings of Islamic fundamentalism, whether Sunni or Shi'ite, does nothing to diminish its utility in the deconstruction of the institutions of the former state and the fact that most of the victims have come from Iraq's three foremost universities, corresponding with the three major political centers of contemporary Iraq, strongly implies a hegemonic political agenda underscores the campaign.

The counter argument to such motivations is that, even if their motives might have been cynical, it must surely be in the interests of the US and UK to establish stability for the purposes of investment. But in the short term there are vast profits to be made from ongoing cycles of reconstruction and private military contracts;[156] in the long term the goal of conquest is the imposition of hegemony: domination that extends from force-escalation superiority and economic subjugation,[157] all the way to a monopoly on the very thoughts that shape society and create political movements. With its new-found "freedom," Iraq, in common with so many of the world's nations, has not reached the end of history, but has begun a new and painful period of struggle in which it finds that its oppressors are those with the motive, the means and the opportunity for ruthless pursuit of their own interests.

Notes

1. See BRussells Tribunal, "List of Killed, Threatened or Kidnapped Iraqi Academics," http://www.brusselstribunal.org/academicsList. htm, accessed December 2008.
2. Annia Ciezadlo, "Death to Those Who Dare to Speak Out," *Christian Science Monitor*, April 30, 2004, http://www.csmonitor. com/2004/0430/p11s01-woiq.html, accessed December 2008.
3. Ahmed Janabi, "Iraqi Intellectuals Appeal for Security," Al Jazeera, May 19, 2004, http://www.brusselstribunal.org/pdf/Academics-Dossier.pdf, accessed December 2008.
4. Tabitha Morgan, "Murder of Lecturers Threatens Iraqi Academia," *Times Higher Education Supplement*, September 10, 2004, http:// www.timeshighereducation.co.uk/story.asp?storyCode=191084& sectioncode=26, accessed December 2008.
5. Ahmed Janabi, "Iraqi Intellectuals Flee 'Death Squads'," Al Jazeera, March 30, 2004, http://www.brusselstribunal.org/pdf/ AcademicsDossier.pdf, accessed December 2008.
6. For instance, the Brookings Institution estimates that some 2,000 of the 34,000 physicians present in Iraq before the war have been killed, http://www.brookings.edu/saban/iraq-index.aspx, accessed December 2008.
7. Alan Sipress, "Iraqis Exact Revenge on Baathists," *Washington Post*, December 20, 2003, http://www.washingtonpost.com/ac2/ wp-dyn/A16407-2003Dec19, accessed December 2008.
8. Zaineb Naji, "Iraq's Scholars Reluctant to Return," *Iraq Crisis Report No. 243*, January 18, 2008, http://www.iwpr. net/?p=icr&s=f&o=342062&apc_state=heniicr2008, accessed December 2008.
9. Andrew Rubin, "The Slaughter of Iraq's Intellectuals," *New Statesman*, September 6, 2004, http://www.newstatesman. com/200409060018, accessed December 2008.
10. Amal Hamdan, "Iraqi Intellectuals Under Siege," Al Jazeera, February 27, 2004, http://www.brusselstribunal.org/pdf/ AcademicsDossier.pdf, accessed December 2008.

11. Lucy Hodges, "Iraq's Universities are in Meltdown," *Independent*, December 7, 2006, http://www.independent.co.uk/news/education/higher/iraqs-universities-are-in-meltdown-427316.html, accessed December 2008.

12. Francis Beckett, "Professors in Penury," *Guardian*, December 12, 2006, http://education.guardian.co.uk/higher/news/story/0,1969718,00.html, accessed December 2008.

13. In July 2008, the Iraqi Ministry of Human Rights claimed that 340 academics had been killed between 2005 and 2007. Although it demanded strict anonymity with regard to sourcing, it insisted it keeps verified information on every individual case and added that the Iraqi government and US occupation authorities have refused to investigate any of the cases. *Azzaman*, "340 Academics and 2,334 Women Killed in 3 Years, Human Rights Ministry Says," July 2, 2008, http://www.iraqupdates.com/p_articlesphp?refid=DH-S-02-07-2008&article=33196, accessed December 2008.

14. Dr. Jalili's analysis of named cases was undertaken in April 2006 based on lists compiled by the Iraqi Teachers Association, the BRussells Tribunal, and data presented at the Madrid International Conference on the Assassinations of Iraqi Academics, April 23–24, 2006, as well as feedback from various Iraqi academics and medics. See *Iraq's Lost Generation: Impact and Implications*, June 15, 2007, http://www.naba.org.uk/content/articles/HR/IraqHRM/Jalili_Report2007_Iraq_LostGeneration.pdf.

15. The latest survey of Iraqi civilian casualties was conducted by Opinion Research Business (ORB). For their January 2008 updated figures, visit: http://www.opinion.co.uk/Documents/New_Casualty_Tabs.pdf, accessed December 2008.

16. These descriptions are drawn from the database of the BRussells Tribunal.

17. Brian Conley and Isam Rashid, "White-collar Iraqis Targeted by Assassins," *Asia Times*, March 3, 2006, http://www.atimes.com/atimes/Middle_East/HC03Ak01.html, accessed December 2008.

18. "Family of Kurdish Historian Accuses Barzani of his Murder," *AINA*, December 28, 2005, http://www.christiansofiraq.com/murder12285.html, accessed December 2008.

19. "The Assassination of Patriotic Iraqi Kurds… Two that we know of," posted on the Free Iraq blogspot, February 17, 2006, http://abutamam.blogspot.com/2006_02_01_archive.html, accessed December 2008.

20. John Akker, "Lecturing in the Iraqi War Zone," *Guardian*, November 17, 2006, http://education.guardian.co.uk/higher/comment/story/0,1950824,00.html, accessed December 2008.
21. Doug Struck, "Professionals Fleeing Iraq as Violence, Threats Persist," *Washington Post*, January 23, 2006, http://www.washingtonpost.com/wp-dyn/content/article/2006/01/22/AR2006012201112_pf.html, accessed December 2008.
22. Matthew Green, "Threats Haunt Iraq's Outspoken Academics," *Arab News*, July 16, 2004, http://www.arabnews.com/?page=4&section=0&article=48422&d=16&m=7&y=2004, accessed December 2008.
23. Jeffrey Gettleman, "The Struggle for Iraq: Killings; Assassinations Tear into Iraq's Educated Class," *New York Times*, February 7, 2004, http://query.nytimes.com/gst/fullpage.html?res=9A02E6D91E3BF934A35751C0A9629C8B63, accessed December 2008.
24. Hugh Sykes, "Iraqi Scholars Fighting for an Education," BBC News, March 24, 2007, http://news.bbc.co.uk/1/hi/world/americas/6491443.stm, accessed December 2008.
25. Sarah Meyer, "Iraq: 'The Occupation is the Disease'," Index Research, May 1, 2006, http://indexresearch.blogspot.com/2006/05/iraq-occupation-is-disease.html, accessed December 2008.
26. Sykes, "Iraqi Scholars Fighting for an Education."
27. Beckett, "Professors in Penury."
28. Howard LaFranchi, "Iraq Losing its Best and Brightest," *Christian Science Monitor*, September 21, 2004, http://www.csmonitor.com/2004/0921/p06s01-woiq.html, accessed December 2008.
29. Gettleman, "The Struggle for Iraq: Killings; Assassinations Tear into Iraq's Educated Class."
30. "A Testimony of an Iraqi Academic," B*Russell*s Tribunal, November 2006, http://www.brusselstribunal.org/ArticlesIraq3.htm#Testimony, accessed December 2008.
31. Sarah Meyer, "We Need International Support, Interview with Eman Khamas," *Foreningen Iraksolidaritet*, http://www.iraksolidaritet.se/index.php?nr=232, accessed December 2008.
32. Sophie Hebden, "Hit List Names Hundreds of Iraqi Scientists," Science and Development Network, June 30, 2006, http://www.scidev.net/en/news/hit-list-names-hundreds-of-iraqi-scientists.html, accessed December 2008; Beckett, "Professors in Penury."
33. Mohammed A. Salih, "Iraqi Professionals a Particular Target," Inter Press Service, December 6, 2006, http://uk.oneworld.net/article/view/143519/1/, accessed December 2008.
34. Beckett, "Professors in Penury."

35. Dirk Adriaensens, "Iraqi Academics in the Killing Zone," B*Russell*s Tribunal, February 2, 2006, http://www.brusselstribunal.org/academicsArticles.htm, accessed December 2008.

36. "Iraq: Higher Education and Academic Freedom in Danger," Joint Statement by MESA, AAUP, AAAS, November 5, 2004, http://fp.arizona.edu/mesassoc/boardletters.htm, 11-05-04, accessed December 2008.

37. Basil Adas, "Dentist Claims Mossad is Behind Scientist Killings," *Gulf News*, August 2, 2006, http://www.worldproutassembly.org/archives/2006/08/dentist_claims.html, accessed December 2008.

38. Zvika Krieger, "Iraq's Universities Near Collapse," *Chronicle of Higher Education*, May 18, 2007, http://chronicle.com/temp/reprint.php?id=t60fms7pmyhdbkklqcbnhqxk6l0jw93q, accessed December 2008.

39. Scott Peterson, "Why Many of Iraq's Elite Don't Flee," *Christian Science Monitor*, June 22, 2006, http://www.csmonitor.com/2006/0622/p01s02-woiq.html, accessed December 2008.

40. Francis Beckett, "Professors in Penury."

41. Gettleman, "The Struggle for Iraq: Killings; Assassinations Tear into Iraq's Educated Class"; Sabrina Tavernise, "Facing Chaos, Iraqi Doctors are Quitting," May 30, 2005, http://www.nytimes.com/2005/05/30/international/middleeast/30doctor.html, accessed December 2008.

42. "Assassins are Targeting University Professors in a Coordinated Liquidation Process," American Association for the Advancement of Science, June 19, 2006, http://www.nearinternational.org/alerts/iraq20060619, accessed December 2008.

43. Matthew Green, "Death Threats, Assassinations Teaching Iraqi Academics to Watch What They Say," *Arab News*, July 16, 2004, http://www.arabnews.com/?page=4&section=0&article=48422&d=16&m=7&y=2004, accessed December 2008.

44. Qais Alazzawy, "30 Medical Doctors Were Killed and 220 Others Were Forced to Immigrate Abroad During the Past Period," *Gulf News*, September 18, 2005, http://www.brusselstribunal.org/Academics.htm, accessed December 2008.

45. "Threatening and Killing of Scientists in Iraq," American Association for the Advancement of Science, updated September 5, 2006, http://shr.aaas.org/emerging_issues/iraq.htm, accessed December 2008.

46. "IRAQ: Threatened Teachers Fleeing the Country," IRIN, August 24, 2006, http://www.irinnews.org/report.aspx?reportid=60564, accessed December 2008.

47. Ralph Greene, "Horrible Tragedies Occur Virtually Every Day in Iraq," GwinnettForum.com, April 20, 2007, http://www. gwinnettforum.com/issue/07.0420.htm, accessed December 2008.

48. Ahmed Mukhtar, "Where Is This Going?" *Al Ahram Weekly*, June 10–16, 2004, http://weekly.ahram.org.eg/2004/694/re7.htm, accessed December 2008.

49. Meyer, "We Need International Support…"

50. Christina Asquith, "Murder, Fear Follow Iraqi Professors on Campus," DiverseEducation.com, November 21, 2006, http://www.diverseeducation.com/artman/publish/article_6690.shtml, accessed December 2008.

51. Akker, "Lecturing in the Iraqi War Zone."

52. "Mandatory University Attendance in Unstable Iraq Angers Many," McClatchy Washington Bureau, December 20, 2006, http://minstrelboy.blogspot.com/2006_12_17_archive.html, accessed December 2008.

53. LaFranchi, "Iraq Losing its Best and Brightest."

54. "Mandatory University Attendance in Unstable Iraq Angers Many," McClatchy Washington Bureau, December 20, 2006.

55. "Rising Threat Against Academics Fuels Brain Drain," IRIN, October 28, 2004, http://www.irinnews.org/report. aspx?reportid=24263, accessed December 2008.

56. Sabrina Tavernise, "Iraq Healers Have Become Targets," *International Herald Tribune*, May 31, 2005, http://www.iht. com/articles/2005/05/30/news/doctors.php, accessed December 2008.

57. Waleed Ibrahim, "Academics Become Casualties of Iraq War," Reuters, March 9, 2006, http://www.warcrimeswatch.org/news_ details_print.cfm?artid=998, accessed December 2008; Struck, "Professionals Fleeing Iraq as Violence, Threats Persist"; Sumedha Senanayake, "Iraq: Brain Drain Poses Threat to Future," Radio Free Europe/Radio Liberty, November 16, 2006, http://www.rferl. org/content/Article/1072793.html, accessed December 2008.

58. Laith Al-Saud, "An Interview with Dr. Saad Jawad: Iraqi Intellectuals and the Occupation," *Counterpunch*, January 3, 2006, http://www.counterpunch.org/laith01032006.html, accessed December 2008.

59. Tom Lasseter and Yasser Salihee, "Sunni Men in Baghdad Targeted by Attackers in Police Uniforms," Knight Ridder Newspapers, June 27, 2005, http://www.mcclatchydc.com/staff/tom_lasseter/ story/11890.html, accessed December 2008; Andrew Buncombe and Patrick Cockburn, "Iraq's Death Squads: On the Brink

of Civil War," *Independent*, February 26, 2006, http://www.commondreams.org/headlines06/0226-01.htm, accessed December 2008; Robert Fisk, "Secrets of the Morgue: Baghdad's Body Count," *Independent*, August 17, 2005, http://www.independent.co.uk/news/fisk/secrets-of-the-morgue-baghdads-body-count-503223.html, accessed December 2008.

60. Haifa Zangana, "The Elimination of Iraq's Academics," *Al Quds Al Arabi*, February 26, 2006, http://www.uslaboragainstwar.org/article.php?id=10268, accessed December 2008.

61. Zeyad, "Meanwhile in Baghdad," Healing Iraq Blog, September 25, 2006, http://iraqsolidaritycampaign.blogspot.com/2006/09/meanwhile-in-baghdad-zeyad-healing.html, accessed December 2008.

62. Francis Elliott, Raymond Whitaker and Kim Sengupta, "British-trained Police in Iraq 'Killed Prisoners with Drills'," *Independent*, November 20, 2005, http://www.independent.co.uk/news/world/middle-east/britishtrained-police-in-iraq-killed-prisoners-with-drills-516158.html, accessed December 2008.

63. A study commissioned by the Feinstein International Center, Tufts University, found that many Iraqis were unable to distinguish clearly between representatives of humanitarian non-governmental organizations and members of the various armed forces. In relation to distinguishing the identities of various armed groups, many of whom may be out of uniform or deliberately attempting to conceal their official identity, it must be imagined that the problem is even more extreme. This is in no way to impugn the faculties of the Iraqi observers, but to highlight a problem of identification and recording that is likely to be drastically exacerbated in zones of conflict. Greg Hansen, "Iraqis Defend Humanitarianism," *Forced Migration Review*, June 2007, p. 31, http://fictufts.edu/downloads/HA2015IraqCountryStudy.pdf, accessed December 2008.

64. Jonathan Steele, "The Iraqi Brain Drain," *Guardian*, March 24, 2006, http://www.guardian.co.uk/world/2006/mar/24/iraq.jonathansteele, accessed December 2008.

65. Ahmed Janabi, "Iraqi Intellectuals Appeal for Security," Al Jazeera, May 19, 2004, http://english.aljazeera.net/archive/2004/05/20084912563384532.html, accessed December 2009.

66. Mukhtar, "Where Is This Going?"

67. LaFranchi, "Iraq Losing its Best and Brightest."

68. Mukhtar, "Where Is This Going?"

69. "Israeli Commandoes in Iraq to Assassinate 500 Scientists," IslamOnline.net, 18 April, 2003, http://www.islamonline.net/

English/News/2003-04/18/article09.shtml, accessed December 2008.

70. Mustafa Amara, "Israeli Secret Agents Killed 310 Iraqi Scientists," *Azzaman*, October 30, 2004, http://www.informationclearinghouse. info/article7199.htm, accessed December 2008.

71. "Castrating Iraq: Mossad has Murdered 530 Iraqi Scientists, Academics," AlJazeera.com, June 8, 2008, http://group121. blogspot.com/2008/06/castrating-iraq-mossad-has-murdered-530. html (this article is becoming harder and harder to find online), accessed December 2008.

72. Julian Borger, "Israel Trains US Assassination Squads in Iraq," *Guardian*, December 9, 2003, http://www.guardian.co.uk/ world/2003/dec/09/iraq.israel, accessed December 2008.

73. Sarah Olmstead, "Emerging Issue: Iraqi Scientists Under Attack," *Report on Science and Human Rights*, Fall/Winter 2005, Vol. XXV, No. 2, American Association for the Advancement of Science, http://shr.aaas.org/report/xxv/iraq.htm, accessed December 2008.

74. Ahmed Janabi, "Everyone is a Target in Iraq," Al Jazeera, September 21, 2005, http://www.brusselstribunal.org/pdf/Aca-demicsDossier.pdf, accessed December 2008.

75. Eventually, the evidence for involvement by Interior Ministry forces in these killings became so overwhelming, (see for example John F. Burns, "Police in Spotlight after Suffocation Deaths," *San Diego Union Tribune*, July 14, 2005, http://www.signonsandiego. com/uniontrib/20050714/news_1n14suffocat.html, accessed December 2008) that the majority of commentators, rather than ask hard questions about British and American responsibility for the institution that they had built from scratch, concluded that Badr had thoroughly infiltrated the ministry. There remains no substantial evidence that Badr controls this ministry, several of whose most senior officers are former military defectors and which continues to include a substantial presence of British and American advisors. For US presence within the Interior Ministry, see John F. Burns, "To Halt Abuses, U.S. will Inspect Jails Run by Iraq," *New York Times*, December 14, 2005, http://www. nytimes.com/2005/12/14/international/middleeast/14abuse. html?_r=1, accessed December 2008; and Solomon Moore, "Police abuses in Iraq detailed," *Los Angeles Times*, July 9, 2006, http://www.globalpolicy.org/security/issues/iraq/election/2006/ 0709policeabuses.htm, accessed December 2008.

76. Gettleman, "The Struggle for Iraq: Killings; Assassinations Tear into Iraq's Educated Class."

77. Lucy Hodges, "It's a Crisis Like That of the 1930s," *Independent*, December 7, 2007, http://findarticles.com/p/articles/mi_qn4158/ is_20061207/ai_n16894379, accessed December 2008.

78. Zvika Krieger, "Iraq's Endangered Schools," *NewsWeek*, August 20–27, 2007, http://www.newsweek.com/id/32291, accessed December 2008.

79. Ralph Peters, "Blood Borders: How a Better Middle East Would Look," *Armed Forces Journal*, June 2006, http://www.armedforcesjournal.com/2006/06/1833899, accessed December 2008.

80. Leslie H. Gelb, "The Three-state Solution," *New York Times*, November 25, 2003, http://www.cfr.org/publication.html?id=6559, accessed December 2008.

81. Mark LeVine, "The New Creative Destruction," *Asia Times Online*, August 22, 2006, http://www.atimes.com/atimes/Middle_East/HH22Ak01.html, accessed December 2008.

82. For example, Zbigniew Brzezinski, *The Grand Chessboard: American Primacy and its Geostrategic Imperatives*, Basic Books, 1997.

83. Since the time of first draft, a similar case has emerged in Sweden, where Dr. Haider Al-Juboori, a lecturer in engineering at Al-Nahrain Uiversity is claiming asylum following his detention and torture after seizure by members of the Interior Ministry's elite counterinsurgency police commando force. Dr. Al-Juboori was eventually released after payment of a large ransom, but was warned to leave the country forthwith on pain of death. The B*Russell*s Tribunal is following the development of Dr. Al-Juboori's case.

84. Max Fuller, "Ghosts of Jadiriyah," B*Russell*s Tribunal, November 14, 2006, http://www.brusselstribunal.org/FullerJadiriyah.htm, accessed December 2008.

85. See, for example, "Iraq Officials Acknowledge New Detainee Abuse, Prime Minister Pledges Investigation," CNN, November 15, 2005, http://edition.cnn.com/2005/WORLD/meast/11/15/iraq.main/index.html, accessed December 2008.

86. See for example "Iraq Detainees 'Found Starving'," BBC News, November 16, 2005, http://news.bbc.co.uk/1/hi/world/middle_east/4440134.stm and Edward Wong, "U.S. Splits with Iraqi Official over Prisoner Abuse," *New York Times*, November 17, 2005, http://www.nytimes.com/2005/11/17/international/middleeast/17cnd-Iraq.html?_r=1, accessed December 2008.

87. Even Bayan Jabr, the then Minister of the Interior, claims to have never received a copy of the report. PBS interview, November

21, 2006, http://www.pbs.org/wgbh/pages/frontline/gangsofiraq/interviews/jabr.html, accessed December 2008.

88. Jim Muir, "Abuse Reports Fuel Iraqi Tensions," BBC News, November 16, 2005, http://news.bbc.co.uk/1/hi/world/middle_east/4443126.stm, accessed December 2008.

89. *UNAMI Human Rights Report 1 July – 31 August 2006*, p. 17, http://www.uniraq.org/documents/HR Report July August 2006 EN.pdf, accessed December 2008.

90. Testimony of Abbas Abid in Kuala Lumpur, February 7, 2007, http://www.brusselstribunal.org/ArticlesIraq3.htm – Abbas, accessed December 2008.

91. Paul Schemm, "Five Police Chiefs Arrested After Mass Kidnapping," News.com.au, November 15, 2006, http://www.news.com.au/story/0,23599,20761611-401,00.html, accessed December 2008.

92. "Twin Blasts 'Kill 27' in Baghdad," BBC News, July 27, 2006, http://news.bbc.co.uk/1/hi/world/middle_east/5219526.stm, accessed December 2008.

93. Kim Sengupta, "Desperate Search After Mass-kidnapping of Sunnis Ends With Hostages Found Alive," *Independent*, November 15, 2006, http://www.independent.co.uk/news/world/middle-east/desperate-search-after-masskidnapping-of-sunnis-ends-with-hostages-found-alive-424342.html, accessed December 2008.

94. "Iraq Hostages 'Freed by Police'," BBC News, November 15, 2006, http://news.bbc.co.uk/1/hi/world/middle_east/6149110.stm, accessed December 2008.

95. "Iraq Ministry Hostages 'Tortured'," BBC News, November 16, 2006, http://news.bbc.co.uk/1/hi/world/middle_east/6153316.stm, accessed December 2008.

96. Bassem Mroue, "Arrest of Sunni Leader Sought in Iraq," *Washington Post*, November 17, 2006, http://www.washingtonpost.com/wp-dyn/content/article/2006/11/16/AR2006111600494_2.html, accessed December 2008.

97. Ibid.

98. *UNAMI Human Rights Report 1 November – 31 December 2006*, p. 10.

99. "Iraq Police Rebrand to Foil Fakes," BBC News, October 9, 2006, http://news.bbc.co.uk/1/hi/world/middle_east/6034975.stm, accessed December 2008.

100. For instance, the *New Statesman* reported in September 2004, well after the purge of academics had become extremely visible and shortly after the transfer of sovereignty, that the Coalition Provisional Authority had neither investigated any of the deaths,

nor made a single arrest, and dismissed the matter as "obscure" (http://www.newstatesman.com/200409060018). A similar point was iterated by Issam al Rawi, head of the Association of University Teachers, in the same month, who stated that, "We don't know who is threatening us, but we do know that when we report killings and kidnappings those responsible are never found" (http://www. csmonitor.com/2004/0921/p06s01-woiq.html). In fact, Brigadier General Kimmit, a spokesman for the occupation forces, had confessed in February 2004 that the military was not involved in any investigations, but assured that advisors from the FBI were helping to train Iraqi detectives. However, Iraqi policemen, left to investigate organized political killings, reported having received no help from American advisors (http://query.nytimes.com/gst/fullpage.html?res=9A02E6D91E3BF934A35751C0A9629C8B63). By March 2006 the Ministry of Higher Education and Scientific Research stated that 89 university professors and senior lecturers had been killed since 2003 and that police investigations had led to nothing (http://www.guardian.co.uk/world/2006/mar/24/iraq.jonathansteele). All websites accessed December 2008.

101. Jeffrey Sluka (ed.), *Death Squad: The Anthropology of State Terror*, University of Pennsylvania Press, 1999.

102. Turi Munthe, "Will Harsh Weed-out Allow Iraqi Academia to Flower?" *Times Education Supplement*, July 25, 2003, http://www.timeshighereducation.co.uk/story.as.p?storyCode=178316&sectioncode=26, accessed December 2008

103. UNESCO and Education in IRAQ Fact Sheet, March 28, 2003, http://portal.unesco.org/es/ev.php-URL_ID=11216&URL_DO=DO_TOPIC&URL_SECTION=201.html, accessed December 2008.

104. Christina Asquith, "Turning the Page on Iraq's History," *Christian Science Monitor*, November 4, 2003, http://www.csmonitor.com/2003/1104/p11s01-legn.html, accessed December 2008.

105. Fuller, "Ghosts of Jadiriyah." Dr. Samarree's first-hand account is reinforced in an SOS issued by "frantic" Iraqi academics very early in the occupation, which describes US soldiers transporting "mobs" to scientific institutions to commit damage and remove documents. See http://www.islamonline/net/englishnews/2003-04/12/article02.shtml. Such mobs are likely to have been formed from the militias of the opposition parties in exile.

106. Coalition Provisional Authority, "Order Number 1: De-Ba'athificaiton of Iraqi Society," http://www.iraqcoalition.org/regulations/20030516_CPAORD_1_De-Ba_athification_of_Iraqi_Society_.pdf, accessed December 2008.

107. Susan Sachs, "A Region Inflamed: Occupation; Baathists, Once Reviled, Prove Difficult to Remove," *New York Times*, November 22, 2003, http://query.nytimes.com/gst/fullpage.html?res=9805 E0DA123BF931A15752C1A9659C8B63, accessed December 2008.

108. Robert Dreyfuss, "Tinker, Banker, Neocon, Spy: Ahmed Chalabi's Long and Winding Road from (and to?) Baghdad," *American Prospect*, November 18, 2002, http://www.prospect.org/cs/articles?article=tinker_banker_neocon_spy, accessed December 2008.

109. Munthe, "Will Harsh Weed-out Allow Iraqi Academia to Flower?"

110. Scott Peterson, "Iraqis Struggle Over Baath Purge," *Christian Science Monitor*, June 26, 2003, http://www.csmonitor.com/2003/0626/p06s01-woiq.html, accessed December 2008.

111. Hamdan, "Iraqi Intellectuals Under Siege."

112. See, for example, Michael Howard, "Mr Fixit Finds His Vision Hard to Sell," *Guardian*, July 1, 2003, http://www.guardian.co.uk/world/2003/jul/01/iraq.michaelhoward, accessed December 2008.

113. Turi Munthe, "Diary: A Weeklong Electronic Journal," Slate.com, July 8, 2003, http://www.slate.com/id/2085234/entry/2085321/, accessed December 2008.

114. Munthe, "Will Harsh Weed-out Allow Iraqi Academia to Flower?"

115. Munthe, "Diary: A Weeklong Electronic Journal."

116. Alan Sipress, "Iraqis Exact Revenge on Baathists," *Washington Post*, December 20, 2003, http://www.washingtonpost.com/ac2/wp-dyn/A16407-2003Dec19, accessed December 2008.

117. Tom Lasseter, "Civilian Violence in Iraq up Sharply since Hussein's Capture," Knight Ridder, December 22, 2003, http://www.commondreams.org/cgi-bin/print.cgi?file=/headlines03/1222-01.htm, accessed December 2008.

118. Joel Brinkley, "Revenge Killings Thin ex-Baathists' Ranks," *New York Times*, November 1, 2003, http://www.sfgate.com/cgi-bin/article.cgi?f=/c/a/2003/11/01/MNGPP2O72B1.DTL, accessed December 2008.

119. "Iraq: Killings of Civilians in Basra and al-'Amara," Amnesty International, May 11, 2004, http://www.amnesty.org/en/library/info/MDE14/007/2004, accessed December 2008.

120. While no accurate figures are available, several commentators have claimed that a high proportion of senior academics were party members. For instance, Robert Fisk states that "all heads of

academic departments were forced to join Saddam's party" (http://www.independent.co.uk/news/fisk/iraqi-academics-targeted-in-murder-spree-553078.html), while Andrew Rubin writes that "former Ba'ath Party members make up the vast majority of professors in postwar Iraq" (http://www.newstatesman.com/200409060018). Andrew Erdmann himself believed that over half of all department heads and the large majority of deans were Ba'athists (http://www.timeshighereducation.co.uk/story.asp?storyCode=178316&sectioncode=26). In this context it is worth emphasizing that many of the academics on the BT list held senior university posts (according to Ismael Jalili some 19 percent of all murdered academics held the post of department head or higher, while professors and assistant professors make up a further 59 percent of all victims – *Iraq's Lost Generation: Impact and Implications*, June 15, 2007). It seems very possible that at least half of all academic victims were members of the Ba'ath Party.

121.   Ahmed Rasheed, "Iraq Law on Baathists Not Being Implemented," Reuters, June 17, 2008, http://www.reuters.com/article/latestCrisis/idUSYAT251579, accessed December 2008.

122.   Seymour M. Hersh, "Moving Targets," *New Yorker*, December 15, 2003, http://www.newyorker.com/archive/2003/12/15/031215fa_fact, accessed December 2008.

123.   These parties included the Iraqi National Congress (INC), the Iraqi Accord (INA), the Supreme Council for Islamic Revolution in Iraq (SCIRI) and the Kurdistan Democratic Party (KDP) and Patriotic Union of Kurdistan (PUK). In fact, it was reported that the US had been training the militias associated with each of these parties prior to the invasion at a military base in Hungary. "Iraqi Exiles to Gather in Hungary for U.S. Military Training," *Chicago Tribune*, January 20, 2003, http://www.blueprint-magazine.de/news/iraq/iraq2.htm, accessed December 2008. It is hardly surprising that these militias should have been earmarked to provide the nucleus for the new security apparatus.

124.   "US Decides to Back Iraqi Militia Force," *Sydney Morning Herald*, November 6, 2003, http://www.smh.com.au/articles/2003/11/05/1068013265653.html, accessed December 2008.

125.   Dana Priest and Josh White, "Before the War, CIA Reportedly Trained a Team of Iraqis to Aid U.S.," *Washington Post*, August 3, 2005, http://www.washingtonpost.com/wp-dyn/content/article/2005/08/02/AR2005080201579.html, accessed December 2008.

126.   Hannah Allam and Warren P. Strobel, "Amidst Doubts, CIA Hangs on to Control of Iraqi Intelligence Service," Knight Ridder,

September 5, 2005, http://www.informationclearinghouse.info/article8792.htm, accessed December 2008.

127. Ibid.

128. The doctrine of counterinsurgeny warfare actually assumes that the "insurgent" enemy has a duel character, in that it is always characterized both by armed militants and a cellular civilian infrastructure (historically, often a communist party). It is the civilian infrastructure that is assumed both to coordinate the military struggle and to pursue the same political objectives (overthrow of the state) by other means. Under the doctrine, this civilian support base subsumes virtually any and all political or rights-based activities that could be interpreted as anti-government, from trades unionists to protest singers (Appendix E: Intelligence Indicators, US Special Forces counterinsurgency manual FMI 3-07-22, http://www.fas.org/irp/doddir/army/fmi3-07-22.pdf). The destruction of this infrastructure is actually seen as a higher priority than the elimination of the armed cells (US Special Forces counterinsurgency manual FM 31-20-3, http://wikileaks.org/wiki/US_Special_Forces_counterinsurgency_manual_leaked). It is not difficult to see how members of the Ba'ath Party or dissenting academics could thus be identified as military targets. A detailed analysis of how such a program aimed at a civilian infrastructure evolved in practice is offered in Douglas Valentine, *The Phoenix Program*, iUniverse.com, 2000.

129. Iraqi Leadership Council statement, May 23, 2003, http://www.aliraqi.org/forums/showthread.php?t=19733, accessed December 2008.

130. Mukhtar, "Where Is This Going?"

131. Scott Wilson, "Chalabi Aides Suspected of Spying for Iran," *Washington Post*, May 22, 2004, http://www.washingtonpost.com/wp-dyn/articles/A46417-2004May21.html, accessed December 2008.

132. "'I Made a Choice to Visit a Country'," *New York Sun*, October 5, 2004, http://www2.nysun.com/article/2675, accessed December 2008; "Iraq Easing Bans on Saddam-era Baath Members," Reuters, January 18, 2007, http://www.iraqupdates.com/p_articles.php/article/13610, accessed December 2008.

133. Kathleen Ridolfo, "A Survey of Armed Groups in Iraq," Radio Free Europe/Radio Liberty, June 4, 2004 (the ULR of this article is no longer valid; a version of the same document can be found on Global Security, but the original reference to Tha'r Allah has been split into a nondescript sentence on Tha'r Allah and a separate entry for "Vengeance Detachments" containing all the

information originally attributed to Tha'r Allah. The version of the document that I first saw can still be obtained as a PDF from SmallWarsJournal.com. Whilst the original document is dated June 4, 2004, the PDF was created on June 11, 2005, which may suggest that the document was altered after that date, http://smallwarsjournal.com/documents/iraqsurvey.pdf, accessed December 2008.)

134. Omar Hasan, "Al-Qaeda Scare has Basra on Edge," Agence France-Presse, November 12, 2003, http://www.iol.co.za/index. php?sf=2813&set_id=&sf=2813&click_id=3&art_id=iol10686 313578161621&set_id=1, accessed December 2008.

135. Jack Fairweather, "Islamic Groups' Rise May Lead to Greater Conflict," *Telegraph*, April 7, 2004, http://www.telegraph.co.uk/ news/worldnews/middleeast/iraq/1458749/Islamic-groups'-rise-may-lead-to-greater-conflict.html, accessed December 2008.

136. According to Michael Knights and Ed Williams, it appears that al-Musawi was actually serving as Basra's deputy governor in February and, by implication, probably at least as far back as early 2006 (*The Calm Before the Storm: The British Experience in Southern Iraq*, Policy Focus 66, Washington Institute for Near East Policy, February 2007, p. 30, http://www.washingtoninstitute. org/pubPDFs/PolicyFocus66.pdf). In fact, al-Musawi is recorded as having been included on Basra's Security Council (*Provincial Politics in Iraq: Fragmentation or New Awakening?*, Michael Knights and Eamon McCarthy, Policy Focus 81, Washington Institute for Near East Policy, April 2008, p. 5, http://www. washingtoninstitute.org/templateC04.php?CID=289), which undoubtedly would have included British and probably American representatives. In counterinsurgency warfare, security committees at local, regional and national levels are deemed to be the necessary locus for orchestrating a strategy that is intended to draw in every sphere of the state (for detailed discussions of counterinsurgency in theory and practice, see Frank Kitson, *Low Intensity Operations: Subversion, Insurgency and Peacekeeping*, Faber and Faber, 1991, and Valentine, *The Phoenix Program*).

137. Jack Fairweather and Haider Samad, "Clerics Become Powerbrokers in the South," *Telegraph*, February 14, 2005, http://www.telegraph. co.uk/news/worldnews/middleeast/iraq/1483509/Clerics-become-powerbrokers-in-the-South.html, accessed December 2008.

138. "Supervisory Commission to Control Checkpoints," *Al-Sabah*, January 16, 2005, p. 3, http://horse.he.net/~swiftpow/phpBB2/ viewtopic.php?t=14632&postdays=0&postorder=asc&start=60

&sid=f92ec77b2b38c3306dfd4d592a504886, accessed December 2008.

139. James Hider, "US Reporter Murdered in Iraq Had Written His Own Epitaph," *The Times*, August 4, 2005, http://www. timesonline.co.uk/article/0,7374-1720268,00.html, accessed December 2008.

140. *Special Report: Testimonials Regarding Human Rights in Basra*, Monitoring of Human Rights in Iraq, April 8, 2006, http://www. brusselstribunal.org/pdf/MHRI080406.pdf, accessed December 2008.

141. Michael Moss, "How Iraq Police Reform Became Casualty of War," *New York Times*, May 22, 2006, http://www.nytimes. com/2006/05/22/world/middleeast/22security.html?, accessed December 2008.

142. "Iraqi secret police force operating in Al-Basrah," Radio Free Europe/Radio Liberty, January 30, 2004, http://www.ecoi. net/189476::iraq/328793.323556.9228...hl.323578/intelligence-secret-service.htm, accessed December 2008.

143. Moss, "How Iraq Police Reform Became Casualty of War."

144. "Death Squad Killings on the Rise in Basra," *Gulf Times*, February 18, 2006, http://www.gulf-times.com/site/topics/ article.asp?cu_no=2&item_no=73241&version=1&template_ id=37&parent_id=17, accessed December 2008.

145. Brinkley, "Revenge Killings Thin ex-Baathists' Ranks."

146. The insistence that kidnapping (abduction) itself represents a form of criminality that lies outside the operation of state terror is contradicted both by the experience and theory of counterinsurgency warfare. For instance a 1962 US Army psychological operations field manual (FM 33-5) stated: "Civilians in the operational area may be supporting their own government or collaborating with an enemy occupation force. An isolation program designed to instill doubt and fear may be carried out, and a positive political action program designed to elicit active support of the guerrillas also may be effected. If these programs fail, it may become necessary to take more aggressive action in the form of harsh treatment or even abductions. The abduction and harsh treatment of key enemy civilians can weaken the collaborators' belief in the strength and power of their military forces. This approach, fraught with propaganda and political dangers, should be used only after all other appeal means have failed. And when used, they [sic] must be made to appear as though initiated and effected by the guerrillas themselves to reduce the possibility of reprisals against civilians" (Michael McClintock, *Instruments of Statecraft: US Guerrilla*

Warfare, Counterinsurgency and Counterterrorism: 1940–1990, 2002, http://www.statecraft.org/chapter10.html).

147. Peter Beaumont, "Revealed: Grim World of New Iraqi Torture Camps," *Observer*, July 3, 2005, http://www.guardian.co.uk/world/2005/jul/03/iraq.peterbeaumont, accessed December 2008.

148. Professor Samarree stated that the purpose of the interrogation sessions that he underwent was to acquire further information about members of the Ba'ath Party (personal communication).

149. As noted above, the strategy of counterinsurgency itself is likely to designate many individuals who would normally consider themselves outside a military conflict as "subversives" and therefore as legitimate military targets. This strategy has been even more baldly stated by members of the US military-intelligence apparatus themselves, who have suggested that the "Sunni [civilian] population is paying no price for the support it is giving to the terrorists... We have to change that equation" (quoted in Tom Regan, "US Considers Salvador Option in Iraq," *Christian Science Monitor*, January 10, 2005, http://www.csmonitor.com/2005/0110/dailyUpdate.html) and that "In almost any counter-insurgency, the basic message the government or the occupiers tries to get across to the population is brutally simple: 'We can protect you from the guerrillas, but the guerrillas can't protect you from us, and you've got to choose sides'." (Christopher Dickey, "Death-Squad Democracy," Newsweek Web Exclusive, October 16, 2007, http://www.newsweek.com/id/47999/output/print).

150. The outgoing United Nations human rights chief in Iraq, John Pace, stated that the majority of extrajudicial killings were being carried out by "militias" attached to the Interior Ministry (Democracy Now! Interview with John Pace, http://www.democracynow.org/2006/2/28/exclusive_former_un_human_rights_chief), while the Iraqi Organization for Follow-up and Monitoring, in a statement published on April 30, 2006, claimed that 92 percent of 3,498 bodies found in different regions of Iraq belonged to victims that had been arrested by officials of the Ministry of Interior (http://www.iraq-amsi.org/news.php?action=view&id=6598&).

151. The fact that what slim evidence exists suggests an Iraqi hand behind the killings of academics does nothing to discredit the thesis that the occupying powers should be held intellectually responsible for these crimes. It is standard procedure to draw the bulk of the various "special operations" groups that carry out the so-called "dirty work" from indigenous "host nation" elements, whether they be existing members of the security forces, recruits in

private armies, former enemy combatants or sentenced criminals. As well as expanding manpower, one of the main advantages of employing local forces is maintaining plausible deniability by placing the maximum distance between the actions and their authorship. Maintaining plausible deniability is also standard operating procedure at the level of command responsibility, where the use of cut-outs and front organizations is cultivated to further displace responsibility (Philip Agee, *CIA Diary: Inside the Company*, Penguin Books, 1975, http://www.thirdworldtraveler. com/CIA/CIA_Diary_Agee.html). For an example of this process in action, see Douglas Valentine's detailed expose of the CIA-controlled Operation Phoenix in Vietnam, *The Phoenix Program*. Thus in Iraq, we should actually expect to find violence conducted by a range of "militia" elements, many of whose operatives may be completely unaware of the agenda they are ultimately serving.

152. As described earlier, the targeted assassinations of academics appear to be based on thorough knowledge of the victim and his or her movements and routine. The physical infrastructure required to conduct such intelligence-based operations lies at the heart of counterinsurgency warfare and, with its network of agents and informers, surveillance hardware, computer databases, individual target files, etc., lies beyond the means of ad hoc and dispersed groups (see, for example, McClintock, *Instruments of Statecraft*). In the end it matters far less which groups, whether they be criminal gangs, fundamentalist militias, mercenaries or disguised special forces personnel, carry out the killings, but from where the detailed intelligence and overarching planning is coordinated.

153. Aaron Mate, "Pillage is Forbidden: Why the Privatisation of Iraq is Illegal," *Guardian*, November 7, 2003, http://www.guardian. co.uk/world/2003/nov/07/iraq.comment, accessed December 2008.

154. Edward Wong, "An American University for Iraq but not in Baghdad," *New York Times*, January 3, 2007, http://www. nytimes.com/2007/01/03/world/middleeast/03university.html?_ r=1&oref=slogin, accessed December 2008. The university, situated at Sulaymania, in the Kurdish part of Iraq, is now enrolling students; the first point in its mission statement reads: "to promote the development and prosperity of Iraq through the careful study of modern commerce, economics, business and public administration."

155. Ian Urbin, "Kurds Vow: '10,000 Men in Baghdad'," *Asia Times*, December 17, 2002, http://www.atimes.com/atimes/Middle_East/DL17Ak01.html, accessed December 2008.

156. Aseem Shrivastava, "The Iraq War is a Huge Success: The Economics of Creative Destruction," Information Clearing House, July 29, 2006, http://www.informationclearinghouse.info/article14267.htm, accessed December 2008.

157. In June 2008 it was reported that the Iraqi government has struck deals with the four oil majors (Exxon Mobil, Shell, Total and BP) that had formed the original consortium evicted from Iraq in 1972. The new deals, displacing Russian and Chinese competition, whilst small, are seen as a very viable foot in the door to the enormous oil bonanza that lies ahead (Andrew E. Kramer, "Deals With Iraq Are Set to Bring Oil Giants Back," *New York Times*, June 19, 2008).

8

DEATH, DISPLACEMENT, OR FLIGHT

Dahr Jamail

Apocalypse is not a moment. Five years of the US led invasion and occupation defines Apocalypse in Iraq, where spring 2003 to spring 2008 has been an unrelieved season of destruction, death and displacement, with no end in sight. The country has witnessed the decimation of natural and economic resources, infrastructure, rule of law, and everything that makes human existence worthwhile. Abduction and indiscriminate killings of civilians, and highly orchestrated ethnic and sectarian cleansing have jointly rendered the country unlivable. A state of explosive anarchy prevails.

A particularly disconcerting facet of this all-encompassing disaster is the targeting of Iraq's intellectuals and professionals. They have been subjected to systemic persecution and elimination. The fortunate ones have met with displacement and those that had the wherewithal have been compelled to leave the country.

Johns Hopkins Bloomberg School of Health, in collaboration with Iraqi doctors from Mustansiriya University in Baghdad, published a study in the *Lancet* medical journal in October 2006 that estimated 655,000 Iraqi deaths, or 2.5 percent of the total population of Iraq, to be the direct result of the US led invasion and occupation. The UK-based polling agency Opinion Research Business updated the figure in September 2007, to a staggering 1.2 million. Currently, the advocacy group Just Foreign Policy also estimates the number of Iraqi dead to be over 1.1 million.[1]

One in five Iraqis has been displaced primarily due to violence. According to the UN Refugee Agency and the International

Organization for Migration, by 2008, the fifth year of occupation, over 5 million Iraqis had been displaced by violence in their country. Refugees International reveals that:

> Over 2.4 million vacated their homes for safer areas within Iraq, up to 1.5 million were living in Syria, and over 1 million refugees were inhabiting Jordan, Iran, Egypt, Lebanon, Turkey and the Gulf States. Most Iraqis are keen to be resettled in Europe or North America, and few consider return to Iraq an option. Iraqis have no legal work options in most host countries and are increasingly desperate and in need of humanitarian assistance. They face challenges in finding housing, obtaining food, and have trouble accessing health and education systems in these host countries. Their resources depleted, small numbers of Iraqis have returned to Iraq in the past few months, between 28,000 to 60,000 people, but Iraq's struggling government recently warned that it cannot accommodate large numbers of returns. Most of those who returned were subsequently displaced again.[2]

Brain Drain

Spokesmen for the Royal Society of London coined the term "brain drain" to describe the outflow of scientists and technologists from the UK to Canada and the United States in the early 1950s. Brain drain occurs when individuals who study abroad do not return to their home country on completing their education. Recent reports show that roughly 80 percent of all Fulbright Scholars do not return to their country of origin. It also occurs when individuals educated in their home country emigrate for higher wages or better opportunities. The second form is arguably worse, because it drains more resources from the home country and is particularly problematic for developing nations.

The phenomenon is also known as human capital flight, as it entails the emigration of trained and talented individuals or "human capital" to other nations or jurisdictions, due to conflicts, lack of opportunity, health hazards or other reasons. It parallels the term "capital flight" which refers to financial capital that is no longer invested in the country where its owner has lived and earned the money. Investment in higher education is also lost when trained individuals leave their home country.

Brain drain is common to all conflicts but is currently most widespread in Iraq where professional certification at a higher level is viewed as one of the few means to escape the war-torn country with life and limb intact. It began during the early days of the occupation. In May 2003, the Bush administration established the Coalition Provisional Authority inside the "Green Zone" in Baghdad under the control of L. Paul Bremer III, who formerly worked for Kissinger and Associates. This body set about dismantling Iraq's state apparatus. Thousands of Ba'ath Party bureaucrats were dismissed from the government; similar large numbers of Iraqi military personnel were discharged from their military positions, and countless workers were laid off from state-owned industries. This mass of freshly unemployed professional and state employees rapidly lost their purchasing power and Iraq's already devastated economy suffered further. Around the same time displacement began to escalate due to several reasons and brain drain was in full swing.

Crime for Wage

The exodus was prompted by an additional menace that came to haunt the educated middle class in Iraq at the time. This was kidnapping. Those of the professional category that did not flee the country sometimes undertook lesser jobs like driving taxis, often using their own cars for the purpose. Baghdad began to face this new threat which became a "hot job" amongst local gangs, foreign infiltrators, and others who realized that professionals in Iraq and their family members fetch the highest ransom. Doctors, professors, lawyers, engineers, and other professionals became easy and immediate targets. The rate of departure of Iraqis fleeing their country accelerated as those who felt threatened fled. This forced exodus saw writers, doctors, scientists, engineers, poets, professors and other professionals and intellectuals flee the country.

By early summer 2004, during and after massive US military operations that targeted portions of Baghdad and nearly the entire cities of Najaf, Kut, and Fallujah, many of Iraq's renowned doctors and professors had fled the country. An alarming number of others were assassinated. While no exact figures are available, it is known for a fact that a large percentage of Iraqis who fled the country at the time belonged to the professional classes, since they happened to have the resources to do so. By doing so they took their professional know-how with them, severely depleting the country of invaluable human capital. Universities and hospitals have borne the brunt of this, with many facilities now reportedly functioning with less than 20 percent of their minimum staff requirement. Even the coveted oil industry in Iraq suffered what the *Wall Street Journal* has referred to as a "petroleum exodus" wherein at least two-thirds of its top hundred managers along with large numbers of its managerial and professional workers have left Iraq.

The sacred Shia shrine of al-Askari in Samarra was bombed on February 22, 2006. As a consequence of this act there was a dramatic upswing in sectarian violence. However, sectarian death squads began to appear in Baghdad while US ambassador to Iraq John Negroponte and a retired colonel, James Steele (who arrived in Baghdad shortly after the invasion of March 2003), held key positions, and US-backed Iraqi forces were involved in the process of "segregating" mixed neighborhoods in Baghdad. The Negroponte–Steele partnership goes back to their days in Central America in the 1980s when Negroponte was Reagan's ambassador to Honduras, at a time when right-wing death squads in the region were instrumental in killing thousands of innocent civilians.[3] Replicating the same policy in Iraq triggered another wave of immigration amongst professionals who, over and above other adversities, now had to contend with systemic sectarian violence.

Surge Purge

In February 2007 the Bush administration launched a "surge" of US forces into Iraq, the stated goals of which were to bring down violence to enable the US backed puppet government in Baghdad to work towards reconciliation of the fragmented population of the country.

The actual effect of the "surge" belies this intent. During 2007, merely 25 of approximately 200 mixed neighborhoods in Baghdad escaped becoming homogeneous. In all others residency came to be determined/permitted strictly on the basis of the Islamic sect that people professed. Minority groups were driven out of these mixed neighborhoods usually by US backed death squads or various militias. They either joined the ranks of the internally displaced people or became refugees in other countries. The Iraqi Red Crescent estimated that by late 2007, one out of every four residents had been displaced from their homes in Baghdad, a capital city of 6 million plus. As on earlier occasions, it was professionals that formed the largest numbers of those who moved to Syria or Jordan, taking not only their skills experience and expertise but also their savings and other resources which are critical to Iraq's future.

Hard Times/Bleak Future

The United Nations High Commissioner for Refugees (UNHCR) figures for Iraq as of January 2008 stand at over 1.5 million refugees in Syria alone, and at least 750,000 in Jordan. Other than these two countries which until recently had the most lenient visa requirements for Iraqis, there were as many as 70,000 refugees in Egypt, another 60,000 in Iran, 30,000 in Lebanon, roughly 200,000 across the Gulf States, 100,000 across Europe, and roughly 50,000 spread across the globe. The American response beggars the imagination. From March 2003 up till mid-2007, the Bush administration had allowed a grand total of 463 Iraqis into the US.[4]

Again, while exact figures are unknown, a large percentage of all of these displaced Iraqis are educated and professionally skilled individuals who have no plans to return home. Many of them have been forced to take up menial jobs, usually in the black market, in order to tend to themselves and their families. It is now commonplace for unemployed scientists, engineers, surgeons and university professors to be driving taxis, selling vegetables and fruit and tea. This leaves little hope for those left behind and makes the future of the country appear bleak indeed.

For most displaced Iraqis, procuring food has become a challenge. The UN has declared half of all displaced Iraqis in need of "urgent food assistance." A substantial portion of adults surveyed in early 2008 reported they were skipping at least one meal in order to be able to feed their children. Others report entire days without food "in order to keep up with rent and utilities."

One fifth of Iraqi children in Syria had diarrhea in the two weeks prior to a McClatchy Newspaper survey in early 2008, and 46 percent of children had dropped out of school. With the younger generations exposed to this level of deprivation what may one envisage of Iraq's future, if there is ever to be reconstruction and resolution in Iraq?

Syria presents the most accurate picture of how Iraq's professional, managerial and administrative sections have been negatively affected by the occupation. Of those that had the wherewithal to leave Iraq approximately one third possessed a university education. Collectively they form a repository of the "human capital" requisite for the reconstruction and restoration of their ravaged country but they are unlikely to return home, ever.

While less than 1 percent of Iraqis left in the country have a postgraduate education, almost 10 percent of the refugees in Syria have advanced degrees, with 4.5 percent having doctorates. In addition, while 20 percent of Iraqis have no schooling, only 3 percent of the refugees in Syria have had no education.

It is not difficult to see what the US neo-liberal policy in Iraq, coupled with the disastrous de-Ba'athification strategy has done to the economy and the future of the country. It has sealed the fate of Iraq by ensuring the decimation, degradation and removal of Iraqis who could have salvaged some degree of order out of the present chaos in their nation.

Underscoring the severity of the crisis, prior to the 2007 exodus from Baghdad, which was a direct result of the "surge," UNHCR issued a clear warning that "the skills required to provide basic services are becoming more and more scarce" in Iraq, referring particularly to doctors, teachers, computer technicians, and even skilled craftsmen like bakers and mechanics.

By the middle of 2007, the catastrophic effects of the brain drain were evident for Iraqi society. Medical facilities were growing increasingly dependent on the services of the family members of patients as nurses, attendants and technicians. People being brought to the hospital had to be carried by relatives because individuals and equipment meant for transportation of patients were no longer at the disposal of hospitals. In the education sector, schools were often closed due to violence and militia activity, and qualified teachers had become scarce at every level ranging from grade schools to universities. Staff shortages of epidemic proportions have made a mockery of exams if they are conducted at all anywhere in the country.

Permanently Disabled

Pathetic as it may sound, the US-backed Iraqi government, which according to polls in Iraq enjoys less than 1 percent support from the population, is not equipped to tackle garbage collection and waste disposal predominantly due to lack of qualified professionals who can plan and execute these essential services and ensure the smooth functioning of a country's infrastructure. The adequate human resource simply does not exist in Iraq anymore. Iraqi cabinet ministers recently admitted to "a shortage of employees trained to write contracts" and also made mention of "the flight of scientific and engineering expertise from the country."[5]

The systematic destruction and elimination of Iraq's human capital has been nearly absolute and obviously deliberate. It has been accomplished through a systematic and irreversible process of liquidating the strongest and the most resourceful members of Iraqi society.

The massive brain drain which has sucked the vast majority of Iraq's trained and highly skilled professionals out of the country is not likely to be reversed anytime soon as there seem to be no plans for a US withdrawal. The longer the occupation persists, the worse life becomes in Iraq. Without Iraq's human capital available, any talk of reconstruction, reconciliation, and a unified future for the country are utterly futile. It is no coincidence that the impossible prospect of Iraq rebuilding herself works in favor of the neo-liberal agenda of the United States. The raging catastrophe provides all the justification it needs for privatizing and outsourcing the country's reconstruction, security, and management of its oil sector.

In the long run the death, displacement and deprivation of its professional class makes Iraq dependent on foreign countries and their interests. One small instance is the oil industry in southern Iraq presently being manned by engineers "imported from Texas and Oklahoma," according to the *Wall Street Journal* in late 2007. According to Michael Schwartz, in his article "Iraq's Tidal Wave of Misery":

> The foreign presence had, in fact, become so pervasive that the main headquarters for the maintenance and development of the Rumaila oil field in southern Iraq (the source of more than two-thirds of the country's oil at present) runs on both Iraqi and Houston time. The American firms in charge of the field's maintenance and development, KBR and PIJV, have been utilizing a large number of subcontractors, most of them American or British, very few of them Iraqi.[6]

This trend has spilled into all of Iraq's crippled infrastructure areas, with unprecedented dependency on foreign assistance in the fields of medicine, food, electricity, the water system, agriculture, textiles, and much else.

With over 4 million Iraqis displaced, over 1 million dead, untold numbers of wounded, and another 4 million in need of emergency assistance according to Oxfam International, the ability of Iraqi professionals to rebuild and lead their country seems remote, if not impossible. This dismemberment of the professional class will have permanent consequences as the spiral of dependence reinforces itself with the passage of time, exponentially deepening Iraq's inability for autonomy and self-rule.

Notes

1. Tom Englehardt, "We Count, They Don't," *TomDispatch*, October 2, 2007, http://www.tomdispatch.com/post/174844/having_a_carnage_party, accessed December 2008.
2. Refugees International, "Iraq," n.d., http://www.refugeesinternational.org/content/article/detail/9679, accessed December 2008.
3. Dahr Jamail, "Negroponte and the Escalation of Death," *Asia Times*, January 11, 2007.
4. Jim Lobe, "Iraq Exodus Ends Four Year Decline in Refugees," Inter Press Service, June 14, 2007, http://www.ipsnews.net/news.asp?idnews=33613, accessed December 2008.
5. James Glanz, "Provinces Use Rebuilding Money in Iraq," *New York Times*, October 1, 2007.
6. Michael Schwarz, "Iraq's Tidal Wave of Misery," *TomDispatch*, February 10, 2008.

9

THE PURGING OF MINDS[1]

Philip Marfleet

In the years following the invasion of 2003, Iraq's academics and professionals have continued to flee from the country. Refugee communities in Arab states receive thousands of university professors, medical doctors, dentists, artists, writers, journalists, teachers and technical experts. Among earlier forced migrants in cities such as Amman, Damascus, Cairo and Beirut few have returned to their former homes. The trajectory of many journeys is away from the region, notably to Europe and North America. In the spring of 2008 one advanced English-language class in Amman contained 45 young Iraqi doctors, all of whom had arrived in Jordan since the invasion; six months later all but three had moved to the United States.[2] Iraq's intellectuals have been scattered worldwide, making the prospect of return and reconsolidation of the country's academic, professional and technical cadres increasingly difficult, leaving a gaping hole in its human resources. A loss of this magnitude will certainly affect the wider society for generations to come. This chapter examines why and how these refugees have been compelled to leave Iraq and what their patterns of movement reveal about the regime of occupation. It suggests that their fate is not an accidental outcome of war and civil conflict: rather it is the result of strategies employed by the United States and its allies to establish a new order in Iraq and the region.

The prevailing discourse of the refugee in the Global North identifies migrants from the Global South who wish for asylum as opportunistic, inauthentic, illicit and likely to be engaged in criminal activity. People from regions in which Islam is the dominant tradition are additionally under suspicion of bearing alien cultural influence. Their religious affiliation is judged to be part of a nexus of threats which must be tackled through regimes of exclusion.[3] In the case of Iraq, refugees are also seen as people contaminated by the conflicts from which they seek to flee. In effect, most governments in North America, Western Europe and Australasia have attempted to displace onto Iraqi refugees their own responsibility for the outcomes of invasion and occupation, notably acute need, social breakdown, communal violence, ethnic cleansing and mass population movements from and within the state. This has not prevented increasingly large numbers of Iraqis attempting to secure refugee status. According to the Office of the United Nations High Commissioner for Refugees (UNHCR) in 2008 applications by Iraqis represented more than one in ten of all claims for refugee status in industrialized states.[4] During the first six months of 2008 their applications by far exceeded all other national groups seeking asylum. Indeed, the number seeking formal refugee status exceeded even the combined total of the second- and third-most important source countries.[5] This total was nonetheless a mere fraction of the number of Iraqis engaged in flight from their former homes. According to UNHCR, by September 2007 some 2.7 million people had been displaced within Iraq, and a further 2 million people had crossed Iraqi borders, the majority to neighboring Arab states in which they lived in large communities of "spontaneously" settled urban refugees, where most were viewed officially as "visitors" or "guests."[6] A number were involved in further movements, so that by 2007 at least 20 states of Europe and North America accommodated significant communities of Iraqi exiles.[7] Despite the reluctance of most governments to accept the refugees, pressures to flee war and occupation had become intense, leading many to seek sanctuary by all means – formal (under the direction of states and migration agencies) and informal.[8]

National Character of Displacement

Most communities of Iraqi refugees originate in migrations which date from the 1960s and 1970s. Chatelard observes that the "refugee-producing phase" in Iraq is not a recent development, noting that throughout the 1990s Iraq vied with Afghanistan to top the list of applications for refugee status in Western Europe.[9] She adds:

> The "refugee crisis" of the past few years is not an entirely new phenomenon and has been overlaid on a continuum of forced or induced migration going back decades and with a marked trend to acceleration as of 1991, and again as of 2005... There has long been an established Iraqi migration order within which Iraqis have migrated for different reasons although instances of forced or induced migration have been predominant.[10]

These important observations help explain the trajectory of recent mass movements. The latter nonetheless have specific features, notably their scale and systemic character. Before 2003, major displacements were the outcome primarily of state offensives against opposition currents and specific ethno-religious groups. Since the invasion, displacement has taken on a *national* dimension. Every region and every ethnic community has been affected and entire socio-cultural, political and professional networks have been disrupted. This outcome is evident in headline statistics for "internal displacement" – forced migration within Iraq's territorial borders. UNHCR noted that by September 2007, people forced from their usual places of residence were to be found across the country: 800,900 internally displaced people (IDPs) were located in the Northern Provinces, 740,500 in the Central Provinces and 714,600 were in the Southern Provinces.[11] Although some governorates such as Baghdad were severely affected, accommodating very large numbers of IDPs, no governorate was unaffected. Displacement has been so widespread that since September 2007 the International Organization for Migration (IOM) has produced regular reports on a governorate-by-governorate basis.[12] These demonstrate complex patterns of flight across the country, with many migrants making lengthy, hazardous journeys. Increasingly, large numbers find themselves marooned at internal borders or in regional centers.[13]

Iraqis of all socio-economic statuses have been affected. One feature of displacement post-2003 has been the progressive involvement in long-distance migration of very poor people. The pattern of mass displacement worldwide reveals that people who are most disadvantaged in terms of economic and social status are most inhibited in their ability to make choices about when, where and how to travel in their journeys of survival.[14] Those with wealth and/or influence are first to migrate and may be able to select routes and destinations. Later migrants include the less privileged, who are often compelled to move more abruptly, with reduced choice of destinations. In the case of the large Iraqi community in Syria, al-Khalidi et al. found that most of those who arrived soon after the 2003 invasion were affluent people.[15] Later all manner of Iraqis came. By 2007, researchers found, "increasingly, those arriving are poor."[16] The same pattern is evident in Egypt, where many of the first post-invasion refugees were wealthy or at least (initially) financially secure. By 2008 refugee support centers in Cairo reported requests for help from impoverished people arriving direct from Iraq.[17]

Recent migrations from Iraq engage people from across the social spectrum. However, people of certain statuses have been disproportionately affected, notably Iraq's academics and professionals. This is consistent with the *national* character of displacement: there is strong evidence to suggest that their journeys of flight are closely associated with an assault upon the structures and ideological resources of Iraq as a national society. Sustained hostility towards people identified with Iraq as an independent nation-state has produced a regime of exclusion in which the intelligentsia is being evacuated: hence the presence in refugee communities of disproportionately large numbers of academics, writers, journalists and artists. As one senior Iraqi academic now living in Amman observes: "They [the occupation authorities and the Iraqi government] have cleared us out."[18] He continues:

> They say, "We [the occupation authorities and the Iraqi government] don't want these people. We"ll prepare a new generation of academics and professionals – people of our own colouring." In order to understand why we [refugee academics] are here [in Amman] you need to know that it's a clear-out of people like me, for whom there is no place in the new Iraq.[19]

"Brain Drain"

The sweeping nature of attacks on Iraq's intellectuals is evident from data on targets of assassinations, disappearances and kidnappings. The BRussells Tribunal, an NGO which monitors the circumstances of Iraqi academics, suggests that the pattern is "non-partisan and non-sectarian, targeting women as well as men, and is countrywide. It is indiscriminate of expertise: professors of geography, history and Arabic literature as well as science are among the dead."[20] The organization's growing list of victims identifies hundreds of highly qualified staff from institutions across the country, many attacked in public by plainclothes killers on or near their university campus. The campaign began shortly after the fall of the Ba'athist regime in April 2003. By December 2006, 470 academics had been eliminated and Iraq's higher education sector was "in meltdown."[21]

Scores of reports in international media, notably in newspapers in Britain and the US, provide compelling evidence of the crisis. In August 2003, only four months after invasion, the *New York Times* identified growing anxieties among Iraqi academics about security on campus.[22] In April 2004, the *Christian Science Monitor* described "a climate of fear" and a "brain drain" of leading academics fleeing the country.[23] In July 2004, Robert Fisk of the *Independent* – an award-winning journalist with a record for accuracy and telling analysis – described the "painful mystery" of assaults on campus, reporting a widespread belief among university staff that the assaults amounted to "a campaign to strip Iraq of its academics."[24] In September 2004, the *Times Higher Education Supplement* reported claims of the Iraqi Union of University Lecturers that 250 academics had been killed since April 2003.[25] In November 2006 the *Boston Globe* produced a lengthy analysis of "Iraq's violent 'brain drain'... an effort to eliminate remaining intellectuals and skilled professionals."[26] In the same month the *Washington Post* carried a lengthy personal account by a refugee professor of his flight from Iraq. Abdul Sattar Jawad, formerly Dean of the College of Arts at Mustansiriya University in Baghdad, observed that "the most dangerous place in Iraq is not the mosque, the marketplace or the military checkpoint, but the classroom."[27] He noted that although attacks on academics had been under way for over three years, "To date, not one person has been arrested for these murders."[28]

Notwithstanding a host of such reports, de facto authorities in Iraq – the national and local administrations and the US military command for example – initially adopted a policy of denial. Between 2003 and 2005 the Coalition Provisional Authority (CPA) failed to investigate any attacks and no arrests were made. When in September 2004 the US State Department was asked to comment, a spokesman described the matter as "obscure."[29] American political leaders have since attributed responsibility to general insecurity and to the activity of "terrorists, insurgents, and the roaming death squads."[30] According to former President George W. Bush, "Shia extremists and al Qaeda terrorists are attempting to reignite sectarian violence through murder, and kidnappings, and other violent activities";[31] they are "different faces of the same totalitarian threat," "violent and malignant ideologies" which encourage "sectarian rage and reprisal."[32] These themes have been repeated *ad extremum* in American media, typically with references to ancient or atavistic religious hatreds, bigotry, "tribalism" and confessional violence.[33]

On this view, it is Islam that cultivates hostility and violence – an explanation that draws on centuries of prejudice and long-discredited Orientalist tropes. Many of those targeted by the assaults have a different view. In November 2006 a panel of Iraqi academics meeting at the Middle East Studies Association (MESA) conference in Washington discussed the problem. They could not attribute responsibility: Asquith notes, "When asked who was behind the killings, the professors' list was long: Sunnis, Shias, radical Islamists, Americans, Iranians, Israelis, Kuwaitis."[34] The B*Russell*s Tribunal also warns against simplistic explanations, in particular, allegations that assassinations are "part of a so-called civil war between Sunni and Shia."[35] The Tribunal's view is that this approach amounts to a "smokescreen" – part of continuing attempts to justify the view that occupying forces should remain in Iraq to restore law and order.[36] Similar skepticism has been expressed in testimony to British parliamentarians. In June 2007 a parliamentary commission composed of members of the main British political parties investigated developments in Iraq.[37] Among materials submitted to the group was a report compiled by Ismail Jalili, former president of the Arab Medical Association. Quoting detailed analysis of attacks on academics and professionals since 2003, Jalili suggested that by mid-2007 some 380 university academics and doctors had been killed, together with 210 lawyers and judges, and 243 journalists/media workers. These deaths, he suggested, were only the tip of an iceberg, as many killings went unreported.[38]

Of particular significance, Jalili maintained, was the geographic distribution of attacks. The majority of assaults on academics had taken place in Baghdad but others were distributed widely across the country in cities in which ethno-religious identities varied widely. Victims also came from a very wide range of academic specialisms. He reported that 31 percent of those affected were scientists, 23 percent were medical doctors, 22 percent were in the humanities, 11 percent in the social sciences, and 13 percent were of unspecified identity.[39] Jalili concluded that they were victims of an assault on the intelligentsia as a whole. This pattern, he maintained, was a novel development intimately associated with the occupation itself: "Targeted assassination of professionals in Iraq is a new phenomenon in Iraq's history. Academia, doctors, indeed knowledge itself, have always been accorded the highest respect. The current problem commenced with the 2003 invasion and continues to escalate."[40]

Investigation by human rights organizations on the ground in Iraq suggests that many political actors may be responsible, notably national and local parties and militias, insurgent/resistance groups and the forces of occupation. Human Rights Watch has observed:

> Responsibility for the abuses...rests with the perpetrators. However, the U.S. and Iraqi governments have committed violations of the laws of war that raise serious doubts about their stated commitment to promoting the rule of law in Iraq...

> The U.S.-backed Iraqi government has committed arbitrary arrests and systematic torture against persons in detention, while militias linked to political parties in the government have been implicated in abductions, torture and assassinations.[41]

Human Rights Watch also notes assertions by senior academics that the very wide spectrum of political views, research interests and religious affiliations of academics who have been targeted implies a systematic attack on Iraq's intellectual elite.[42] It quotes the Vice Chancellor of al-Nahrain University in Baghdad to the effect that, "The only common demoninator is [the victims'] excellence."[43]

Emergency

Some academic networks have identified the seriousness of the assaults. In the US, the Scholar Rescue Fund (SRF) sees a problem of startling proportions – "one of the greatest academic crises of our time."[44] SRF is associated with the US government, administering Fulbright Student and Scholars Programs on behalf of the State Department; it nonetheless observes that "hundreds if not thousands of Iraqi scholars have been killed," specifically targeted by groups which are intent on destroying the intellectual capital of Iraq.[45] According to SRF, "Untold thousands have been threatened and forced to flee while others are trapped in the country, unable to teach, conduct research, or carry out productive academic work."[46] The organization has established an Iraq Scholar Rescue Project to assist 150 senior academics by creating temporary academic positions for Iraqis at universities and colleges in the Middle East and North Africa. Its aim is "to contribute to the preservation of Iraq's vital intellectual capital."[47]

In Britain, the Council for Assisting Refugee Academics (CARA), an organization of concerned scholars, has declared an emergency. In 2006 it launched a campaign to support Iraqi colleagues, creating a special fund to assist those reaching Britain. According to John Withrington, chairman of CARA's British Universities Iraq Consortium, "What we are seeing today in Iraq is a cynical and ruthless strategy of destabilisation... The strategy is to intimidate, to introduce anarchy instead or order, despair instead of hope."[48] CARA was founded in the 1930s by distinguished academics such as John Maynard Keynes and John Rutherford, with the aim of helping the Jewish intelligentsia then under persecution in Germany. According to its president, John Ashworth, "Now we have a crisis that is comparable in magnitude to the 1930s... In the 1930s Jews were not only being encouraged to emigrate but were also being murdered. We intend to support Iraqi academics wherever they may be."[49] He called on all universities in the UK and on student unions to "adopt" an Iraqi, i.e. to give an Iraqi academic work or to give a student a place at a British university.

In 2006 CARA made contact with British Prime Minister Tony Blair, expressing its concerns and asking for support of Iraq academics. It also changed rules in place for decades, whereby CARA was only to support people granted formal refugee status in the UK. The organization now assists Iraqis not officially classified as refugees – a policy that challenges the British government, which has for years rejected claims by most Iraqis for asylum rights. The CARA position signals that many have good reason to seek refuge, asserting that events in Iraq do have implications for refugee policy in states such as Britain.[50]

Repression and Refuge

There is a complex relationship between state powers and intellectuals. The latter have long been targets of repression. They may enjoy special personal status and/or be part of institutions and networks which enjoy some independence of local or central authority. As potential focal points for dissent or even resistance, they attract disproportionate interest from those in positions of power or who aspire to power. They have long been prominent among the excluded, becoming exiles – or in the modern usage, refugees.

Anderson has established the importance to the modern state of an educated cadre within which ideas about nation, national belonging and national culture are developed and embellished.[51]

In the early modern era, networks of scholars, clerks and teachers were integral to state-building in Europe. They facilitated processes of monitoring and surveillance associated with efforts by new political authorities to assure control over increasingly volatile populations. At the same time they provided resources for the elaboration of novel national/nationalist ideologies. Increased literacy and the development of "print capitalism" made the intelligentsia a vital but also more dangerous resource.[52] Intellectuals in general became more important to the state and potentially more subversive of it. For this powerful reason, they were also closely monitored and were often key targets of campaigns of repression. When the new states excluded certain groups as part of processes integral to nation-state formation the intellectuals were prominent among those expelled.[53] Among the Jews and Muslims of Spain and Portugal, for example, many leading intellectuals were driven from religious institutions and centers of learning in exemplary actions *pour encourager les autres*: hundreds of thousands of their co-religionists subsequently fled. In the seventeenth century the Bourbon regime in France expelled similar numbers of religious dissenters by focusing upon the ideologues of Calvinism, notably writers and priests. These Huguenots became the archetypal *refugies*, people who had been excluded and who sought security in *la refuge*, communities of exile.[54]

Regulation of population movement, suggests Soguk, is part of "statecraft" in the modern era.[55] In the case of the Huguenots the emerging Bourbon state asserted its authority by marginalizing and then excluding Calvinists as a means of articulating "a novel organization of polity."[56] This marked out "statist territoriality," securing internal and external borders "to serve the felicity of the state."[57] Over the next two centuries there were many similar episodes. As the old empires of Europe resolved into a host of nation-states, nationalist intellectuals were in the vanguard of change. As leading figures in movements for self-determination they were often expelled or forced to flee: hence the majority of refugees in nineteenth century Britain, the refugee capital of Europe, were "political exiles" from Italy, Hungary, Poland and Germany.[58] Some were also victims of authorities *within* the new states – like the Huguenots they were people whose cultural markers (religion, language, "ethnicity") identified them as different and as appropriate for exclusionary measures which were integral to consolidation of the nation-state.[59]

Somewhat similar developments were under way in Africa, Asia, Latin America and the Middle East. Here European states had developed cadres of local military men, administrators, teachers and technical experts to enable commercial activity and mediate relations with subordinate populations. From these milieux emerged radical thinkers whose ideas about rights and self-determination were subversive of European rule. The pattern was particularly striking during the last phases of the colonial era, when in the Middle East European dominance was contested by proponents of national and regional independence who emerged primarily from within the structures of the colonial state, notably from the education system and the armed forces. They had in effect been instruments of state-building who turned their efforts as intellectuals and activists to the project of self-determination. Pan-Islamism, Pan-Arabism and a host of movements for national independence were shaped within such networks.

These developments became more marked as the project of independent national development was linked to the state itself. By the mid twentieth century, agendas for change in the "Third" world were focused upon the state as an agency for liberation and social progress. In the Middle East a series of upheavals brought to power governments committed to sweeping change, including nationalization of foreign capital, collectivization of land, and independent industrial development. In the case of Egypt, said Gamal Abdel-Nasser, the state of the colonial era had been no more than "a group of clerks" charged with maintaining order and issuing documents; after the revolution of 1952, he observed, its activities vastly increased.[60] In newly independent states education was high on the agenda. Universities were directed to produce a new generation of intellectuals who would serve as leaders in politics, the armed forces and civil administration. In the case of Egypt, observes Baker, there were "monumental efforts" to advance higher education.[61] So too in Iraq, where the

University of Baghdad – the country's first modern university – was established shortly before the nationalist revolution of 1958. During the 1960s five more universities were established: the University of Technology and Al-Mustansiriya University in Baghdad, and institutions in Basra, Mosul and Sulaymania. Over the next two decades higher education grew fast: by 2003 there were 14 public universities, among them institutions widely viewed as pre-eminent in the Arab world, and which became integral to the Ba'athist project.[62]

Persecution

Arab regimes share the experiences of political authorities worldwide. Intellectuals are at once essential to the life of the state and potentially subversive of it. Notwithstanding a comprehensive regime of repression under the Ba'ath, Iraq's academics, writers and artists retained a margin of independence within which they maintained creative activity. Reviewing the history of modern Iraq, Tripp comments on the "creative and independently minded intellectuals associated with the remarkable flowering of artistic talent in Iraq."[63] For an increasing number of Iraqis, however, the price of independence has been exclusion. Tripp also comments on those compelled to leave, "when exit was often the only way to ensure that their voices did not become drowned in the barked commands of the centre."[64] From the 1960s, Iraqi refugees were widely dispersed across the Arab world and during the 1970s and 1980s exile communities grew rapidly. In the 1990s there was continuing migratory movement, especially to Jordan.[65] In this respect Iraq's academics, professionals and artists have undergone experiences similar to those of refugee intellectuals worldwide. They are part of processes of formation and consolidation of modern states, and also among the state's most prominent victims. Since 2003, however, they have suffered a different fate. The marginal space within which some survived has finally closed, as the intelligentsia faces an onslaught without precedent in Iraqi history.

The most significant aspect of the recent crisis is its systemic character. Each and every university has come under attack and academics and specialists from a wide range of disciplines and professions have been targeted. This reality cannot be isolated from assaults on the Iraqi state initiated in the early 1990s through sanctions and international efforts at isolation. Higher education and research were easy targets for those organizing sanctions: they banned dispatch of academic journals to Iraq, prevented Iraqi delegates attending most international conferences, and inhibited individual and institutional involvement in collaborative projects. In 2003 the process was intensified when de-Ba'athification placed all academics under suspicion as enemies of the new order. This was a direct outcome of policies adopted by the US which aimed to cleanse Iraq of influences said to have deformed the society at large. Of these the most damaging, argued American strategists, was the notion that the state should be a core component of national life.

The US has long intervened in the affairs of Arab states with the aim of compelling them to conform to a specific vision of development. In the mid-1970s American officials secured agreement of the Sadat regime in Egypt to introduce "market" reforms. Encouraged, they pressed for privatization, cuts in subsidies and welfare provision, and free policies for trade and investment across the region. By the 1980s this program was being pursued formally as "neo-liberalism," with a global agenda for change. Endorsed by key financial institutions, notably the International Monetary Fund (IMF) and the World Bank, it was imposed by all means, including structural adjustment policies and instrumental use of military support and development "aid." State-centered economic policies were meanwhile declared unacceptable and those attached to them deemed enemies of progress. As neo-liberalism was complemented by neo-conservative views on political and social order, the US became a self-appointed "geopolitical manager," distributing aid and favors and – where local regimes did not behave as required – declaring them "rogue" states and imposing punitive measures.[66] After September 11, 2001 and declaration of a war on terror, a series of such states (including Iraq, Iran, Syria, Libya and Sudan) were also linked to alleged terrorist conspiracies, becoming part of a nexus of threats to world order.

American political leaders were convinced (at least publicly) that such threats were to be identified primarily with the Middle East. The key feature of states in this region, they maintained, was recalcitrance in relation to economic and political reforms – what Klein calls a "deficit in free-market democracy" – which should be corrected by exemplary interventions aimed to set off "democratic/ neoliberal waves" of reform.[67] Klein observes: "Within the internal logic of this theory, fighting terrorism, spreading frontier capitalism and holding elections were bundled into a single unified project."[68] The initial target for corrective measures was Iraq, which was to be turned into a "model state." Iraq would be a base for reforms which would ripple across the Middle East in a comprehensive process of economic and political cleansing.[69]

Assault on the State

Thomas Friedman has argued that "we [Americans] are not doing nation-building in Iraq. We are doing nation-creating."[70] Invasion of Iraq aimed to make a national society fit for the contemporary era, with the state itself the main target of reconstruction. In 2003 CPA chief Paul Bremer embraced de-Ba'athification as an exemplary statement about US intentions, telling the Pentagon that he wanted his arrival in Iraq to be marked by "clear, public and decisive steps to reassure Iraqis that we are determined to eradicate Saddamism."[71] In this scenario all material and human resources associated with the old order were legitimate targets: as one senior official attested, the public sector as a whole was now under suspicion.[72] Following the invasion, US forces stood by as looters removed all manner of goods from state properties – from ministries, agencies, depots, colleges and university campuses. Klein quotes Peter McPherson, senior economic advisor to CPA head Paul Bremer, to the effect that this was part of the process of change: "I thought that the privatisation which occurs sort of naturally [sic] when somebody took over their state vehicle, or began to drive a truck that the state used to own, was just fine."[73]

Pillage of public resources, he said, was a legitimate form of public sector "shrinkage."[74] McPherson's job, comments Klein, was "to radically downsize the state and privatise its assets, which meant that the looters were really just giving him a jump-start."[75]

As an integral part of the independent state, Iraq's academic institutions were to be subject to sweeping change. In 2003 John Agresto was appointed Senior Advisor to the Ministry of Higher Education and Scientific Research, reporting directly to Bremer. He told the *Washington Post* that before leaving for Iraq he knew "next to nothing" about Iraq's universities but that he accepted the position because, "This is what Americans do: They go and help... I guess I just always wanted to be a good American."[76] Agresto (formerly responsible for a minor liberal arts college in the US) was put in charge of the entire Iraqi higher education system with its 375,000 students. His aim was "to reconstruct Iraq's decrepit [sic] universities and create an educational system that would nurture and promote the country's best minds."[77] He regarded the post-invasion looting of campuses as beneficial, saying that it provided "the opportunity for a clean start."[78]

The attack on physical structures of the state was paralleled by an assault on its human resources. De-Ba'athification removed hundreds of thousands of state employees, including in primary and secondary education where 10,000 to 15,000 teachers immediately lost their jobs, leaving schools in some regions stripped of staff.[79] In an early report the *Times Higher Education Supplement* described "a devastating impact on academe."[80] It noted the assertion of leading academics that they had been "professors first and Ba'athists a very distant second," observing that under the Saddam regime junior members of university staff had been compelled to carry party cards even to enter their institutions. As Sassoon observes, academics with even the most tenuous links to the Ba'ath Party became targets. De-Ba'athification identified them officially with the core of the old regime and, at a stroke, removed a host of people whose qualifications and experience were already in short supply.[81] Klein comments that the purges cut away people viewed officially as "dead wood" and who were judged likely to oppose the new agenda of free-market reform and democratic change.[82] It is in this context that the CPA approved a wholesale assault on academic and professional networks. In effect it declared open season on professors, medical doctors, dentists, pharmacists, engineers, writers, artists – the "old" intelligentsia. They were guilty by association for having worked within the apparatus of state, for having remained in Iraq through the years of sanctions and hardship, and for not having become exiles. Most important, they were deemed to be people of influence who did not have a place within the new order and who could be targeted with impunity. As a result the Iraqi diaspora, like many others before it, soon contained unprecedented numbers of the country's intellectuals, "looted" like their libraries, offices, classrooms, studios and laboratories. Had they too become objects of contemporary statecraft – marginalized and excluded during reconstruction of the nation-state?

State of Terror

There is circumstantial evidence to suggest involvement of all manner of internal and external forces in attacks on the intelligentsia. Sassoon notes that from 2006 it became increasingly difficult to distinguish between incidents involving armed opposition to the American occupation, communal hostilities and freelance "mafia-style" kidnappings and killings.[83] Other contributors to this book examine in detail questions about *who* perpetrated the assaults. Here, it is useful to consider aspects of the crisis which can be placed in a comparative context.

Arbuthnot comments on the gruesome methods in use in Iraq since 2003:

> [P]eople from the entire spectrum of Iraq's professional class [are] dragged from homes, offices and consulting room. Tortured, shot, ambushed or simply disappeared, they are found dumped outside hospitals, morgues, slumped over car wheels, on refuse dumps, or in the streets.[84]

For researchers who have examined other such crises this is a familiar scenario. Summerfield comments on the use of "states of terror" in campaigns of violence.[85] The aim, he says, is to affect "grassroots social relations, as well as subjective mental life, as a means of social control":

> It is to these ends that most acts of torture are directed, rather than to the extracting of information. The mutilated bodies of those abducted by security agents, dumped in a public place, are props in a political theatre meant to render a whole society a stunned audience.[86]

These tactics are often associated with blanket denials of responsibility. The identity of perpetrators is concealed by the authorities, which maintain an official posture of denial. Ignacio Martin-Baro, a priest-academic murdered in El Salvador in 1989, wrote of "institutionalized lies" and of "circles of silence" which accompany disappearances and arbitrary killings and which are part of efforts to create feelings of intense insecurity, leading to mass displacement.[87] Atrocities are planned by state agencies, political movements and militias with the aim of producing a "demonstration" effect, forcing people onto the move and clearing communities and social networks, sometimes whole regions. During conflicts associated with partition of India in 1947 millions of people fled in the face of attacks in which extremes of violence were used.[88] In Palestine, Pappe relates how Zionist militias used similar methods to precipitate mass flight of the Arab population.[89] Morris asserts that those responsible aimed "to encourage the population to take to the roads," projecting "a message of transfer [of the Palestinians]."[90] Ethno-nationalist organizations in Central Asia, East and West Africa and the Balkans have since used a similar approach.

In recent decades instrumental use of terror has been formalized by American intelligence agencies, notably the CIA. During the 1950s the organization worked closely with pro-American regimes and movements in Central America with the aim of fragmenting dissident communities and political networks, and clearing territories in order to pursue commercial and/or strategic interests. Using a strategy it described as "demobilization," the agency aimed "to atomise and make docile the ordinary citizenry."[91] In Guatemala, it targeted left-wing activists and peasant and labor unions, compiling lists of suspects to be targeted by death squads composed of plainclothes soldiers or police. Thousands of people were killed and "disappeared" and much larger numbers fled. This approach was later formalized as "counterinsurgency," becoming a key element in US strategy for conflicts involving large civilian populations.[92] In the 1970s it was repackaged as "low intensity conflict" (LIC), a strategy for intervention in the "Third" world which combined economic pressures with psychological warfare.

In Nicaragua the CIA provided pro-American Contra forces with a handbook, *Psychological Operations in Guerrilla Warfare*.[93] This explained how "techniques of persuasion" could be used by covert groups with the aim of generating "justified violence" against target communities and stimulating a "whiplash" effect which would "shake up" and "replace" undesirable aspects of Nicaraguan society.[94] Selected targets were to be "neutralized"; allies including "professional criminals" should be hired to carry out "specific jobs."[95] The publication confirmed suspicions that intelligence agencies had long worked systematically across Central America to disseminate fear and prompt crises in which hundreds of thousands of people became migrants. Academics had been key targets. In 1980 the US-backed Duarte junta in El Salvador organized an attack on the San Salvador campus of the country's leading educational institution, the National University. Some 30 faculty members, including the Rector, were killed or disappeared and buildings were burned and looted. The Dean of Science and Humanities reported:

> The army burned complete libraries; in the law school, where we once had about 100,000 volumes, we now have only 3,000. In the first days of the occupation, the officers of the army grabbed as much of the equipment, furniture, medical supplies [as] they could, and the rest they destroyed. Whatever equipment they didn't understand, they ruined.[96]

Such attacks aimed at the cumulative collapse of academic networks deemed to contain human materials uncongenial to the junta. Almost 20 years before similar events in Iraq, Chomsky described them as efforts "to destroy the national culture by violence."[97]

Salvador Option

The US has not pioneered use of terror. The latter has a long history including, in the twentieth century, in states under fascist or Stalinist control or influence. Since the 1950s, however, successive American administrations have used intelligence agencies to disseminate worldwide the practices rehearsed in Central America. States which have embraced these methods or refined existing practice on the US model, include Turkey, Egypt, Indonesia, the Philippines, Kenya, Colombia and Peru. In some cases there have been admissions of responsibility, as when in 1999 President Clinton apologized to the people of Guatemala for US involvement in "violence and widespread repression."[98] Under the influence of neo-conservative strategists, however, LIC has been refurbished with methods including intensified state terror, "extraordinary rendition" and extremes of torture such as those which became public at Abu Ghraib Prison in Iraq. Chomsky comments that, "Washington [has] waged its 'war on terrorism' by creating an international terror network of unprecedented scale, and employing it worldwide with lethal and long lasting effects."[99]

In evidence to the British parliamentary commission Jalili maintains that the US has implemented a "Salvador" option in Iraq. He observes that atrocities which followed the invasion, aimed at Iraq's intelligentsia, "followed a methodical period of looting and destruction of Iraq's heritage, infrastructure, universities and libraries."[100] He concludes:

> Many Iraqis, together with sections of international academia, believe this to be highly indicative of a plan to drain Iraq of its intellectuals and experts and dismantle its infrastructure along a pattern known as "El-Salvador Option" used in that country by the Pentagon.[101]

Has the US implemented such a strategy in Iraq – or have its aims been more modest, to prompt uncertainty and instability, inhibiting the development of independent alternatives to those now in authority? Saad Jawad was formerly Professor of Political Science at the University of Baghdad: he is now a research fellow at the University of Exeter, UK. Analyzing the progress of the occupation in 2006, he observed that intellectuals were among the main victims of a general crisis of insecurity:

> The problem of security, or the lack of it, is the main reason why intellectuals have become such easy targets [of kidnapping or assassination]... precisely because of the chaos, the systematized assassinations of Iraqi intellectuals have gone largely unnoticed in the outside world. Iraq is being drained of its most able thinkers, thus an important component to any true Iraqi independence is being eliminated.[102]

It may be many years before responsibility can be attributed with confidence, especially for specific attacks. It does seem likely, however, that strategies rehearsed elsewhere have been applied with special ferocity in Iraq, where – uniquely – the state itself has been under assault. Klein describes the CPA's approach to the Iraqi economy as a Year Zero agenda – an attempt to sweep away obstacles to free-market relations as part of a millenarian vision of what US-led "liberation" was to deliver. As neo-liberalism fused with neo-conservatism both US forces and their proxies within Iraq's new, confessionally based political order were presented with the spectacle of an intelligentsia contaminated by its association with the state.[103] Academic and professional relations – which had operated on a largely secular basis – violated the new arrangements in which loyalty to political parties, militias and networks of patronage was to be organized through ethno-religious affiliation. It is in this sense that, when President George W. Bush resolved to attack Iraq, a purging of minds became inevitable.

The offensive has been successful, producing cumulative effects which lead thousands of people and their families to flee. It has scattered people whose institutional and professional networks are in disrepair. Academics in particular are separated from the human resources which facilitate their work, including colleagues, students and wider professional relationships. A professor of science from Baghdad laments the outcome: "It took decades of painful work to establish our universities – now they are ruined. Why? Because Bush and his friends said: 'You are *all* guilty' and condemned us to death or to leave Iraq. What choice did we have?"[104] Further testimony comes from an unlikely source: since ending his tenure as CPA advisor on universities, John Agresto has reflected on the fate of higher education in Iraq. He told the *Washington Post* of his disillusion and anger, concluding: "I'm a neoconservative who's been mugged by reality."[105] Agresto lived to tell his tale: many Iraqi intellectuals "mugged" by the realities of invasion and occupation have suffered a different fate.

Notes

1. Thanks to Raymond Baker for comments on this chapter in draft.
2. Interview with NGO official in Amman, October 2008.
3. For a fuller development of this argument see Philip Marfleet, *Refugees in a Global Era*, Basingstoke: Palgrave Macmillan, 2006.
4. UNHCR, "Iraqis Still at the Top of the Asylum Seeker Table, Despite Drop," 2008, http://www.unhcr.org.uk/press/PR20October08. htm, accessed December 2008.
5. According to the UNHCR's asylum trends report, the number of claims made by Iraqis (19,500) during the first six months of 2008 was higher than the combined number of asylum claims submitted by citizens of the Russian Federation (9,400) and China (8,700), the second and third most important source countries. See UNHCR, "Iraqis Still at the Top of the Asylum Seeker Table, Despite Drop."
6. Refugees not placed formally in camps or other sites are usually known as "spontaneous" or "self-settled" refugees.
7. UNHCR, *Statistics on Displaced Iraqis around the World*, 2008, http://www.unhcr.org/cgi-bin/texis/vtx/home/opendoc.pdf?tbl=S UBSITES&id=470387fc2, accessed December 2008.
8. There is growing evidence to suggest that Iraqis denied admission to states in which they seek sanctuary use clandestine means of travel and of entry. Iraqi refugees in Cairo, for example, have increasingly used informal migration routes to reach states of Western Europe and North America. Information obtained through personal interviews with NGO officials in Egypt, November 2008.
9. Geraldine Chatelard, "Constructing and Deconstructing 'the Iraq Refugee Crises'," paper presented to the conference of the

International Association of Contemporary Iraqi Studies, London, July 2008.

10. Ibid.
11. UNHCR, *Statistics on Displaced Iraqis around the World*, 2008.
12. See IOM reports provided in the IOM-Iraq General Library, at: http://www.iom-iraq.net/library.html.
13. Philip Marfleet, "Iraq's Refugees: War and the Strategy of Exit," *International Journal of Contemporary Iraqi Studies*, Vol. 1, No. 3, 2007.
14. Marfleet, *Refugees in a Global Era*.
15. Ashraf al-Khalidi, Sophia Hoffman and Victor Tanner, *Iraqi Refugees in the Syrian Arab Republic: A Field-Based Snapshot*, Washington, DC: Brookings-Bern, 2007, p. 10.
16. Ibid.
17. Interview with officials of St. Andrew's Church refugee services, Cairo, January 2008.
18. Personal interview with a former senior academic from Baghdad now living in Jordan; Amman, October 2008.
19. Ibid.
20. B*Russell*s Tribunal, "Stop the Assassination of Iraqi Academics," http://www.brusselstribunal.org/Academics.htm, accessed December 2008.
21. Lucy Hodges, "Iraq's Universities are in Meltdown," *Independent*, December 7, 2006.
22. Christina Asquith, "Righting Iraq's Universities," *New York Times*, 3 August 2003.
23. Annia Ciezadlo, "Death to Those Who Dare to Speak Out," *Christian Science Monitor*, April 30, 2004.
24. Robert Fisk, "Academics Targeted as Murder and Mayhem Hits Iraqi Colleges," *Independent*, July 14, 2004.
25. Tabitha Morgan, "Murder of Lecturers Threatens Iraqi Academia," *Times Higher Education Supplement*, September 10, 2004.
26. Bryan Bender and Farah Stockman, "Iraq's Violent 'Brain Drain' Called a Threat to Future," *Boston Globe*, November 30, 2006.
27. Abdul Sattar Jawad, "Iraq's Deadliest Zone: Schools," *Washington Post*, November 27, 2006.
28. Ibid.
29. Andrew Rubin, "The Slaughter of Iraq's Intellectuals," *New Statesman*, September 6, 2004.
30. White House, "State of the Union Address," January 23, 2007, Washington DC: White House, Office of the Press Secretary.

31. White House, "President Bush Visits Naval War College, Discusses Iraq, War on Terror," June 28, 2007, Washington DC: White House, Office of the Press Secretary.

32. White House, "State of the Union Address," January 23, 2007.

33. Most media analyses follow this lead. In March 2007 *Time* magazine, for example, declared that US hopes of building a stable Iraq had been ruined by "toxic" hatreds between Iraq's Sunni and Shia communities (Bobby Ghosh, "Why They Hate Each Other," *Time*, March 12, 2007). The mass of Iraqis were divided by an "unbridgeable chasm," it asserted, suggesting that the loss of loved ones, jobs, homes and entire communities should be attributed to the "venom," "bloodlust," "fury" and "rage" of Iraqi Muslims.

34. Christina Asquith, "Murder, Fear Follow Iraqi Professors on Campus," *Diverse Issues in Higher Education*, November 21, 2007.

35. Dirk Andriaensens, "About the Assassination of Iraqi Academics," Report of an International Seminar in Madrid 2006, http://www.uruknet.info/?s1=1&p=22885&s2=27, accessed December 2008.

36. Ibid.

37. The Commission was jointly chaired by the former Liberal Democrat leader Lord Ashdown; a former Labour Leader of the House of Lords, Baroness Jay; and a former Conservative Defence Secretary, Lord King. It was set up by the Foreign Policy Centre, in partnership with Channel 4, with an aspiration to be the British equivalent of the US Iraq Study Group. See the Commission's website at: http://www.channel4.com/news/microsites/I/the_iraq_commission/index.html.

38. Ismail Jalili, *Iraq's Lost Generation: Impact and Implications*, 2007, p. 2, http://www.brusselstribunal.org/pdf/alJalili170607.pdf, accessed December 2008.

39. Ibid., p. 8.

40. Ibid., p. 14.

41. Human Rights Watch, *A Face and a Name: Civilian Victims of Insurgent Groups in Iraq*, New York: Human Rights Watch, 2005, p. 1.

42. Ibid., p. 93.

43. Ibid.

44. Scholar Rescue Fund – Iraq Scholar Refugee Project, http://www.scholarrescuefund.org/iraq/pages/about-us.php, accessed December 2008.

45. Ibid.

46. Ibid.

47. Ibid.
48. Hodges, "Iraq's Universities are in Meltdown."
49. Ibid.
50. Between September 2006 and September 2007 only 55 of 780 applications for asylum processed by the British government were successful (Tom Porteous, "The Refugees Fleeing Iraq Are Our Responsibility," *Independent*, March 6, 2007). CARA's executive secretary, John Akker, has commented: "The UK government is hung up on its policy on Iraq... Because it believes things will be settled in Iraq and that there are some safe areas, they [the government] are not giving any kind of refugee status to those who have genuine fears for their lives" (Zvika Krieger, "Iraq's Universities Near Collapse," *Chronicle of Higher Education*, May 18, 2007).
51. Benedict Anderson, *Imagined Communities: Reflections on the Origin and Spread of Nationalism*, London: Verso, 1983.
52. Ibid.
53. For a fuller account of this argument see Marfleet, *Refugees in a Global Era* and Philip Marfleet, "Refugees and History: Why We Must Address the Past," *Refugee Survey Quarterly*, Vol. 26, No. 3, 2007.
54. The term *refugie* may first have been used by Calvinists fleeing the Netherlands during the sixteenth century but, suggests Cottret (*The Huguenots in England*, Cambridge: Cambridge University Press, 1991), it was not used systematically until after the Huguenots' mass flight from France in 1685.
55. Nevzat Soguk, *States and Strangers: Refugees and Displacements of Statecraft*, Minneapolis: University of Minnesota Press, 1999.
56. Ibid., p. 72.
57. Ibid., p. 73.
58. Bernard Porter, *The Refugee Question in mid-Victorian Politics*, Cambridge: Cambridge University Press, 1979.
59. These developments later resolved into wholesale population movements which sometimes affected entire regions, notably Eastern Europe and the Balkans, where large groups of people were "cleansed" on the basis of ethnic identification. By the early twentieth century state formation in Europe and the Middle East was associated with complex processes in which large populations were "unmixed" – Turkification, Russification, Hellenization and eventually Arabization.
60. Quoted in Raymond W. Baker, *Egypt's Uncertain Revolution under Nasser and Sadat*, Cambridge, Mass.: Harvard University Press, 1978, p. 60.

61. Ibid., p. 73.

62. There were in addition 47 technical institutes.

63. Charles Tripp, *A History of Iraq*, Cambridge and New York: Cambridge University Press, 2002, p. 294.

64. Ibid.

65. Chatelard, "Constructing and Deconstructing 'the Iraq Refugee Crises'."

66. Richard Falk, *The Great Terror War*, Moreton-in-Marsh, UK: Arris, 2003.

67. Naomi Klein, *The Shock Doctrine: The Rise of Disaster Capitalism*, London: Penguin, 2007, p. 328.

68. Ibid.

69. Ibid.

70. Thomas Friedman, "What Were They Thinking?" *New York Times*, October 7, 2005.

71. Rajiv Chandrasekaran, *Imperial Life in the Emerald City*, London: Bloomsbury, 2006, p. 78.

72. "No One Believes in the Private Sector": Mohamed Tofiq of the Industry Ministry interviewed by Naomi Klein, in Klein, *The Shock Doctrine*, p. 349.

73. Klein, *The Shock Doctrine*, p. 337.

74. Ibid.

75. Ibid.

76. Chandrasekaran, *Imperial Life in the Emerald City*.

77. Ibid and pp. 31–5. In the CPA some of the new officials appeared to believe the rhetoric of change. Agresto anticipated securing hundreds of millions of dollars for the universities. He was eventually allocated $8 million (reduced by $500,000 of "administrative fees") for the entire sector: when he left Iraq after almost a year in office his attempts to obtain even elementary science lab equipment had failed and he was left with "pocket change" for reconstruction.

78. Ibid., p. 184. Agresto says that later he regretted the destruction: "What the looting did to the capacity to teach was incredible… The Americans don't want to talk about it because we did so little to stop the looting."

79. Under the previous regime the Ministry of Education had instructed teachers in certain schools to join the ruling party as a condition of employment. See Chandrasekaran, *Imperial Life in the Emerald City*, ch. 4.

80. Turi Munthe, "Will Harsh Weed-out Allow Iraqi Academia to Flower?" *Times Higher Education Supplement*, July 25, 2003.

81. Joseph Sassoon, *The Iraqi Refugees: The New Crisis in the Middle East*, London: IB Tauris, 2008, p. 140.

82. Klein, *The Shock Doctrine*, p. 352.

83. Sassoon, *The Iraqi Refugees*, p. 141.

84. Felicity Arbuthnot, "Tortured, shot, ambushed, victims are found dumped outside morgues. What is happening to Iraq's intellectuals is chilling," *Times Higher Education Supplement*, March 10, 2006.

85. Derek Summerfield, "Addressing Human Response to War and Atrocity: Major Challenges in Research and Practices and the Limitations of Western Psychiatric Models," in R.J. Kleber, C.R. Figley and B.P.R. Gersons (eds.), *Beyond Trauma: Cultural and Societal Dynamics*, New York: Plenum Press, 1995, p. 17.

86. Ibid.

87. Ignacio Martin-Baro, *Writings for a Liberation Psychology*, Cambridge: Harvard University Press, 1994.

88. Gyanendra Pandey, *Remembering Partition: Violence, Nationalism and History in India*, Cambridge: Cambridge University Press, 2001.

89. Ian Pappe, *The Ethnic Cleansing of Palestine*, Oxford: Oneworld, 2006, p. 110.

90. Benny Morris, "On Ethnic Cleansing," *New Left Review*, Second Series, Vol. 26, March–April 2004, p. 40.

91. John A. Booth and Thomas W. Walker, *Understanding Central America*, Boulder: Westview, 1993, p. 146.

92. For a fuller account see Marfleet, *Refugees in a Global Era*.

93. CIA (Central Intelligence Agency), *Psychological Operations in Guerrilla Warfare*, 1984, http://www.freewebs.com/moeial/CIA's%20Psychological%20Operations%20in%20Guerrilla%20Warfare.pdf, accessed December 2008.

94. Ibid., pp. 7 and 47.

95. Ibid., p. 51.

96. Quoted in Noam Chomsky, *Turning the Tide: US Intervention in Central America and the Struggle for Peace*, Boston, Mass.: South End Press, 1985, pp. 105–6.

97. Ibid.

98. Quoted in Human Rights Watch, *World Report 2000*; New York: Human Rights Watch, 2000: 133.

99. Noam Chomsky, "Who are the Global Terrorists?," in Ken Booth and Tim Dunne, *Worlds in Collision: Terror and the Future of Global Order*, Basingstoke: Palgrave Macmillan, 2002, p. 132.

100. Jalili, *Iraq's Lost Generation*, p. 14.

101. Ibid. Others have explored this analysis. See, for example, Robert Dreyfuss, "Phoenix Rising," *American Prospect*, January 1, 2004, and observations of the B*Russell*s Tribunal at: http://orogenysound. net/files/Download/iraqi-adaemics-assassination_2006.htm.

102. Laith Al-Saud, "Iraqi Intellectuals and the Occupation," *Counterpunch*, January 3, 2006.

103. On the architecture of Iraq's post-2005 political order see Marfleet "Iraq's Refugees: War and the Strategy of Exit."

104. Personal interview, Amman, October 2008.

105. Chandrasekaran, *Imperial Life in the Emerald City*, p. 4.

10

MINORITIES IN IRAQ:
THE OTHER VICTIMS[1]

Mokhtar Lamani

Introduction

Until my resignation in January 2007 from my position as the Arab League ambassador and Special Envoy to Iraq, I witnessed that all Iraqis from different ethnic, religious and sectarian backgrounds were not only suffering but were also victims to the collapse of the foundations of their societies rooted in Mesopotamian heritage. The Iraqi crisis becomes a question of life or death for hundreds of thousands of people; it is also a threat to a critical part of human history and civilization. The purpose of this chapter on minorities is not to further divide the Iraqi people; but to illuminate their suffering, which all endure, albeit differently. The chapter was originally published as a special report of the Centre for International Governance Innovation (CIGI), a Canadian-based, independent, nonpartisan think tank that addresses international governance challenges. It represents the first fruits of a collective and ongoing effort, supported by the Centre.

Where the term "minorities" is used in this chapter, it refers to the dozen ethnic and religious groups that are apart from what was established by the occupying forces as an atypical division (Shia, Sunni and Kurd). This political system based on ethnic and religious quotas has emphasized the other minorities' vulnerability to the dangers that have persisted since then.

It is clear that the findings of this chapter cannot be considered final. The evolution of the situation on the ground in Iraq, and its implications for all Iraqis, is so rapid and so often contradictory that this chapter should stay open for future updating, corrections and judgments. Our intention is to present a portrait that is as accurate as possible, to update our conclusions as the situation continues to evolve and to assess the direction of events. We also offer suggestions for action to alleviate the very difficult circumstances in which minorities find themselves. Mesopotamia has been the birthplace and, for millennia, the home of dozens of ethnicities and religions, which together formed a delicate and beautiful cultural, religious and social mosaic that later came to be an important part of the identity of the modern state of Iraq. For thousands of years, under countless regimes and through successive conflicts, these minority groups have persisted and the mosaic of Iraq has flourished.

The ongoing sectarian violence and the inability of the current Iraqi leadership to achieve national reconciliation and a secure social environment threatens to destroy the mosaic that has persisted for all this time. Iraqi minorities are facing a disproportionate level of violence and instability, which threatens to drive them out of Iraq permanently. While Iraqi minorities make up only 5 percent of the total population, they comprise more than 20 percent of the displaced population.[2]

The question of minorities is always a very sensitive issue in the Middle East. Our original plan was to conduct field research on Iraqi minorities in Iraq, Jordan, Syria and Egypt in November and December 2008. Unfortunately we couldn't include Syria; I was informed that this specific mission was not welcome at this time and therefore my assistant, a Canadian, was unable to get a visa. We were able to meet with leaders and individuals in Iraq, Jordan, and Egypt.

The Middle East comprises a myriad of different religious, ethnic, and tribal minorities, all of which have coexisted down through history and preserved their rich identities and traditions over the centuries. Despite their significant cultural and intellectual contributions to the diversity and prosperity in the communities in which they reside, minority groups are the focus of much of contemporary conflict in the Middle East. Many Middle Eastern minorities are facing increasing hostility at the hands of extremist groups and even government bodies. Ironically, even groups that are a physical majority in their countries can sometimes be a political minority in their governments and face similar minority pressures.

We still have not seen a constitution that is based on equal citizenship implemented in the whole region. An example of this is the requirement that citizens of most Middle Eastern countries declare their ethnic or religious background, or both, on their identification cards or official papers. In some cases they are even forced to indicate an affiliation that doesn't reflect reality because their governments do not recognize their religion or ethnic group.

We have chosen to focus on the Iraqi case not only because it is a question of life or death for hundreds of thousands of people, but also because the crisis there threatens a critical part of human history and civilization.

Iraq has crystallized strong geopolitical and geostrategic tensions that are marked by three layers of complexity:

- The first is the unfolding of the internal Iraqi socio-political crisis and its different aspects.
- The second has at its root the extremely complex nature of the regional dimension and its interplay with the internal aspects of the Iraq crisis.
- The third is the international interactions inherent in Iraq's position in the region, compounded by its importance to the international economy because of its oil resources and its position in the Middle East.

These geopolitical and geostrategic tensions lie at the heart of the threats that minorities face. They are pawns, used by all parties on the chessboard that is the new Iraq. Little if any attention is paid to their genuine needs; rather their suffering is used to advance other agendas.

If there was ever a need for dynamic new thinking to address to governance challenges in Iraq, it is now. By sounding the alarm over the desperate plight of Iraq's minorities, this project can hopefully begin to stimulate much needed, serious dialogue that can advance positive change for and protection of Iraq's numerous, endangered minorities.

Field Research

This first section focuses on the minority groups that reside or have taken refuge in Iraqi-Kurdistan. The rise of sectarianism in other parts of the country has reduced formerly mixed communities into Shia and Sunni enclaves. Many of the religious minorities cannot find protection in either of these and as a result have attempted either to flee the country or to move north to Iraqi-Kurdistan where religious identity is less of a determining factor in security.

A total of five days were spent in Iraqi-Kurdistan where Prime Minister Barzani facilitated our visit and provided logistical support and security. We were free to travel and meet with anyone we requested; no officials were required to accompany us to these meetings. Numerous meetings were conducted with people displaced by the ongoing violence across Iraq; these included Mandaean families who had fled to Erbil in 2006 as well as Christian families that had fled to Ankawa from Mosul during the second peak of violence there in 2008. We also traveled to visit the Yezidi communities in Qal'at Shihan and Lalish. Meetings took place there with the Yezidi Mîr (or prince) and the Baba Sheikh (or pope) as well as a visit to their holy temple in Lalish.

Following our trip to Iraqi-Kurdistan, eight days were spent meeting with different representatives and displaced Iraqi minorities in Amman and Cairo. We met with several Iraqi families who had been forced to flee the country and have found refuge in Jordan. We also met with various officials from the United Nations, Iraqi Members of Parliament, as well as Iraqi leaders from inside and outside the existing political process in Iraq.

A significant volume of information was received from many different sources during our research, all of which had to be independently verified before it was included in this chapter.

Current Situation of Minorities

All Iraqis are suffering but there are specificities to the case of minorities that put them at exceptional threat. It has been estimated that because of sectarianism and recent changes to Iraqi society, as many as 25–30 percent of the population have been forced to leave their homes and are either internally or externally displaced. However, for minorities the percentage of those displaced is actually much higher. More than 80 percent of the Mandaean population has been forced to flee; for Christians and other ethnic or religious groups, nearly 60 percent of their populations are displaced.[3]

Iraqi minorities are at risk of extinction. As one inter-faith expert we consulted stated, "when a Muslim is driven from his home, he usually plans on returning once the situation has stabilized; when a Christian or other minority leaves, they never want to come back." Sadly, the evidence collected to date would seem to support this view; the UNHCR states that in 2007 less than 1 percent of the displaced were able to return, but even among this paltry number not a single minority person was counted.[4]

The situation of minorities has become worse as a result of the 2003 Iraq war and subsequent occupation. The problems facing minorities, not just in Iraq but across the whole Middle East, have existed long before 2003. One example is the expulsion of the Faili Kurds from Iraq during the Iran–Iraq war. However, the war and occupation have led to dangerous new changes to the local environment that have had a negative impact on the already tenuous situation of many of Iraq's minorities. The persistent climate of fear and insecurity as well as the entrenchment of sectarianism in the emerging Iraqi political process has spurred massive population displacement, sectarian strife and far-reaching instability. The situation in the country is so fragile that this instability threatens to spiral and engulf the entire region.

Violence and displacement have been ongoing and constant in Iraq since 2003, but they reached two peaks that are worth mentioning, when large waves of people suffered multiple acts of violence and forced displacement. In 2006, the Sunni–Shia violence reached its peak and forced thousands of minority families to flee the ethnic cleansing that was taking place to create homogeneous Sunni and Shia neighborhoods, predominantly in and around Baghdad. This time saw most minorities across the country being forced to flee abroad or to the north. Later in 2008, a second wave of violence against Christians in Mosul saw thousands of Christian families flee the city and go to Iraqi-Kurdistan. During these periods, Iraq witnessed extensive displacement of people that fundamentally altered the demographic makeup of some parts of the country. It is important to note that these two waves of displacement in 2006 and 2008 were simply the peaks in the ebb and flow of constant violence; people continue to suffer from insecurity and violence at all times.

The flight to Iraqi-Kurdistan of those minorities that cannot escape the country has created enormous pressure on the governance institutions within the Kurdish region. In particular, the government there struggles to provide protection and basic services to the large numbers of displaced that are fleeing towards its borders. One example is in basic education where minority groups have had difficulty finding spaces; we have been told by Kurdish officials that they have over 10,000 Kurdish students without spaces in schools. The lack of capacity makes it extremely challenging to provide basic services to the local population, let alone to tens of thousands of displaced people.

Every minority group that was met with during our research was asked if they would stay in Iraq if the constitution offered equal citizenship to all Iraqis irrespective of their ethnic or religious affiliation; unanimously they said that they didn't believe it was possible in Iraq. Although they want to stay, the situation is too dangerous. For many, the only solution is to get out and settle in another country. In addition to the general despair and fear felt by these minorities, there were several specific problems that they all shared regardless of whether they were displaced internally in Iraq or externally in Jordan or elsewhere:

- A lack of basic education opportunities for their children
- A lack of access to universities

- A lack of access to employment opportunities
- A lack of integration into the broader community
- A very high level of frustration at the lack of interest from the outside about their situation.

Yezidis

The Yezidis are an excellent example of a specific group with some very specific concerns. They almost all live together in Iraqi-Kurdistan and the so-called disputed territories that border it; even though they are minorities at the regional or national level, they are majorities inside their own villages. This has meant that they have not been forced to leave their homes in the same percentages as other groups that are more thinly spread and exposed across Iraq, such as the Mandaeans or the Christians.

However, this does not mean that they have escaped persecution. We were informed that, because of the violence from extremist groups, there have been no Yezidis left in Mosul since 2007. Unlike Christians who can pay a tax to stay in their homes, the Yezidis can only choose between conversion, expulsion, or execution. In 2007, suspected al-Qaeda affiliated militants targeted Yezidis, shooting dead 23 on a bus and bombing several villages resulting in hundreds of deaths.[5] Many extremists consider the Yezidis devil worshippers and extremist imams have openly called for their killing if they refuse to convert. We were given a recording of Imam Mullah Farzanda making statements in his Friday sermon that it was the duty of good Muslims to kill all Yezidis in Iraq if they refused to convert to Islam. Despite their relative isolation and small numbers, extremists have made the Yezidis a direct target.

According to their beliefs, Yezidis can only be baptized in their temple at Lalish; the temple is the center of their religion and critical to their religious rites. This explains their extreme attachment to their land. The social chaos that has spread throughout Iraq threatens to undermine this attachment and therefore their ability to practice their religion. In the village of Qal'at Shihan Yezidis have traditionally been the majority; now they are moving towards becoming a minority in their own village because of the huge influx of displaced peoples fleeing sectarian violence in other parts of the country. This new demographic balance is difficult for the Yezidis who have expressed anxiety about this new exposure to potentially hostile groups.

The Yezidi community is also vulnerable because of their delicate demographic balance. Their religion does not allow intermarriage with non-Yezidis; even further, there is a caste system within the Yezidi faith that discourages marriage between the different castes. These strict rules around marriage for Yezidis, combined with their already small population, make the forced displacement of their people very harmful to the fragile demographic balance that sustains their numbers.

Due to the already small size of their population, their attachment to their land, and their strictly closed ranks, the violence and dispersal they are enduring could lead to the extinction of this millennia old group. The Yezidis CIGI I spoke to want their unique cultural identity recognized and protected by the regional and national governments. In particular they want their religious places in Lalish and their villages protected. Because of their religious attachment to their land they do not want to leave; the best solution in their eyes is a secular government that will protect their rights equally to the rights of other groups.

Mandaeans

The Mandaeans also have some very specific concerns. Mandaeans are not concentrated in a few villages; until the outbreak of sectarian violence in 2006 they were spread across several urban centers in Iraq, particularly Baghdad. Their thin distribution made them especially vulnerable to sectarian violence between larger groups and they have fled the country by the tens of thousands; those that could not escape Iraq fled north and took refuge in Erbil. It is estimated that there were as many as 70,000 Mandaeans worldwide and most lived in Iraq before the 2003 war; less than 5,000 now remain.[6]

Like the Yezidis, Mandaeans do not intermarry and their beliefs are considered heretical by the extremist groups who target them.

However, it is not only extremists who target Mandaeans; they have a reputation of being wealthier than ordinary Iraqis because many formerly traded in alcohol, jewelry and other profitable businesses. This has made them the target of criminal gangs conducting kidnappings for ransom.[7]

All of the Mandaean families that CIGI interviewed said that it was their strong desire to remain in Iraq but their security was too greatly endangered. They did not believe that a constitution based on equal citizenship would ever happen or that their security needs could be met in the short or medium term. They wanted help getting out of Iraq and settling in a safe country such as Australia or the United States. Their religion requires that they live near running water and conduct their baptisms there but the location of the river itself is not important; for them security is the primary concern.

In discussion with Mandaean refugee groups in Jordan it was disclosed that approximately 650 Mandaean families have been forced to flee to Jordan and a further 2,100 to Syria. Of the 650 families that fled to Jordan only 202 families remain; the rest have already relocated to the US and Australia. Of those 202 remaining families, 172 have already received approval to transfer to other countries and the remaining 30 are still waiting on their papers to transfer outside.

One of their fears as a closed religious group is that they might be spread too thinly across the world and that their religion would simply disappear over time. They consider dispersion to be a threat to their existence and are trying to facilitate their emigration to one country as a group, so that they do not become overly separated. They would prefer to stay in Iraq, but failing that, they are trying to flee as a group to a safe place where they can practice their religion in security and maintain their identity.

Christians

Twenty years ago, there were approximately 1.4 million Christians in Iraq; today there are fewer than 700,000.[8] Since the 2003 war,

Christians have faced ongoing violence that has peaked twice; the first in 2006 when sectarian violence reached its peak across the country and the second in 2008 when most were driven from Mosul to Ankawa and other parts of Iraqi-Kurdistan. Like the Mandaeans, Christians were spread thinly across Iraq and have been caught between larger extremist groups as they fought one another. Many Christians, like those in Mosul, reside within the so-called "disputed territories" and this has added an internal political dimension to their persecution. In several interviews Christians discussed how they had been assaulted, killed, forced to pay the *jeziya*, and in some cases had been threatened even after paying the tax. Most have tried to leave the country and those that cannot have taken refuge in Iraqi-Kurdistan.

The Christian identity is not as homogeneous as some of the other Iraqi minority identities. Many Christians not only consider themselves a religion, but also as part of one of four distinct ethnicities as well; Chaldean, Assyrian, Armenian, or Syriac. Chaldeans follow an eastern right of the Catholic Church; Syriacs consider themselves Eastern Orthodox; Armenians are part of either the Roman Catholic or Eastern Orthodox Churches; and Assyrians are part of the Church of the East or Nestorian. Still other Christians consider themselves Arab-Christians, a religious minority but not a separate ethnicity. The Christian community is one of the largest of the minority communities in Iraq and it is difficult to achieve a consensus approach to their problems.

Beyond the internal complexities of the Iraqi Christian identity, there is a strong external component in the powerful Christian diaspora communities in other states. These groups have helped to raise awareness about the circumstances of Christians in Iraq; however they have also added an international layer of complexity to the internal problems Iraqis face. In particular, the support foreign groups have given to politically contentious positions, such as the Nineveh plains proposal to create a separate autonomous region administered by and catering to minorities, has further complicated an already fragmented political scene.

Turkmen

The Turkmen are a distinct ethnic group; approximately 60 percent are Sunni, just fewer than 40 percent are Shia, and the remainder are Christians. Like the Christians of Mosul, the Turkmen also reside within the so-called "disputed territories" and have been put under pressure from several groups trying to gain political advantage over each other. Approximately 85 percent of their Iraqi population lives in the regions around Mosul, Kirkuk, Erbil and Tel Afar; the rest are in Baghdad and smaller villages, such as Tuz Khurmato.[9]

The Turkmen, like other ethnic minorities, did not have their unique culture recognized by past regimes. "Arabization" and "correction" campaigns refused to acknowledge the Turkmens' distinctiveness.

Presently, the Turkmen community finds itself at the center of one of Iraq's most contentious political questions, the fate of oil-rich Kirkuk. Some Turkmen support the Kurdish claim and would like to become a part of the Kurdistan region. Others strongly oppose this for fear of being assimilated into the Kurdish identity. They therefore oppose the creation of autonomous regions and favor a strong central government that respects their cultural heritage. As the major parties position themselves to seek maximum advantage against the others in this debate, the Turkmen community is often used by different internal and external parties without any regard for their own concerns.

Other Minorities[10]

The minorities discussed above are just some of the many groups that make up Iraq's mosaic. Others not specifically mentioned include the Shabaks, Bahá'is, Faili Kurds, and Kaka'is (Yaresan) among others. Our access to these groups was limited and some do not reside in the so-called "disputed territories." However, they share some of the same vulnerabilities as the other minority groups that we have discussed and they have an equal stake in the evolution of a national identity in Iraq that is based on equal citizenship, not sectarianism.

Like other groups they have been targeted because of their ethnic or religious identity and forced to leave their homes as majority communities try to create religious and ethnically homogeneous enclaves. The toll that violence has taken on these groups is similar to that of the other minorities covered in this chapter. The Shabaks are mostly located within the so-called "disputed territories" of Mosul and the Nineveh plain; like the Christians and Turkmen who also reside there, they have been caught in the violent political gamesmanship between majority parties over territory. Both the Shia Shabak and the Shia Turkmen have endured a lot of suffering from al-Qaeda from 2006 to 2008 in the areas around Mosul. The Bahá'i religion is still not recognized by the majority of Middle East governments and they have no right to express their identity. The Faili Kurds, who experienced expulsion during the *Anfal* campaign, are still struggling to return to their expropriated homes.

All these problems have at their root the lack of a common Iraqi identity. A governance approach is needed that emphasizes equal citizenship based on respect for human rights, not sectarian affiliation. Ultimately an equal national identity is the only long-term solution that can address all the problems raised by Iraq's minorities. Unfortunately, this approach has not been adopted by the major political and religious parties, and governance challenges have grown worse over time.

Governance Challenges

The relations between the various Iraqi political or religious groups are marred by a high level of mistrust. Since the future is so uncertain, all groups are making maximum demands to try to ensure that their minimum objectives are met; however, this approach is causing more problems than it solves for all concerned. Numerous meetings with politicians confirmed the highly politicized nature of the issues surrounding minorities.

Each party is trying to use these issues to condemn other parties. Their competing political demands make the situation even worse for minorities because many of them live in the so-called "disputed territories." Minorities in Iraq are the victims not only of sectarianism and extremism but of competing political agendas; their displacement is a consequence of both.

All parties are essentially reacting instead of acting and this has had profoundly negative consequences. There is little regard for the deep level of suffering that these minority communities are facing; rather than seeking to address the root causes of their misery, major political parties are using this suffering to advance their own political agendas.

Minorities have been caught in between; their identity receiving only limited or conditional recognition as they are first told that they are in fact Arab, or that they are Kurd, or that they must change their religion depending on the political demands of the majority group at any given time. The rising influence of religious political parties does not make Iraq's minorities any more optimistic that the future Iraq will recognize and fully respect their identities and treat them equally to the majority communities.

This situation in Iraq stands in stark contrast to the United Nations Universal Declaration of Human Rights. Two clauses stand out in particular:

Article 3: Everyone has the right to life, liberty and security of person

Article 18: Everyone has the right to freedom of thought, conscience and religion.

Furthermore, the United Nations Declaration on the Rights of Indigenous Peoples, adopted by the UN General Assembly in September 2007, clearly lays out numerous protections for indigenous cultures in Article 8:

1. Indigenous peoples and individuals have the right not to be subjected to forced assimilation or destruction of their culture.

2. States shall provide effective mechanisms for prevention of, and redress for:

    (a) Any action which has the aim or effect of depriving them of their integrity as distinct peoples, or of their cultural values or ethnic identities;

(b)   Any action which has the aim or effect of dispossessing them of their lands, territories or resources;

(c)   Any form of forced population transfer which has the aim or effect of violating or undermining any of their rights;

(d)   Any form of forced assimilation or integration;

(e)   Any form of propaganda designed to promote or incite racial or ethnic discrimination directed against them.

It is clear that none of these conventions is being respected in Iraq today. Minorities in particular are constantly under threat and, while immediate violence may be down temporarily, the central government has thus far proved incapable of dealing with the root causes of this discrimination. This leaves a significant likelihood that violence will resume in the not too distant future, particularly as contentious questions are addressed such as the fate of regional boundaries and the future return of some of the displaced. No solution can provide lasting security if it does not strive for the human rights protections expressed by these UN conventions.

In this context, the debate about Article 50 of the Iraqi Constitution has been a flashpoint for anxieties relating to the place of minorities in the Iraqi political system and society. Article 50 provided for minimum representation of minorities in elected positions to the provincial governments; it was removed from the provincial election laws in the lead up to the referendum to ratify the law. This prompted a huge backlash from minority and international groups. Ultimately, the President of Iraq intervened personally to ensure its reinstatement into the law. The fact that this controversy occurred in the midst of ongoing violence against religious and ethnic minorities sent a powerful signal to those groups that the majority parties are not interested in their well-being. This crisis over the election law risked pushing minorities out of the political process and leaving them with only very limited or symbolic representation at a time when they are threatened with extinction.

The debate surrounding Article 50 should at best be a temporary one. The best protection is equal, non-sectarian citizenship. Legislation that provides quotas for each minority should only serve as a temporary measure until equality is achieved. This is to say that every Iraqi, regardless of his or her religious or ethnic background, should be free to strive for any position within the political process and not be limited to seats set aside for specific groups.

Conclusions

All Iraqis are caught in multiple and contradictory narratives about violence and victimhood. The US occupation and its mistakes that have led to the destruction of the fragile Iraqi social tissue and the new political class in Iraq is not yet in a conciliatory mood. Its posture is still essentially reactive in an atmosphere of total mistrust. This atmosphere is complicated by two emerging trends: first, the ongoing and unsustainable fragmentation within the political and social arena has reached a point where it is impossible to even identify all the actors; second, the narrow focus of the major parties on consolidating their power bases rather than adhering to a real national process of reconciliation, the only guarantee for the future of Iraq.

If nothing is done, the extremist danger from one side could lead to the extermination of some of these minorities as well as the destruction of the millennia-old cultural heritage of the Mesopotamian civilization. On the other side, the emergence of religious parties as the main political actors in the new Iraq has left minorities in a very insecure situation and casts doubt on the current government's ability or willingness to address any of these new challenges alone.

The solution cannot be only partial. It cannot seek to address the minority issue without putting it in the broader frame that is the Iraqi national crisis, the historically fragile position of minorities in Iraq, the catastrophic consequences of the US invasion and the resulting destruction of the Iraqi social tissue. The way forward must also take into consideration the dangers inherent in the present situation as well as the conflicting agendas of both internal and external actors.

The transition to a new US administration based on promised change may offer a possibility of sober reflection on previous US policy towards Iraq. This change in the US administration may present a tangible opportunity to implement much needed corrections that can more effectively address the whole Iraqi crisis, including a real effort towards national reconciliation. Consequently, the issues of minorities could be better managed.

For all these reasons, the establishment of an independent international monitoring committee would be a helpful first step in addressing these complications and in bringing forward practical and constructive proposals. A committee comprised only of Iraqi actors would be limited by the conflicting agendas and mistrust that permeate the present atmosphere. This international monitoring committee would have to be made up of very senior figures known for their professionalism and credibility that would have easy access to the key decision-makers locally, regionally, and internationally.

The complexities associated with the Iraqi crisis continue to multiply at an exponential rate; the standard mechanisms are proving unable to address this crisis in a fashion that can lead to a durable solution that will correct the current situation and also be acceptable to all actors. It goes without saying that the extinction of Iraqi minorities is not only a tragedy for them or a loss for Iraq, but for all mankind.

Notes

1. This chapter draws from a special report of the Centre for International Governance Innovation, a Canadian-based, independent, nonpartisan think tank that addresses international governance challenges.
2. Kathryn Westcott, "Iraq's Rich Mosaic of People," BBC News, February 27, 2003, http://news.bbc.co.uk/2/hi/middle_east/2783989. stm, accessed December 2008.
3. Preti Taneja, "Assimilation, Exodus, Eradication: Iraq's Minority Communities since 2003," Minority Rights Group International, http://www.minorityrights.org/?lid=2805, accessed December 2008.

4. UNHCR, "Second Rapid Assessment of Return of Iraqis from Displacement Locations in Iraq and from Neighbouring Countries," February 2008, p. 13, http://www.reliefweb.int/rw/RWFiles2008. nsf/FilesByRWDocUnidFilename/SHIG-7CEDPJ-full_chapter. pdf/$File/full_chapter.pdf, accessed December 2008.

5. "Iraq Bomb Toll Reaches 344," BBC News, August 17, 2007, http:// news.bbc.co.uk/2/hi/middle_east/6951221.stm, accessed December 2008.

6. Angus Crawford, "Iraq's Mandaeans Face Extinction," BBC News, March 4, 2007, http://news.bbc.co.uk/2/hi/middle_east/6412453. stm, accessed December 2008.

7. Taneja, "Assimilation, Exodus, Eradication."

8. Phebe Marr, introduction to *Iraq's Refugee and IDP Crisis: Human Toll and Implications*, Washington, DC: Middle East Institute, http://www.mideasti.org/files/iraqs-refugee-and-IDP-crisis.pdf, accessed December 2008.

9. Gilles Munier, "Les Turcomans Irakiens: un people oublié ou marginalisé," *Le blog de France-Irak Actualité*, May 31, 2007, www.gmunier.blogspot.com/2007/05/turcomans-irakiens.html, accessed December 2008.

10. Some intensive analysis of the humanitarian crisis facing a broad range of Iraqi minority groups has been undertaken by Minority Rights Group International. Those desiring more detailed background information regarding specific humanitarian issues relating to a broad range of Iraqi minorities should consult Taneja, "Assimilation, Exodus, Eradication."

APPENDIX 1:
REFLECTIONS ON DEATH ANXIETY AND UNIVERSITY PROFESSORS IN IRAQ

Faris K.O. Nadhmi

Spinoza (1632–1677) wrote in hopeful insight: "A free man scarcely thinks of death, because his wisdom is to contemplate life, not death." But what if death thinks of the free man non-stop, follows him in the city streets, lurks in the ally next to his home, comes out even in his sleep and deepest apprehensions, while he is keeping to his room, wondering if life has any meaning? What if a whole nation waits in a queue with an invisible end, but with a guillotine at the beginning, going up and down with the time pendulum?

Is it a universal irony or psycho-historic that the "death anxiety" is connected with "eternity anxiety" for the Iraqis, and with the tragic search for a coherent explanation of the existence-annihilation absurdum? When Gilgamesh found out he is two thirds god and one third human destined to die, like his friend Enkido, he sadly said:

> Death frightened me, so I wandered aimlessly about,
> If I die, would not my destiny be like Enkido's,
> To Otonabishtim, I took the way, and hurried
> To ask about the life-death enigma!

Death Psychology

Apart from death essence, its religious or philosophical root, whether it is annihilation or a face of another life, modern psychology has dealt with death as "total stopping of consciousness or feeling, the brain stops its work as a maestro of all lower sense and movement, and upper mind functions," there is the human response to death, studied clinically and on the ground, the responses of those who lost a supporter or a loved one. These responses can be sadness and mourning, or depression and suicide, explaining the movement and feelings phenomenon which accompany these responses, its effect on psychological, body, and professional health, their negative attitudes to death, what in general we call "death anxiety." Dickstein defined it as "conscious contemplation in the reality of death, and the negative estimation of this reality."

Some psychoanalysts went further. Melanie Klein found that the fear of death is the origin of all anxieties, the root of all human aggressive behaviors. Freud (1856–1939) wrote on death and war: "we can not really imagine our death, and if we do, we do it as living audience...." For this reason, Freud concluded that deep inside, man has an unconscious feeling and belief in eternity.

Death anxiety has three dimensions: fear of dying, fear of what happens after death, and fear of life stopping. On the other hand, four aspects of death could be distinguished: fear of death of the ego, dying of ego, others' death, and others dying. Accordingly, four independent factors were generated: fear of the unknown, suffering, loneliness, and personal vanishing.

Death Anxiety in Iraq

These four aspects and factors of the psychology of death anxiety have now become the most impressing phenomenon in the Iraqi reality; indeed we can say that most daily life details were diverted and deformed in their biological, social, and psychological contents to suit the idea of death's inevitability and its overwhelming dominion. The Iraqi individual, no matter what of what class or affiliation, realizes that the highest or most precious goal of life becomes just "to survive," "not to die," instead of "to live," with full realization that death means assassinations, explosions, and rains of stray bullets.

The educated and the technocrat are among the first who look for ways "not to die." It is extremely difficult to get precise numbers, but events and studies indicate that medical doctors and academics are especially targeted. In a report for Human Rights Watch in November 2005, some academics explained that it is a way of eliminating the educated elite in Iraq. One vice president of an Iraqi university said "the victims are among different scientific interests, political directions, and religious sects, the only thing common among them is their distinguished scientific achievement. I think this is a plan to evacuate Iraq of its scientific backbone."

According to the Iraqi Ministry of Health, between April 2003 and June 2006, 720 medical doctors and health professionals were killed. Other unofficial estimations said that 2,000 Iraqi doctors emigrated from the country fleeing from killing and kidnapping.

According to a previous study by the Iraqi Ministry of Health, by April 2005, 160–300 Iraqi medical doctors were kidnapped by armed groups which killed 25. Up to that date, 1,000 doctors left the country, an average of 30 monthly.

In a statement of the "Voices of Iraq" news agency, the head of the Association of University Teachers in Iraq said that by summer 2006, 172 university teachers had been killed. However, if we add the numbers of lecturers and the consultants, it would exceed 300. This number does not include the medical doctors, engineers, religious teachers with higher degrees in religious studies.

Dr. Ismail Al-Jalili, a medical consultant, indicated in a study presented at the April 2006 Madrid International Conference on the Assassinations of Iraqi Academics that statistics show that 80 percent of the assassinations targeted people working in the universities, and that half of them are either professors or professor assistants, that half of the assassinations happened in Baghdad university, a third of them were in Basra, then Mosul and Al-Mustansiriya University. The study mentioned that 62 percent of the assassinations were PhDs.

One third of them are specialized in natural sciences and medicine, 17 percent are practicing doctors, and three quarters of those who were exposed to attempted assassination were actually killed. This "systematic" killing confirms Dr. Jalili's belief that these assassinations and kidnappings are similar to the El Salvador death squads, which was in fact, a series of assassinations supervised by the CIA in many Latin American countries.

Without going into analyzing the political and security dimensions, these data and statistics present a primary indicator of the destructive psychological impacts that anxiety causes university professors because of kidnapping and killings. Studies done in relatively stable eastern and western societies show that death anxiety is in direct proportion with depression, unsociability, over sensitivity, tension, obsessions, phobias; but it is in contrary proportion with self confidence, social skills, extroversion, endurance, self respect, self accomplishment, positive attitude to one's self, strong ego, sense of the purpose of life.

Other studies show that the more intelligent a person is, the less he is frightened of death, that the middle class are more afraid of dying pains, that the more educated a person is the less he is afraid of death, and that women are more afraid of death than men. There is no agreement on the relation between death anxiety and age or religion.

As a pioneer contribution in investigating the psychological paths that death anxiety would take within the Iraqi educated personality, we established 15 questions with a choice of 5 answers ranging between "totally agree" and "totally disagree," and gave it to the Baghdad and Mustansiriya university professors, who all had an MA, MSc, or PhD and were of varying ages and scientific degrees (professor, assistant professor, teacher and assistant teacher). The results were as follows:

- All professors suffer death anxiety
- Afraid of painful death (91%)
- Thinking of death of loved ones (81%)
- Afraid of body deterioration that accompanies slow death (72%)
- Worried about dying very painfully (69%)
- Feeling that death is everywhere (66%)

- Terrified of seeing a dead body (66%)
- Obsession with getting killed any minute (66%)
- Thinking of my personal death (53%)
- Prefer not to attend a dying friend (53%)
- Would avoid death no matter what it takes (50%)
- Think of death directly before going to bed (47%)
- Death is better than a painful life (38%)
- Feel closer to death than to life (31%)
- Extremely afraid to die (31%)
- Terrified by the idea of decomposition after death (28%)

Conclusions

Death anxiety is spread among this sample of Iraqi university professors, regardless of age and scientific degree which signifies that its effect is widely spread. Women were more worried about death than men. This result is consistent with the psychological literature mentioned above which says that women feel less secure; hence their death anxiety is higher. Gender rules, too, demand that men should be "brave" and not show fear or anxiety in this sense. In addition to that, women's death anxiety is related to themselves personally and to their husbands.

The fear of dying painfully is high among the sample individuals, as is their fear of the death of loved ones, signifying the psychological agony and tense feeling of threat that a professor has on his way from home to class.

More than two thirds of the sample have anxiety of painful death or of seeing a dead body, in addition to compulsive thoughts that death is surrounding them and that they could be exposed to death at any minute. This signifies that obsessive and oppressive elements are pervading the university professors' thinking.

One quarter to half of the sample's thoughts were centered on avoiding death, thinking of it, fearing it, and how close they are to it, signifying a relative carelessness about the conventional concept of death if mentioned without the idea of pain and threat of killing.

The essential task of the academic personality is to create life in its highest aims, beginning with lectures, scientific research, whether theoretical or inside laboratories or in the field, and to accumulate the eternal truths in the human mind library. Is it possible for such a creator of life to coexist with deep and objective anxiety of assassination and death pain?

Today, the Iraqi situation proves that death anxiety does not dissuade Iraqi university academics from their deep civilized awareness that desperately defending life culture is the only effective way to pull out death's treacherous fangs, and to rehabilitate the concept of "eternity" as an alternative to all cultures of annihilation and elimination.

APPENDIX 2:
LIST OF MURDERED ACADEMICS

The following table is an edited version of the list maintained by the B*Russell*s Tribunal, originally based on data provided by the Iraqi Association of University Teachers. The full B*Russell*s Tribunal list can be viewed at http://www.brusselstribunal.org/ pdf/academicsBT151108.pdf. The list includes some teachers, medical professionals and government officials who, though not strictly defined as academics, were felt to fall within the broader terms of an assault on Iraq's educational base. Efforts have been made to eliminate duplications, though some may remain due to variation in the translation of Arabic names. Due to the difficulty of reporting, it is almost certain that the list, though the best we have, is incomplete.

Name	Profession	University	Date
Aalim Abdul Hameed	Dean of Medicine College	Mustansiriya	Unknown
Abbas Kadhem Al-Hashimi	Professor Dr., Baghdad University	Baghdad	Unknown
Abbass al-Attar	Professor in Humanities	Baghdad	Unknown
Abbas al-Attar	Professor and specialist in gynaecology	Baghdad	Unknown
Abdel Al Munim Abdel Mayad	Lecturer	Basra	Unknown
Abdel Gani Assaadun	Lecturer	Basra	Unknown
Abdel Husein Jabuk	Doctor and professor	Baghdad	Unknown
Abdel Jabar Al Naimi	Dean of College of Humanities	Mosul	Unknown
Abdel Salam Saba	Professor of Sociology	Baghdad	Unknown
Abdl-Kareem Mekhlef Salih	Lecturer in College of Education	Al-Anbar	Unknown

Name	Profession	University	Date
Abdul Aziz El-Atrachi	Professor in College of Agriculture and Forestry	Mosul	Unknown
Abdul Azizi Jassem	College of Islamic Sciences	Baghdad	Unknown
Abdul Hadi Al-Anni	Consultative Doctor	Unknown	Unknown
Abdul Rahman saed	University Professor	Unknown	Unknown
Abdul Sameia al-Janabi	Professor in Education	Mustansiriya	Unknown
Abdul Yabar Mustafa	Dean of the faculty of political sciences	Mosul	Unknown
Ahlam Alghureri	Professor of pharmaceutical chemistry	Baghdad	Unknown
Ahmad Abdl-Hadi Al-Rawi and his wife	Lecturer in College of Agriculture	Al-Anbar	Unknown
Ahmad Abdul-Alrahman hameid Al-Khbissy	Lecturer in College of Medicine	Al-Anbar	Unknown
Ahmad Abdul Raziq	PhD in medicine	Unknown	Unknown
Aki Thakir Alaany	Professor in the faculty of literature	Mustansiriya	Unknown
Akil Abdel Jabar al-Bahadili	Deputy dean of medicine college	An-nahreen	Unknown
Ali Abdul-Hussein Kamil	Professor of physics	Baghdad	Unknown
Ali al-Maliki	PhD	Baghdad	Unknown
Amir al-Mallah	Oculist	Unknown	Unknown
Amir Mizhir al-Dayni	Professor of Communications Engineering	Unknown	Unknown
Ammar Al-ani	PhD in medicine	Unknown	Unknown
Aziz Ali	Dean of law department, chairman of Red Crescent Society	Unknown	Unknown
Basil al-Karkhi	Professor of chemistry	Baghdad	Unknown
Bassam Kubba	Advisor at the Ministry of Interior	Unknown	Unknown
Emad Sarsam	Professor in medicine	Unknown	Unknown
Fadel Trad Alyasari	School principal at Kerbala School	Kerbala	Unknown
Faidhi al-Faidhi	Professor of social sciences	Mustansiriya	Unknown
Falah Al-Dulaimi	Assistant Dean	Mustansiriya	Unknown

Name	Profession	University	Date
Faysal Al Assadi	Professor at the College of Agronomy	Basra	Unknown
Faysal Al-mash-hadani	PhD	Unknown	Unknown
Galib Lateef Al Zuhair	Sheikh, teacher and religious scholar	Dyala	Unknown
Hafez Al-hafez	Paediatrician	Unknown	Unknown
Haidar al Ba'aj	Director of educational hospital	Basra	Unknown
Haidar Taher	Professor at the College of Medicine	Basra	Unknown
Haithem Ooda	Deputy head of chemical engineering department	Basra	Unknown
Hamad Faysal Fahdawi	Unknown	Al-Anbar	Unknown
Hazim Abdul HadiTae	Professor in medicine	Baghdad	Unknown
Hisham Charif	Head of Department of History	Baghdad	Unknown
Hussam Al-Ddin Ahmad Mahmmoud	Chairman of the College of Education	Mustansiriya	Unknown
Hussam al-Din Juma'	Professor of agriculture	Baghdad	Unknown
Ibrahim Al-rashed	Ministry of Science and Technology	Unknown	Unknown
Ihsan Abed Ali Rabiei	Deputy dean of medicine college	Baghdad	Unknown
Ihsan Karim Alghazi	Directorate of Financial Control Bureau	Unknown	Unknown
Imad Nasir Al-foadi	Faculty of political science	Mustansiriya	Unknown
Iman Younis	Head of translation department	Mosul	Unknown
Isam Said Abd al-Halim	Geological expert at the Ministry of Construction	Unknown	Unknown
Ismael Yousef	Deputy at the appeal court	Unknown	Unknown
Jafar Sadeq Naqeeb	Neurologist	Unknown	Unknown
Jalil Ismail Abd al-Dahri	Professor of physics	Baghdad	Unknown
Jameel Aboud al Baydani	School principal	Unknown	Unknown
Jasim Abdul Kareem	Professor of humanities	Mustansiriya	Unknown
Jasim Mohemed Achamri	Dean of College of Philosophy	Baghdad	Unknown

Name	Profession	University	Date
Jawad Ashakraji	Venereologist	Unknown	Unknown
Kadhem Asaydae	Vice Dean, faculty of sciences	Nahrain	Unknown
Kamal al-Jarrah	General Manager at Ministry of Education		Unknown
Karim Ghayith Dama	Practicing lawyer	Unknown	Unknown
Karim Hassani	Lecturer at the College of Medicine	Basra	Unknown
Khalid Ibrahim Sa'id	Professor of engineering	Unknown	Unknown
Khalid M. al-Janabi	Professor of Islamic history	Babylon	Unknown
Khalid Shrieda	Dean of the Engineering College	Basra	Unknown
Kilan Mahmud Ramez	Professor of political science	Baghdad	Unknown
Laith Abdul Aziz Abbas	Sciences college	An-nahreen	Unknown
Maha Abdel Kadira	Lecturer at College of Humanities	Baghdad	Unknown
Majeed Hussein Ali	Professor of physics	Baghdad	Unknown
Makki Dashar Gharbawi	Surgeon	Unknown	Unknown
Marwan al-Rawi	Professor of engineering	Unknown	Unknown
Marwan Rasheed	Vice Dean of Engineering College	Baghdad Engineering College	Unknown
Mehned Al-Dulaimi	Lecturer in mechanical engineering	Baghdad	Unknown
Mohamad Abd Al Husein Wahed	Lecturer at the Institute of Administration	Baghdad	Unknown
Mohamad Al Adramli	PhD in chemical sciences	Unknown	Unknown
Mohamad Al Hakim	Dean of College of Pharmacy	Basra	Unknown
Mohamad Kasem	Professor of engineering	Basra	Unknown
Mohamad Yassem Badr	Chairman	Basra	Unknown
Mohammed Al-Erdhroumly	Expert at the Iraqi atomic agency	Unknown	Unknown
Mohammed Ali Jawad Ashami	Dean of Law Faculty	Mustansiriya	Unknown
Mohammed Al-Kissi	Lecturer	Baghdad	Unknown
Mohammed Falah Al-Dulaimi	Lecturer in physical sciences	Baghdad	Unknown

Name	Profession	University	Date
Mohammed Munim al-Izmerly	Professor of chemistry	Unknown	Unknown
Mohammed Yaqoub Al Obaidi	Unknown	Baghdad	Unknown
Mohammed Yaqoub Asaidi	Unknown	Unknown	Unknown
Mouloud Hassan Albardar Aturki	Professor of theology of the faculty Al Imam Al Aadam	Baghdad	Unknown
Mudher al-Ani	Faculty of medicine	Baghdad	Unknown
Muhannad Abbas Khudaire	Faculty member at the Technology University	Baghdad Engineering College	Unknown
Muhannad Al-Dilami	Faculty member	Baghdad Technology College	Unknown
Muhey Hussein	Faculty member of the mechanical engineering department	Baghdad Technology College	Unknown
Muneer al-Khiero	Professor of law	Mosul	Unknown
Mustapha al-Mashadani	Professor of religious studies	Baghdad	Unknown
Nafia Aboud	Professor of Arab literature	Baghdad	Unknown
Najim Karboul Alyasari	School principal	Kerbala	Unknown
Nazar Abdul Amir Al Ubaidy	Professor	Baghdad	Unknown
Noel Butrus S. Mathew	Professor at the Institute of Health	Mosul	Unknown
Omer Fakhri	Professor of biology	Basra	Unknown
Qusai Salah Deen	Head of students council	Mosul	Unknown
Raad okhssin Al-binow	Lecturer in College of Medicine	Al-Anbar	Unknown
Reyad Khalid Waleed	Electronics engineer	Unknown	Unknown
Saad Alrubaiee	Biology	Basra	Unknown
Sabah bahnam	Ministry of Interior Affairs	Unknown	Unknown
Sabah Hachim Yaber	Professor at Technical College	Basra	Unknown
Sabah Hashim	Teacher at the Administration Institute	Basra	Unknown

Name	Profession	University	Date
Sadiq Al-Baaj	Director of the military hospital, Annasereya	Unknown	Unknown
Sadiq al-Ubaidi	Neurologist	Unknown	Unknown
Sahera Mohammed Mash-hadani	Technology University	Baghdad Engineering College	Unknown
Salah Bandar	School principal, al Kindi Preliminary	Unknown	Unknown
Shaker falah Hasan	Engineer at South Gaz company		Unknown
Shakier al-Khafaji	Professor of administration; Director of the Standardization and Quality Control Council	Unknown	Unknown
Shakir Mahmmoud Jasim	Assistant professor in College of Agriculture	Al-Anbar	Unknown
Suhad al-Abadi	Physician	Unknown	Unknown
Tamer Abdulateef	General manager at Ministry of Science and Technology	Unknown	Unknown
Yaddab Al-Hajjam	Lecturer at the College of Education	Basra	Unknown
Zanubia Abdel Husein	Lecturer at the College of Veterinary Medicine	Basra	Unknown
Wajeeh Mahjoub	General director of physical education at the Ministry of Education	Unknown	04/09/2003
Khalid Faisal Hamid Al-Sheekho	Assistant professor in College of Physical Education	Mosul	04/11/2003
Mohammed Falah Ali Hussein	Vice Dean of the College of Science	Mustansiriya	05/10/2003
Sabah Mahmoud al-Rubaie	Dean of the College of Education	Mustansiriya	05/16/2003
Ghassab jabber Attar	Assistant lecturer in College of Engineering	Basra	06/08/2003
Rafi Sarcissan Vancan	Lecturer in the College of Women's Education	Baghdad	06/09/2003
Mohammed Najeeb Al-Qissi	Assistant professor in research department	Mustansiriya	06/20/2003
Human Al-Din Ahman Mahmoud	Head of department	Mustansiriya	07/11/2003

Name	Profession	University	Date
Mohammed Abdallah Falah al-Rawi	President of Baghdad University	Baghdad	07/27/2003
Haifa Alwan Al-Hill	Lecturer in the College of Science for Women	Baghdad	09/07/2003
Abdullah al-Fedhil	Professor of chemistry	Basra	09/30/2003
Asaad Salem abdul qader Shrieda	Dean of the Engineering College	Basra	10/15/2003
Essam Sharif Mohammed	Assistant professor in College of Arts	Baghdad Art College	10/25/2003
Abdul Sattar Jeid Al-Dulaimy	Professor of microbiology at the veterinary faculty	Baghdad	11/01/2003
Abdul wahab Salman	PhD	Unknown	12/09/2003
Nafeaa Mahmoud Khalaf	Professor in College of Arts	Baghdad	12/13/2003
Amal Maamlaji	IT professor at al-Mansour University	Baghdad	2004
Adel Jabar Abid Mustafa	Dean of political science	Mosul	01/01/2004
Mohammed Abd-AlHussein Wahed	Lecturer in Administrable Institute	Baghdad Engineering College	01/09/2004
Abdul-Latif al-Mayah	Chairman of the research department	Mustansiriya	01/19/2004
Mohammed younis Thanoon	Assistant lecturer in College of Physical Education	Mosul	01/27/2004
Huseín Yasín	Lecturer in sciences	Basra	02/18/2004
Majeed Hussein Mahbouba	Assistant professor of medicine	Al-Qadisiya	03/10/2004
Marwan G. Mudh'hir al-Hetti	Professor of chemical engineering	Baghdad Engineering College	03/16/2004
Saadi Ahmad Zidaan Al-Fahdawi	Lecturer in Islamic Science College	Baghdad	03/26/2004
Ali Ghalib Abd-Ali	Assistant lecturer in College of Engineering	Basra	04/12/2004
Kefaia Hussein Salih	Lecturer in College of Education	Basra	05/28/2004
Qahtan Kadhim Hatim	Assistant lecturer at College of Engineering	Baghdad	05/30/2004
Sabri Mustapha al-Bayati	Professor of geography	Baghdad	06/13/2004

Name	Profession	University	Date
Lyla Abdullah al-Saad	Dean of the Law College	Mosul	06/22/2004
Fathal Mosa Hussine Al-Akili	Professor in College of Physical Education	Tikrit	06/27/2004
Bassem al-Mudares	Professor of chemistry	Tikrit	07/21/2004
Saadi Dagher Morab	Assistant professor in College of Fine Arts	Baghdad	07/23/2004
Ismail Al-Kilabi	Head of the Mamouduyah Teachers Institute	Baghdad	07/30/2004
Aamir Ibrahim Hamza	Assistant lecturer, Engineering College	Baghdad	08/17/2004
Mohamed Salih Mahdi	Assistant lecturer in Cancer Research Center	Baghdad Engineering College	08/17/2004
Eman Abd-Almonaom younis	Lecturer in College of Arts	Mosul	08/30/2004
Mahmoud Ibrahim Hussein	Assistant professor in College of Education	Tikrit	09/03/2004
Mohammed Tuki Hussein al-Talakani	Nuclear scientist	Unknown	09/04/2004
Zaki jabar Laftah Al-Saedi	Assistant lecturer in veterinary medicine	Baghdad	10/16/2004
Khalil Ismail abdAldahri	Assistant professor in College of Physical Education	Baghdad	10/17/2004
Faidhy al Faidhy	Religious scholar	Mosul	11/22/2004
Qassem Muhawi Hassan	General manager of telecommunications company	Ministry of Communication	12/16/2004
Muwafaq Yaha Hamdoun	Deputy Dean of Agricultural College	Mosul	12/18/2004
Mahfoudh al-Qazzaz	Professor of Islamic history	Mosul	12/20/2004
Taleb Ibrahim al-Daher	Professor of physics	Dyala	12/21/2004
Hassan Abd-Ali Dawood Al-Rubai	Dean of the College of Dentistry	Baghdad	12/25/2004
Omar Mahmoud Abdullah	Retired pharmacist	Unknown	01/04/2005
Madloul al-Bazi	Unknown	Tikrit	01/06/2005
Ahmed Nassir Al-Nassiri	Professor of education	Baghdad	02/01/2005
Ahmed Saadi Zaidan	Professor of education	Al-Anbar	02/01/2005

Name	Profession	University	Date
Hareth Abdul Jabbar Assamrani	Graduate student, Engineering College	Tikrit	02/12/2005
Seif Zaki Saadi	PhD	Unknown	02/12/2005
Wannas Abdulah Al-Naddawi	Professor of education	Baghdad	02/18/2005
Wa'adullah Abdulqader	Professor	Mosul	03/29/2005
Natiq Sabri Hasan	Head of agricultural mechanics department	Mosul	04/12/2005
Bassem Habib Salman	Medicine College	Mustansiriya	04/15/2005
Hussam Karyaqoush Thomas	Professor at Medicine College	Mustansiriya	04/15/2005
Fouad Abrahim Mohammed Al-Bayati	Head of German department	Baghdad	04/19/2005
Naef Sultan Saleh	PhD	Mosul	04/26/2005
Raad Abdul-Latif Al-Saadi	Ministry of Higher Education and Scientific Research	Unknown	04/28/2005
Abdl-Hussein Nasir Khalaf	PhD in Research Center of Date Palm	Basra	05/01/2005
Basil Abbass Hassan	Professor of medicine		05/01/2005
Abdulla Saheb Younis	Specialist doctor, Anoaman Hospital	Baghdad	05/11/2005
Kadum Allwash	General manager of Karama Hospital	Baghdad	05/11/2005
Mustapha Mohammed Amin Al-Hitti	Dean of the Pharmacy College	Baghdad	05/11/2005
Sami Aymen	Specialist in the field of malignant and chronic diseases	Unknown	05/11/2005
Sinan Mu'yad	Hamdanya town Hospital	Mosul	05/11/2005
Reda Refat Amin	Doctor of medicine	Unknown	05/13/2005
Qasim Mohammed Al-Umari	Professor	Baghdad	05/19/2005
Abdul Hussein Nasir	Unknown	Basra	05/22/2005
Musa Saloum Al Ameer	Vice Dean of Education College	Mustansiriya	05/27/2005
Abdul As Satar Sabar Al Khazraji	PhD in history	Mustansiriya	06/19/2005
Abdul Sattar Sab'ar Al-Khazraji	Professor of engineering	An-nahreen	06/19/2005
Jassim Al-Issawi	Professor of law	Baghdad	06/21/2005
Salah Jmor	Professor	Unknown	06/28/2005

Name	Profession	University	Date
Jumhour Karim Khamass	Arabic language professor	Basra	07/08/2005
Alaa Daud Salman	Professor of history	Basra	07/18/2005
Ala'a Dawood Salman	Assistant scientific president	Basra	07/20/2005
Damen Hussien Al-Obaidi	Professor of law	Tikrit	07/23/2005
Mojbil Achaij Issa Al Jaburi	Lecturer in international law	Tikrit	07/23/2005
Hakim Malik Al Zayadi	Lecturer of Arabic literature	Al-Qadisiya	07/24/2005
Jamhour Karim Kammas Al Zargani	Department head at the College of Education	Basra	08/19/2005
Adel Jabar Abid Mustapha	Chairman of science department	Mosul	08/24/2005
Wissam Al-Hashimi	Chairman of Arab Geologists Union; senior expert on oil reservoirs	Unknown	08/24/2005
Hashim Abdul Kareem	Lecturer in College of Education	Mustansiriya	08/28/2005
Samir yield Gerges	Vice dean in Administration and Economy College	Mustansiriya	08/28/2005
Zaki Thakir Alaany	Lecturer in College of Literature	Mustansiriya	08/28/2005
Abdul latif Attai	PhD	Baghdad	09/05/2005
Mohammed Al-mash-hadani	Member of National Dialogue Committee	Unknown	09/19/2005
Mawlood Hassan Albarbar Alturki	Professor of Islamic science	Baghdad	09/25/2005
Umran Hamed	Lecturer	Tikrit	10/12/2005
Mustafa Al Hity	Faculty member at the College of Medicine	Baghdad	11/14/2005
Jasim al-Fahaidawi	Lecturer in Arabic literature	Mustansiriya	11/15/2005
Mohammed Al Jazairi	Faculty member at the College of Medicine	Nahrain	11/15/2005
Raad Muhsin Mutar al-Mawla	Faculty member at the College of Science	Baghdad	11/16/2005
Amir Al Khazragi	Faculty member at the College of Medicine	Baghdad	11/17/2005
Haikal Mohammed al-Moosawy	Faculty member at the El-Kendi Medicine College	Baghdad	11/17/2005

Name	Profession	University	Date
Raad Shlash	Head of the Biology department	Baghdad	11/17/2005
Saad Yaseen al-Ansary	Faculty member at the College of Science	Baghdad	11/17/2005
Kadhim Talal Husain Allami	Vice Dean of the College of Education	Mustansiriya	11/23/2005
Abdel Majed Hamed al-Karboli	Professor	Al-Anbar	12/01/2005
Hamed Faisal Antar	Lecturer in the College of Law	Ramadi	12/01/2005
Kadhum Mashhut Awad	Dean of agriculture faculty	Basra	12/01/2005
Mohammed Fathi Mjamed	Directorate of roads and bridges	Unknown	12/05/2005
Firas Anoaimi	PhD in medicine, Al Falluja Hospital	Unknown	12/13/2005
Omar Miran	Professor	Mosul	12/23/2005
Mohsin Sulaiman Al-Ajeely	Professor at the Agriculture College	Babylon	12/24/2005
Nawfal Ahmed Hassan	Professor of the Institute of Fine Arts	Baghdad	12/25/2005
Youssef Salman	Engineering professor	Basra	2006
Abdullah Hamed Al-Fadel	Vice Dean of the College of Medicine	Basra	01/01/2006
Naser Abdel Karem Mejlef al-Dulaimi	Physics professor	Al-Anbar	01/16/2006
Nasar Al Fadhawi	Unknown	Al Anbar	01/16/2006
Atheer Husham Abdul-Hameed	Veterinary surgeon	Unknown	01/22/2006
Abdulrazzaq Al-Naas	Political analyst	Baghdad	01/28/2006
Haitham Al-Azzawi	Teacher from the Islamic University	Baghdad	02/13/2006
Abdul Qadir Miran	Unknown	Mosul	02/14/2006
Bassem al-Muddaris	Professor of philosophy	Baghdad	02/28/2006
Fuad Al-Daján	Lecturer in gynaecology	Basra	03/01/2006
Saad Al-Shahín	Lecturer in internal medicine	Basra	03/01/2006
Yasoob Sulaiman	Skin specialist	Mosul	03/02/2006
Ali Husain Muhawish	Dean of Engineering	Baghdad	03/09/2006
Faiz Ghani Aziz allousi	Director-general of the Vegetable Oil Company	Unknown	03/09/2006
Khalil Ibrahim Al-Mishari	Professor	Basra	03/20/2006

Name	Profession	University	Date
Kays Hussam Al Den Jumaa	Professor of agriculture	Baghdad	03/26/2006
Kazim Batin Zahir al-Hayyani	Professor	Mustansiriya	03/27/2006
Salah Abdul-Aziz Hashim	Professor	Basra	04/05/2006
Darb Muhammad Al-Mousawi	Director of the Ear, Nose and Throat center	Baghdad	04/09/2006
Abdul Karim Hussein Naser	Professor of agriculture	Basra	04/10/2006
Kasem Mohamad Ad Dayni	Lecturer in psychology	Kerbala	04/17/2006
Laith Muhsin	Professor	Baquba	04/19/2006
Mis (surname unknown)	Lecturer	Baquba	04/19/2006
Salam Ali Husein	Unknown	Baquba	04/19/2006
Bashshar Hassan	Doctor of veterinary medicine	Unknown	04/22/2006
Abdul Salam Ali Al-Mehdawi	Professor	Baquba	04/26/2006
Mais Ganem Mahmud	Lecturer	Baquba	04/26/2006
Meshhin Hardan Madhlom Al-Dulaimy	Professor	Baquba	04/26/2006
Mohamad Abdul Rahman Al Ani	Lecturer at the College of Law	Mustansiriya	04/26/2006
Satar Jabar Akool	Lecturer	Baquba	04/26/2006
Hussain Al Sharifi	Professor of urinary surgery	Baghdad	05/01/2006
Fadhel Izzildeen Al-Obaidi	Pharmacist	Unknown	05/08/2006
Waled Kamel	Professor	Basra	05/08/2006
Sulaiman Jadaan al-Jubouri	Director of Al-Skaikhan Hospital, near Mosul	Unknown	05/10/2006
Qassim Mohammed	Psychology teacher	Kerbala	05/10/2006
Khalaf al-Jumaili	Professor of Islamic law	Al Fallujah	05/11/2006
Riadh Abbas Saleh	Lecturer at Centre for International Studies	Baghdad	05/11/2006
Hamed Faisal Antar	Professor of physical education	Al-Anbar	05/12/2006
Khawla Mohammad Taqi Zwain	Lecturer at College of Medicine	Kufa	05/12/2006
Ali Hasan Mauch	Dean of Engineering	Mustansiriya	05/12/2006

Name	Profession	University	Date
Adnan Abbas al-Hasjimi	Consultant orthopaedic surgeon	Mosul	05/15/2006
Abbas Al Amery	Head of Department of Administration and Business	Baghdad	05/16/2006
Riyad Abbas Salih al Juburi	Academic researcher	Unknown	05/17/2006
Ali Ahmed Hussein	Professor, Engineering College	Baghdad	05/22/2006
Sabah al-Jaf	Official at the Education Ministry	Unknown	05/22/2006
Jasim Fiadh Al-Shammari	Speciality in psychology	Mustansiriya	05/23/2006
Majid Jasim Al Janabi	Technology College	Baghdad	05/23/2006
Nabil Hujazi	Lecturer at the College of Medicine	Ramadi	06/01/2006
Ahmad Abdulkader Abdullah	Professor at the College of Science	Basra	06/09/2006
Ahmad Abdul Wadir Abdullah	Professor of chemistry	Basra	06/10/2006
Hani Aref Al-Dulaimy	Lecturer in the department of computer engineering	Baghdad College of Engineering	06/13/2006
Kasem Yusuf Yakub	Head of mechanical engineering department	Basra	06/13/2006
Muthana Harith Jassim	Professor	Baghdad	06/13/2006
Modhaer Zayed Al-Dabagh	Lecturer	Mosul	06/18/2006
Hadi Muhammad Abub Al Obaidi	Lecturer in the department of surgery	Baghdad	06/19/2006
Hamza Shenian	Professor of veterinary surgery	Baghdad	06/21/2006
Jassim Mohama Al-Eesaui	Professor of political science	Baghdad	06/22/2006
Amira al-Rubaie	Professor at the College of Medicine	Tikrit	July 2006
Name unknown	Lecturer	Baghdad University of Technology	06/27/2006
Barak Farouk	Professor	Baghdad	06/26/2006
Noel Petros Shammas Matti	Lecturer at the Medical Institute	Mosul	08/04/2006
Shukur Arsalan	Professor at the faculty of medicine	Baghdad	08/05/2006

Name	Profession	University	Date
Ali al-Kafif	Professor	Baghdad	08/05/2006
Adil al-Mansuri	Professor at the College of Medicine	Baghdad	08/06/2006
Karim al-Saadi	Lecturer	Baquba	08/06/2006
Mohamed al-Tamimi	Head of the College of Education	Baquba	08/06/2006
Uday al-Beiruti	Professor	An-Nahrein	08/06/2006
Muhammad Abbas	Head of the computer department	Baquba	08/19/2006
Kreem Slman Al-Hamed Al-Sadey	Professor in the department of Arabic language	Baquba	08/19/2006
Ahmed Abdul Qadil Al-Rifaee	Specialist in breast cancer	Unknown	09/01/2006
Khalid Ibrahim Mousa	Professor at the faculty of medicine	Baghdad	09/06/2006
Shukir Mahmoud As-Salam	Lecturer at College of Medicine	Baghdad	09/06/2006
Tawfeeq Al-Khishaky	Medical doctor	Unknown	09/06/2006
Mahdi Nuseif Jasim	Professor of oil engineering	Baghdad	09/13/2006
Yahya Al-Janabi	Doctor in General Hospital, Sadr City	Baghdad	09/18/2006
Kemal Nassir	Professor of history	Mustansiriya, Kufa	10/01/2006
Nadjat Al-Sahili	Professor of psychology	Mustansiriya	10/01/2006
Yaqdan Sadún Al Dhalmi	Professor in the College of Education	Baghdad	10/16/2006
Hassib Aref Al Obaidi	Professor of political science	Mustansiriya	10/22/2006
Saad Mehdi Shalash	Professor of journalism	Baghdad	10/25/2006
Fadhil Al-Dulaimi	Vice Dean of the Baghdad College Preparatory School	Baghdad	10/29/2006
Issam al-Rawi	Professor of geology and head of the Iraqi Lecturers Association	Baghdad	10/30/2006
Mohammed Jassim Al Thahbi	Dean of the administration and economy faculty	Baghdad	11/02/2006
wife of Mohammed Jassim Al Thahbi	Professor in the administration and economy faculty	Baghdad	11/02/2006

Name	Profession	University	Date
Dhia Al Deen Mahdi Hussein	Professor of international criminal law	Mustansiriya	11/04/2006
Unknown university professor	Unknown	Unknown	11/06/2006
Abdul Hamid Al Hadizi	Professor	Baghdad	11/13/2006
Abdul Salam Suaidan Al Mashhadani	Lecturer in political sciences and head of the scholarships section of the Ministry of Higher Education	Baghdad	11/13/2006
Mohamed Mehdi Saleh	Lecturer	Baghdad	11/14/2006
Ali Kadhim Ali	Professor, Engineering College	Baghdad	11/16/2006
Mahmud Mohammed al-Mohamadi	Unknown	Anbar	11/16/2006
Ahmed Hamid al-Taie	Head of clinic department	Mosul	11/20/2006
Ali al-Grari	Professor	Babylon	11/20/2006
Fleih Al Gharbawi	Lecturer at the College of Medicine	Babylon	11/20/2006
Hussein Qader Omar	Director of administration at College of Education	Kirkuk	11/20/2006
Izi Al Deen Al Raui	President of the Arabic University's Institute of Petroleum, Industry and Minerals		11/20/2006
Farhan Mahmud	Lecturer at the College of Theology	Tikrit	11/24/2006
Ahmed Mehawish Hasan	Lecturer in the department of Arabic	Baquba	12/01/2006
Kathum Mashhout	Lecturer in edaphology at the College of Agriculture	Basra	12/01/2006
Hedaib Majhol	Head of Students Club	Baghdad	12/03/2006
Al Hareth Abdul Hamid	Head of the Department of Psychology	Baghdad	12/06/2006
Mohammed Haidar Sulaiman	Professor at Sports Education College	Mosul	12/07/2008
Hassan Ahmed	Professor of Arabic language	Diyala	12/08/2006
University professor (unknown)	Unknown	Baquba	12/08/2006

Name	Profession	University	Date
Ali Jassam	Lecturer in the law department	Mustansiriya	12/20/2006
Muntathar al-Hamdani	Vice Dean of law department	Mustansiriya	12/20/2006
Anas al-Jomaili	Professor at medical school	Nahrain	12/22/2006
Khalil al-Jomaili	Professor at medical school	Nahrain	12/22/2006
Kamil Abdul Hussein	Deputy Dean of Law College	Mosul	01/12/2007
Majid Nassir Hussein	Lecturer in the Medicine College	Baghdad	01/17/2007
Anwar Abdul Hussain	Lecturer at the College of Odontology	Baghdad	01/21/2007
Diya Al-Meqoter	Professor of economics	Mustansiriya	01/23/2007
Abedasamia Al Jenabi	Deputy president of the Baghdad University of Technology	Mustansiriya	01/23/2007
Abdul Mutalib Abdul Razaq al-Hashmi	Lecturer in law	Nahrain	01/28/2007
Adnan Mohammad Saleh al-A'abid	Professor of law	Nahrain	01/28/2007
Ali Abdul Mutalib Abdul Razaq al-Hashmi	PhD student, son of Abdul Mutalib Al Hashmi	Nahrain	01/28/2007
Amir Kasim al-Kaisi	Lecturer in law	Nahrain	01/28/2007
Walhan Hameed Faris al-Ruba'aee	Dean of Physical Education College	Diyala	02/01/2007
Ahmed Izaldin Yahya	Lecturer in the College of Engineering	Kirkuk	02/16/2007
Majid Naser Husien al-Ma'amoori	Professor at the Veterinary College	Baghdad	02/17/2007
Kareem Ahmed Al-Timmi	Head of the department of Arabic language	Open University	02/22/2007
Ameer Mekki El Zihairi	Lecturer, Technology Institute	Baghdad	03/01/2007
Khalid al-Naid	Vice Dean of the Medical College	Nahrain	03/29/2007
Ridha Abdul Hussein Al Qureaishi	Assistant to Dean of the Management and Economics College	Mustansiriya	03/29/2007
Sami Sitrak	Acting Dean of the College of Law	Nahrain	03/29/2007
Munthir Ahmed Al Ani	Unknown	Unknown	03/31/2007

Name	Profession	University	Date
Khalid AL Hassan	Secretary to Dean of Political Science College	Baghdad	04/02/2007
Thair Ahmed Jebr	Physics department	Nahrain	04/05/2007
Abdul Ghabur Al-Qasi	Lecturer in history	Baquba	04/10/2007
Jaffer Hasan Sadiq	Professor of history	Mosul	04/16/2007
Talal Al-Jalili	Dean of faculty of political sciences	Mosul	04/16/2007
Ali Mohamed Hamza	Professor of Islamic studies	Baghdad	04/17/2007
Khalid Jubair al-Dulaimi	Professor at College of Engineering	Al Anbar	04/27/2007
Abdul Wahab Majid	Lecturer at College of Education	Baghdad	05/02/2007
Ismail Taleb Ahmed	Lecturer at the College of Education	Mosul	05/02/2007
Nidal al-Asadi	Professor, computers department	Mosul	05/02/2007
Sabah Al-Taei	Vice Dean of the College of Education	Baghdad	05/07/2007
Saad Jassim Muhammad	Professor at the University of Islamic Science	Baghdad	05/11/2007
Mahdi Saleh al-Any	Professor	Unknown	05/12/2007
Mohammad Aziz Alwan	Lecturer of art and design	Basra	05/26/2007
Khalil al-Zahawi	One of the Muslim world's leading calligraphers	Unknown	05/27/2007
Abdel-Rahman Al-Issawi	Journalism professor	Baghdad	05/29/2007
Qais Sabah al-Jabouri	Professor at the Islamic University, al-Adhamiya	Baghdad	06/06/2007
Alaa Jalel Essa	Unknown	Baghdad	06/07/2007
Unknown	Professor	Baghdad	06/07/2007
Unknown	Head of the Education Ministry's department of research and development	Baghdad	06/07/2007
Alaa Shakir Mahmoud	Chancellor	Diyala	06/14/2007
Muhammad Kasem Al-Jeboory	Lecturer at the College of Agriculture	Baghdad	06/22/2007
Nihad Mohammed Al-Rawi	Vice chancellor	Baghdad	06/26/2007

Name	Profession	University	Date
Samir (rest of name unknown)	Professor at the Faculty of Management and Economics	Baghdad	06/28/2007
Zeki Al-Fadaq	Surgeon	Basra	07/16/2007
Firas Abdul Zahra	Lecturere at Physical Education College	Basra	07/18/2007
Shahlaa al-Nasrawi	Professor of law	Kufa	08/21/2007
Abdul Qadir Ali Abdullah	Education College	Mosul	08/25/2007
Muayad Ahmad Khalaf	Literature College	Basra	09/11/2007
Unknown	Professor	Mosul	09/30/2007
Yasir Al Yasiri	Lecturer at Al Sadr religious university	Basra	10/05/2007
Ali Sabeeh al-Sa'idi	Law professor	Unknown	10/06/2007
Amin Abdul Aziz Sarhan	Professor	Baghdad	10/15/2007
Mohammad Kadhem Al-Atabi	Former professor	Baghdad	10/18/2007
Adel Abdul Hadi	Professor of philosophy	Kufa	10/28/2007
Jamal Mustafa	Head of the history department	Baquba	10/29/2007
Sabri Abdul Jabar Mohammad	Open College for Education	Kirkuk	11/01/2007
Haitham Abdel Salam	Academic	Kirkuk	11/12/2007
Musa Ja'afar	Head of Iraqi Geological Survey	Unknown	11/20/2007
Mustafa Khudhr Qasi	Professor	Tikrit	11/21/2007
Ali al-Naimi	Unknown	Baghdad	12/17/2007
Mohammad Al-Miyahi	Dean of Al-Maamoun private college, Baghdad	Baghdad	12/19/2007
Sulaym Khalil an-Nu'aymi	Professor of accounting	Mosul	01/21/2008
Aziz Sulaiman	Lecturer of sociology	Mosul	01/22/2008
Munther Murhej Radhi	Dean of the College of Odontology	Baghdad	01/23/2008
Khalil Ibrahim al Nuaymi	President of Islamic jurisprudence in Islamic science faculty	Mosul	01/30/2008
Abdel Sattar Tahir Sharif	Academic and founder of pro-government Kurdistan Revolutionary Party in the 1970s	Kirkuk	03/05/2008

Name	Profession	University	Date
Jaled Naser Al-Miyahi	Professor of neurosurgery	Basra	03/12/2008
Mundir Marhach	Dean of faculty of stomatology	Baghdad	03/12/2008
Iyad Hamza	Academic assistant to the president of Al-Nahrein University	Al Nahrein	05/04/2008
Mahmoud Talb Latif Al-Jumaily	Member of the Commision of Muslim Scientists		05/15/2008
Taha AbdulRazak Al-Ani	Professor in Islamic studies	Tikrit	05/15/2008
Fares Younes Abdul Rahman	Vice Dean of the Agriculture Faculty	Mosul	06/02/2008
Walid Saad Allah al-Mouli	Professor	Mosul	06/15/2008
Salih Abed Hassoun	Dean of College of Law at Al Qadisiyah University	Baghdad	07/07/2008
Khaldoun Sabry	Professor	Unknown	08/25/2008
Salam Rasheed	Medical professor	Baquba	09/01/2008
Saleh al-Auqaeili	Former professor	Unknown	10/09/2008
Faiz Saheb Ghali	Dean of the faculty of science	Muthanna	10/02/2008

NOTES ON CONTRIBUTORS

Dirk Adriaensens is coordinator of SOS Iraq, an organization that campaigned against the sanctions imposed on Iraq (1990–2003). He is also a member of the executive committee of the B*Russell*s Tribunal, an international network of intellectuals, artists and activists who denounce and organize against the logic of permanent war promoted by the American government and currently targeting the Middle East. The B*Russell*s Tribunal launched the World Tribunal on Iraq and it continues to serve as a bridge between the intellectual resistance in the Arab World and Western peace movements. The B*Russell*s Tribunal initiated the global campaign against the assassinations of Iraqi academics.

Zainab Bahrani is the Edith Porada Professor of Art History and Archaeology at Columbia University, New York. She is the author of *Women of Babylon: Gender and Representation in Mesopotamia* (Routledge, 2001), *The Graven Image: Representation in Babylon and Assyria* (University of Pennsylvania Press, 2003), *Rituals of War: The Body and Violence in Mesopotamia* (Zone Books, 2008). In 2004, as the Senior Advisor to Iraq's Minister of Culture, she initiated Iraq's official demand for the removal of the US and coalition military base from the ancient city of Babylon. Bahrani is the recipient of awards from the Metropolitan Museum of Art, the Kevorkian Foundation, the Getty Foundation, the Mellon Foundation, and the Guggenheim Foundation. In 2008 she was awarded the Distinguished Columbia Faculty Lenfest prize.

Raymond William Baker is College Professor of International Politics at Trinity College, USA, and an adjunct Professor of Politics at the American University in Cairo. Baker was designated as a Carnegies Scholar in Islamic Studies for 2006–08. His most recent book is *Islam Without Fear*, published originally by Harvard Press and this year in Egypt and Jordan in an Arabic version. A past president of the International Association of Middle East Studies, Baker is currently a governing board member of the World Congress of Middle East Studies. He is also a founding member of the International Association of Contemporary Iraqi Studies.

Max Fuller is an independent researcher who has specialized in examining Iraq's extrajudicial violence, including so-called sectarian violence, in relation to the counterinsurgency strategies of the US and UK, drawing on his background as a human rights activist for Colombia. His essays, including "For Iraq the Salvador Option Becomes Reality" and "Crying Wolf: Death Squads and Disinformation in Occupied Iraq" are published by the Centre for Research on Globalization. He has been a member of the Advisory Committee for the B*Russell*s Tribunal since 2006 and is the co-author, with Tareq Y. Ismael, of "The Disintegration of Iraq: The Manufacturing and Politicization of Sectarianism," published in the *International Journal of Contemporary Iraqi Studies*.

Abbas al-Hussainy was Director-General of the State Board of Antiquities and Heritage of Iraq. He was also a member of the Department of Archaeology at Al-Qadissiyah University in Iraq, specializing in Islamic archaeology. Hussainy has guest lectured in numerous American and European universities on the state of affairs of Iraqi antiquities following the Anglo-American occupation. He is the author of numerous publications on the archaeology and antiquities of Iraq. In 2007–08 Hussainy was a visiting scholar in the department of Archaeology, University College, London.

Shereen T. Ismael is Associate Professor of Social Work and MSW Field Coordinator in the School of Social Work, Carleton University. In addition to her book *Child Poverty and the Canadian Welfare State: from Entitlement to Charity* (2006), she is the editor of *Globalization: Policies, Challenges and Responses* (1999). She has published numerous articles on Canadian and international social welfare issues. Her latest journal articles have appeared in the *Journal of Comparative Family Studies*, *Arab Studies Quarterly* and *The International Journal of Contemporary Iraqi Studies*.

Tareq Y. Ismael is Professor of Political Science at the University of Calgary, Canada. He also serves as president of the International Center for Contemporary Middle Eastern Studies, Secretary General of the International Association of Middle Eastern Studies and is author and editor of numerous works on Iraq and the Middle East, including *Middle East Politics Today: Government and Civil Society* (2001), *Iraq: The Human Cost of History* (2003), *The Iraqi Predicament: People in the Quagmire of Power Politics* (2004), *The Communist Movement in the Arab World* (2005), and *The Rise and Fall of the Communist Party in Iraq* (2008).

Dahr Jamail is an independent journalist who has been covering the Middle East for more than five years. He currently writes for the Inter Press Service, *Le Monde Diplomatique*, and *The Progressive*. His stories have also been published with *The Nation, The Sunday Herald* in Scotland, Al-Jazeera, the *Guardian, Foreign Policy in Focus*, and the *Independent*. Jamail also wrote *Beyond the Green Zone: Dispatches from an Unembedded Journalist in Occupied Iraq* (2007). Jamail's reporting won the prestigious 2008 Martha Gellhorn Award for Journalism, the James Aronson Award for Social Justice Journalism, the Joe A. Callaway Award for Civic Courage, and four Project Censored awards.

Mokhtar Lamani is a Senior Visiting Fellow at the Centre for International Governance Innovation (CIGI). Previously, he served as Special Representative of the Arab League in Iraq. He worked to reconcile fractious parties and sectarian groups in Iraq while building peaceful relations between Iraq and neighboring countries. Earlier Mr. Lamani served as Ambassador of the Organization of the Islamic Conference to the United Nations as well as Deputy Permanent Observer to the UN, Officer in Charge of Iraq–Kuwait dispute, Coordinator of Secretariat Reform, and Coordinator of the Euro-Arab Dialogue and Afro-Arab Cooperation.

Philip Marfleet is Reader in Refugee Studies and Director of the Refugee Research Centre at the University of East London in the UK. He is the author of numerous works on globalization, migration and the refugee experience and has published widely on Middle East politics and society. His most recent book is *Refugees in a Global Era* (Palgrave Macmillan, 2006) and *Egypt: The Moment of Change* (co-edited with Rabab El Mehdi, Zed Books, 2009).

Faris Nadhmi, who holds PhD and MA degrees in social psychology from the University of Baghdad, has been an instructor and researcher at the university since 2002. He writes on issues of death anxiety in the context of war. Dr. Faris is a founding member of the Iraqi Psychological Association.

Glenn E. Perry received his PhD in Foreign Affairs from the University of Virginia in 1964 and did further work in Arabic and Middle East Studies at Princeton. He has taught Political Science, particularly courses on the Middle East, at Indiana State University since 1970. He also taught at the American University in Cairo. Reflecting his interdisciplinary interests in the region, he has published several books – including *The Middle East: Fourteen Islamic Centuries* (1997) and *The History of Egypt* (2004) – and dozens of articles and chapters, all dealing with Middle Eastern politics, history, and religion. In recent years, much of his work has focused on the paucity of Middle Eastern democracy.

Nabil al-Tikriti was a member of the team that operated the Catholic Relief Services humanitarian assistance project in Iraq in 1991–92, and later served with Medécins Sans Frontières as a relief worker in Somalia, Iran, Albania, Turkey, and Jordan. After serving as a field administrator and election monitor in various program assignments, he joined the Department of History at the University of Mary Washington in Fredericksburg, Virginia in 2004. He has been awarded a US Institute of Peace Senior Fellowship, two Fulbright grants, and research support from both the University of Chicago and the University of Mary Washington.

INDEX

Compiled by Sue Carlton

DATE DUE

BRODART, CO.   Cat. No. 23-221